THE POLITICS OF
OIL

A SURVEY

THE POLITICS OF
OIL

A SURVEY

FIRST EDITION

Edited by Bülent Gökay

Routledge
Taylor & Francis Group

LONDON AND NEW YORK

Published 2006 by Routledge
2 Park Square, Milton Park, Abingdon, Oxon, OX14 4RN
52 Vanderbilt Avenue, New York, NY 10017

First Edition 2006

First issued in paperback 2018

Routledge is an imprint of the Taylor & Francis Group, an informa business

Development Editor: Cathy Hartley
Copy Editor and Proof-reader: Simon Chapman

Typeset in Times New Roman 10.5/12

Typeset by AJS Solutions, Huddersfield – Dundee

ISBN 13: 978-1-85743-754-6 (pbk)
ISBN 13: 978-1-85743-340-1 (hbk)

Foreword

The Politics of Oil aims to provide up-to-date information on and analysis of essential aspects of oil politics, with the intention that it should serve as a reference book.

The volume is divided into four parts. The first consists of essays which endeavour to present some of the latest research findings, and in this way to initiate further enquiry into the topic. An Introduction, followed by a piece on oil and the global political economy by Darrell Whitman, set the scene for the subsequent essays. The second essay, by Emre Iseri, provides an account of the geopolitics of oil and pipelines in the Eurasian Heartland. Erin Mofford, in the third contribution, examines oil and power in the Caspian Sea region, focusing on supermajor oil companies and geopolitics. Production Sharing Agreements and oil nationalism in the context of Iraq are the subject of the fourth essay, by Vassilis Fouskas. Øystein Noreng's essay focuses on the subject of oil and Islam, and the section concludes with Chukwumerije Okereke's examination of oil politics and environmental conflict in Nigeria.

The second part of the book provides an extensive A–Z glossary section, prepared by Bülent Gökay. This glossary provides essential factual and analytical information on relevant terms, issues and personalities in the area of world oil politics. Entries are cross-referenced for ease of use.

The third section consists of a number of maps and statistical tables, which furnish the reader with an important guide to understanding the politics of oil in relation to various production regions and key issues.

The final section contains a select bibliography organized into specific fields of interest. This bibliography is not in any respect comprehensive—a select bibliography is, by definition, limited. The aim of the bibliography is to guide those who are interested in studying the politics of oil towards the main books and articles, which, it is hoped, will both inform and entertain them. It is dedicated to those who have an interest in the subject but who do not know precise bibliographic details of the key sources.

August 2006
Bülent Gökay
Reader in International Relations
Keele University

Contents

CONTENTS

Acknowledgements

The editor, authors and publishers are most grateful to the Cartographic Unit at the University of Southampton for drawing up the maps for this edition. They are also indebted to those organizations which kindly allowed their data to be reproduced in this volume, and especially to the *BP Statistical Review of World Energy*, 2005 and 2006 editions.

The editor wishes to thank the contributors to the volume, from whom he learned a tremendous amount in the editing process. In particular, he appreciated the comments of Eric B. Mofford (Project Manager for BP), who read some of the essays and offered numerous suggestions. The editor is also grateful to Simon Chapman, the copy editor, for making the text more readable and fluent, and would like to thank Cathy Hartley at Routledge for her helpfulness, efficiency and her dynamic editorial style.

The Contributors

Vassilis K. Fouskas is Senior Lecturer in International Relations at the University of Stirling. He is the founding editor of the *Journal of Southern Europe and the Balkans* and the author of *Zones of Conflict: U.S. Foreign Policy in the Balkans and Greater Middle East* (2003) and *Italy, Europe, and the Left* (1998), and co-author of *The New American Imperialism: Bush's War on Terror and Blood for Oil* (Praeger, 2005, with Bülent Gökay).

Bülent Gökay is a Reader in International Relations at Keele University. He is the author (or co-author) of many books on global politics and oil, including *The Politics of Caspian Oil* (2001), *Kosovo: Politics of Delusion* (2001), *11 September 2001: War, Terror and Judgement* (2003) and *The New American Imperialism: Bush's War on Terror and Blood for Oil* (Praeger, 2005, with Vassilis K. Fouskas).

Emre Iseri has studied international relations and politics at Bilkent University, Marmara University and the University of Kent, and published articles on the security of Europe and the Middle East. He is currently undertaking research at Keele University on 'US Global Hegemony and the Eurasian Heartland in the Post-Cold-War Era, with special reference to the main Caspian oil export pipeline: Baku–Tbilisi–Ceyhan (BTC)'.

Erin K. Mofford has undertaken extensive research on the role of multinational oil companies and just finished her fieldwork in Baku, Azerbaijan. She is currently completing a research project at Keele University on 'Supermajor Oil Companies and Geopolitics in the Caspian Sea Region'.

Øystein Noreng is Professor for Petroleum Economics and Management at the BI Norwegian School of Management. He is the author of a number of publications, including *Crude Power: Politics and the Oil Market* (I. B. Tauris, second edn, 2005).

Chukwumerije Okereke is a Senior Research Associate at the Tyndall Centre Headquarters, Zuckerman Institute for Connective Environmental Research, School of Environmental Sciences, University of East Anglia. His latest work, *Global Justice and Neoliberal Environmental Governance: Ethics, Sustainable Development and International Co-operation*, will be published by Routledge in 2007.

Darrell Whitman is a licensed attorney, community activist and educator. He holds advanced degrees in law, social science, government and international relations, and has taught political sociology, international political economy and media studies at university level. He has worked professionally in practiced electoral, community and environmental politics, and served as an advisor on climate change issues to the State of California. Currently, he is conducting research into the politics of the Intergovernmental Panel on Climate Change and the relationship between oil and the global financial system, which he plans to publish in 2007.

Abbreviations

b/d	barrels per day
bbl	barrels of oil
c.	circa
Cent.	Central
DC	District of Columbia
Dr	Doctor
Ed	Editor
Edn	Edition
Gen.	General
m.	million
OECD	Organisation for Economic Co-operation and Development
OPEC	Organization of the Petroleum Exporting Countries
Rep.	Republic
Rev.	Revenue
S.	South
UK	United Kingdom
UN	United Nations
US	United States
USA	United States of America

Essays

Introduction: How Oil Fuels World Politics

BÜLENT GÖKAY

'*Standard Oil (now ExxonMobil) and Shell seat and unseat kings and presidents, finance palace plots and coups d'états, have innumerable generals, ministers and James Bonds at their command . . . make decisions about peace or war in every field and every language.*' (Eduardo Galeano, *Open Veins of Latin America*)[1]

Oil is the most strategic raw material. It can hardly be overstated how crucial petroleum is to our modern industrial society. Virtually every aspect of modern industrial life requires oil, gas and—largely created from these fossil fuels—electricity. The economic history of the last 200 years has been a succession of technological transformations in the way of finding and delivering energy to production, transport and communications—first based on coal and steam, then on petroleum, then on electricity and electronic communications—which is also based on a mixture of fossil fuels (oil, gas and coal) and nuclear power. This is the story of how our modern system of production has evolved essential material characteristics, most critically those of the carbon economy. How have we become so dependent upon oil?

The story starts in AD 347 in China, where the first oil wells were drilled. These wells were 240 m deep and bamboo poles were used to extract the oil. The first modern oil well, however, was drilled in the Tsarist Russian Empire in 1848. According to the Azerbaijan Academy of Science, this well was prepared in what is now known as the giant Bibi-Eibat field in Baku. This was not even intentional! Oil was discovered during drilling for water. However, mechanical drilling did not substitute digging by hand until drilling machinery was imported to Baku in 1871, which was followed by the opening of large flowing wells in 1873.

The modern history of the oil industry began in 1853, with the discovery of the process of oil distillation. Crude oil was first distilled into kerosene by Ignacy Łukasiewicz, a Polish pharmacist. He also invented the petroleum kerosene lamp, which he used in 1853 to light a local hospital in Lvov so that an emergency surgical operation could be performed. As a result, the first 'rock

---

[1] Eduardo Galeano, *Open Veins of Latin America: Five Centuries of the Pillage of a Continent*, (Translator: Cedric Belfrage), Monthly Review Press, 25th anniv. Edition, 1998.

oil' mine was opened in Bóbrka (near Krosno) in southern Poland in the following year and the first oil refinery was constructed in Ulaszowice, also by Łukasiewicz. Six years after Łukasiewicz's refinery was constructed, Edwin L. Drake drilled the first modern technological oil well, which was about 21 m deep, near Titusville in north-western Pennsylvania. The invention of the kerosene lamp, by Łukasiewicz in Poland, had ignited strong demand for oil world-wide. By drilling an oil well, Drake was keen to profit from the growing demand in the USA for oil for lighting and industrial lubrication. His business quickly made huge profits. Drake's success encouraged hundreds of entrepreneurs and small companies to search for oil in the USA. As a result, in 1860, world oil production reached 500,000 barrels; and by the 1870s oil production had climbed to 20m. barrels annually.

The distinguished Russian chemist Dimitri Mendeleyev, who was commissioned to analyse technological development in the Caspian-Caucasus oil region, attended the US Centennial Exposition at Philadelphia in 1876 as a member of the official Russian delegation. This offered him the opportunity to visit the Pennsylvanian oil-producing region. He was impressed by the fact that the Pennsylvania oil belt and the principal axes of the Alleghany mountains bore a remarkable resemblance to the Baku fields and the Caucasus mountains. After this visit, more collaboration between the Russian oil industry and its US counterpart took place in the field of technological know-how.[2]

As oil production exploded, prices fell and oil industry profits dropped—basic economics. In 1882, John D. Rockefeller, the US industrialist who set up the Standard Oil company, worked out a solution to the problem of unrestrained competition in the oilfields: he managed to establish a kind of monopolistic control, and the Standard Oil trust was born, which brought together 40 of the USA's foremost refiners. Through its control of refining, Standard Oil trust was temporarily able to regulate the price of oil and restore high profits.

Up until the 1910s, it was the USA which produced 60%–70% of the world's oil supply. As fear intensified that US oil reserves were becoming depleted, the search for oil turned to the rest of the world. Oil was discovered in Mexico at the beginning of the 20th century, in Iran in 1908, in Venezuela during the First World War, and in Iraq in 1927. Many of the new oil discoveries took place in areas controlled by the British and Dutch empires. Indeed, in the early years of the 20th century, when Great Britain had converted its naval fleet from coal to oil propulsion, the relationship between oil and military power had become the central driver of imperial policies. Lacking any petroleum reserves of its own, the British Empire found itself dependent on rich oil resources in the Middle East. During the First World War, keeping those oil-rich lands under British control became a crucial war goal for Britain. As a result, by 1919, Britain found itself practically controlling 50% of the world's proven oil reserves. Therefore, it was not surprising to see the start of a bitter battle for control of world oil reserves in the aftermath of the the First World War. Britain, Holland and France disallowed

---

[2] B. Gökay (Ed.), *The Politics of Caspian Oil*, Palgrave, 2001, pp. 5–6.

US companies from purchasing (or operating in) oilfields in territories under their domination. The US Congress struck back in 1920 by introducing the Mineral Leasing Act, which denied right of entry to US oil reserves to any foreign country that limited US access to oil reserves under its control. The quarrel was partly resolved during the 1920s when some US oil companies were finally permitted to drill in the British Middle East and the Dutch East Indies.

In the USA, during the early 20th century, despite earlier fears, oil production continued to climb. By 1920, it had reached 450m. barrels, which again prompted fears that the nation was about to run out of oil. Government officials predicted that US oil reserves would not even last for another 10 years. However, the discovery of enormous new oilfields in Texas, Oklahoma, and California in 1924 ended the fear that US oil reserves were nearly exhausted. As a result of these discoveries, together with production from new fields outside the USA, most importantly in Mexico, the Soviet Union and Venezuela, oil prices again declined drastically. By 1931, with crude oil selling for 10 US cents a barrel, US oil producers were calling for restrictions on production in order to raise prices to a profitable level. In response, Texas and Oklahoma passed state laws and stationed militia units at oilfields to prevent drillers from exceeding production quotas. Despite these measures, prices continued to fall.

During the Second World War, however, the oil surpluses of the 1930s quickly disappeared. The heavy war machine of the Allied forces was consuming huge quantities. Six thousand million of the seven thousand million barrels of petroleum used by the Western allies during the war came from the USA. In the 1940s, the USA began to rely on foreign oil to fulfil rising energy demand. There emerged serious worries once again that the USA was running out of oil.

After the war, it seemed imperative that the USA secure access to foreign oil reserves. Energy security became an essential dimension of state security. Increasingly, policy-makers and the oil industry focused their attention on the Middle East, particularly the Persian (Arabian) Gulf, which they rightly believed would become the centre of post-war oil production. As early as the 1930s, Britain had gained control over Iran's oilfields and the US companies discovered oil reserves in Kuwait and Saudi Arabia. After the war ended, Middle Eastern oil production maintained its upward surge. From that point on, gradually, US dependence on Middle Eastern oil increased.

During the 1950s, a mixture of cheap fuel and a rapidly increasing consumer culture led to frantic indulgence in consumption. With only 6% of the world's population, the USA accounted for one-third of global oil consumption. Foreign oil was so cheap that coal-burning utilities led the expensive shift to oil and natural gas. But this optimism based on readily available cheap oil did not last. Initially, in 1960, low oil prices pushed Iran, Venezuela, and Arab oil producers to group together to form the Organization of Petroleum Exporting Countries (OPEC), a producers' cartel, to negotiate higher oil prices. OPEC was fashioned after the thinking of Argentinian economist Raúl Prebisch, who chaired the UN Economic Commission for Latin America and promoted the idea that national sovereignty over natural resources was essential for successful development.

OPEC was organized as a producers' bloc that could collectively bargain for the price of oil and thus enhance oil's value for the producing countries. Several large oil-producing countries, however, including the Soviet Union and the USA, remained outside of OPEC and actively worked to undermine its power to control oil prices.

By the early 1970s, the USA depended on the Middle East for one-third of its oil. Foreign oil producers were finally in a position to raise world oil prices. The oil embargo of 1973 and 1974, during which oil prices quadrupled, and the oil crisis of 1978 and 1979, when oil prices doubled, graphically demonstrated how vulnerable the USA (and Europe) had become to foreign producers. In response to this situation, US President Jimmy Carter introduced the so-called 'Carter Doctrine', labelling access to Middle Eastern oil resources as a vital US security interest. In order to implement this doctrine, Carter established the Rapid Deployment Joint Task Force and initiated a web of US military and intelligence base arrangements in the Middle East oil region.

The oil crises of the 1970s were a painful reminder of the critical role that oil plays in the global political economy. These crises had also an unanticipated side effect. Rising oil prices stimulated conservation and exploration for new oil sources. As a result of increasing supplies and declining demand, oil prices fell from US $35 a barrel in 1981 to US $9 a barrel in 1986. The sharp slide in world oil prices was one of the factors that led Iraq to invade neighbouring Kuwait in 1990, in a miscalculated attempt to secure control over 40% of Middle Eastern oil reserves. The expulsion of Iraqi forces from Kuwait in February 1991 produced a degree of stability, for about 10 years, in this strategic oil region. The same events, however, underlined once more the growing reliance of the Western industrial-ized economies on foreign oil.

Despite these ups and downs in oil prices, it is an unquestionable fact that the petroleum industry is among the most rewarding and most important in the world, and its impact on international politics is colossal. We live in a petroleum landscape, in the sense that the advance made in industry and technology over the last 150 years and the luxury we enjoy every day have been made possible by one thing and one thing only: cheap energy, in the form of oil. The whole success of the world economic system, the so-called prosperity of the 20th century, was driven by cheap, oil-based energy. Oil fuels the economy. If gold was the standard for currency and economic progress for much of the 19th and early 20th centuries, it has now been replaced by oil. The ability to set the price of gold against a particular currency, as happened with the post-Second World War dollar, has now been replaced by the ability to set the price of oil against a particular currency. But, unlike gold, oil has the added power of being central to the industrial processes of modern economies: it does not rely on a perception of value, but on its actual instrumental value as an essential commodity. Thus, holding the power of setting oil's value against a currency means that transactions in oil will naturally gravitate toward that currency as the most stable indicator of its value. This logic is fully played out when oil contracts are required to be valued in a particular currency, whose strength is then reinforced by the demand for the currency created by the contracting parties. Since 1975, when the USA concluded an agreement with Saudi Arabia (OPEC's most powerful member), OPEC has been committed to pricing oil exclusively in dollars. This understanding, much of it never publicized and little understood by the public, provided the Saudi ruling family the security it craved in a dangerous neighbourhood while ensuring that the USA had a reliable and very important ally in OPEC.[3] Since then, practically all oil has been traded in US dollars. Hence the oil standard became the dollar standard. In 2002, a former US ambassador to Saudi Arabia told a committee of the US Congress: 'One of the major things the Saudis have historically done, in part out of friendship with the US, is to insist that oil continues to be priced in dollars. Therefore the US Treasury can print money and buy oil, which is an advantage no other country has.'[4]

Oil is also a determinant of national security. Today's modern armies are entirely dependent on oil-powered ships, planes, helicopters and armoured vehicles. A defining characteristic of the second half of the 20th century was very swift, accelerating, inescapable technological change. At the same time, rapid societal change and organizational adaptations by military forces were also taking place. The military establishments of the industrialised countries are making the most of the new technology that they are introducing, and have energetically exploited and experimented with it in military campaigns since the end of the Cold War. All of this new technology, including high-tech precision weaponry and new information systems, however, is exclusively based on oil-based energy. Modern military technology is exclusively dependent on oil. Oil has become the pivot upon which the axis of war and peace rests. This is consistent with a historical pattern in which control of precious minerals has directly or indirectly led to war. In the last century alone, oil played a key role in at least 10 of the 12 major conflicts. It seems that of all the resources that are critical to modern industrial society in the 21st century, none is more likely to provoke a major war between states than oil, and as oil reserves decline its importance will only grow in the decades ahead.[5]

As a result, over the last century, the demand for oil has risen dramatically and the physical structure of our society is organized around the assumption that there will always be plenty of it. What makes it possible that we do what we do? What makes us have jobs? How can we buy anything we want? What powers all the conveniences we enjoy in our houses? What fuels our cars and airplanes? What makes the water flow? Why are the supermarkets always full of food? What is this magical thing?

It is energy. Massively available, cheap energy. Cheap energy is essential for the world economic system. Even to produce food we need to burn oil: 17% of our energy is used for producing food. Modern agriculture makes heavy use of oil

---

[3] R. G. Kaiser and D. Ottaway, 'Oil for Security Fueled Close Ties', *Washington Post*, 11 February 2002.

[4] In S. Nixon, 'What's that in euros?', *The Spectator*, 18 October 2003.

[5] V. K. Fouskas and B. Gökay, *The New American Imperialism*, Praeger Security International, 2005, pp. 79–86.

in a variety of ways. We use oil for fertilizers, pesticides, and for the packaging and distribution of food. Since the beginning of the 20th century, global trade and a global economy have developed, and our population has grown in size from 1,000m. to 6,000m. by drawing down a massive natural gift of energy in the form of cheap crude oil. Indeed, all economies are energy-dependent. There are no exceptions.

Up until early modern times, miners, scientists, natural philosophers and other 'experts' believed that gold, silver and other minerals were vegetable-like in that, when mined, they would literally grow back like mown grass. This belief was not wrong in principle in the case of coal and its hydrocarbon cousins in gaseous and liquid form, because they are the remains of ancient organisms. As a practical maxim, however, it was completely mistaken, because the time it would take normal geological processes to transform organic matter into coal, natural gas and petroleum is of the order of millions of years. Therefore, for all practical purposes, these fuels are finite, non-renewable energy resources.

In 1956, much to the surprise of most oil experts and industry executives, M. King Hubbert, a geophysicist working as an oil consultant to Shell Oil Company, developed a simple model of US oil production which predicted that the USA would peak in its oil production in the next 10–15 years (i.e. in 1966–71) and enter a permanent decline. This model was considered highly contentious for that era, and most economists and other experts, who thought the analysis failed to take the effects of market prices into consideration, rejected Hubbert's results. Many others, including Shell executives, also thought Hubbert's analysis was invalid and defeatist and would damage support for the home-based, US oil industry. Just before the time that the real price for petroleum inflated following the attempted oil embargo related to the October 1973 Arab–Israeli War, US oil production did indeed peak and entered a permanent decline. Hubbert was proved right. Since then many petroleum experts and economists have used Hubbert's method to predict the timing of the oil peak world-wide.

More than a quarter of a century later, similar questions to those asked earlier about the USA are now being asked about oil production world-wide. Is world production of so-called 'easy oil' approaching its peak? If world oil production does reach a peak, will it straight away begin to trend downwards, and, if so, how does this affect oil prices? Most predictions made in advance of the peak are likely to be highly unreliable, mainly because production and resource figures from many countries are not reliable. Both oil companies and countries have financial and political incentives to either over- or underestimate the amount of oil reserves under their control. The real world peak point can only be empirically visible when world oil production passes its highest point. Once the world-wide peak takes place, how steep will the curve of decline be thereafter? These questions, whose answers are at present all perplexing, are seriously worrying. Oil-producing countries that have peaked already are the United Kingdom, Norway, China, Mexico, Venezuela, Indonesia, Russia, Syria, Libya, Nigeria, Qatar and many others. Only part of the Middle East and the Caspian Sea region have spare capacity, and their reserve figures are not very transparent.

Today, it seems that the idea that the world may have hit 'peak oil' seems to be taking hold; and oil and gas experts around the world are growing alarmed not just at future scarcity, but also at who is in control of the remaining 'black gold'. As demand for energy explodes world-wide, there is less of it available and, it seems, less exploration for it. According to many estimates, world oil production will peak between 2004 and 2008, which means that the world is depleting oil reserves at an annual rate of 6%. At the same time, growth in demand is rising at an annual rate of 2%. All this means that the world's oil industry would have to find the equivalent of 8% a year in newly discovered oil reserves to maintain an orderly oil market. Unfortunately, discoveries are lagging behind, primarily because new large oil deposits are not being found, but also because even if they were there is a considerable time lag between a discovery and turning the oil into a usable energy product. While conservation and renewable energy are much in the news, the reality is that neither of these factors are likely to have any significant impact on the steadily growing demand for oil products. As an essential energy source, oil is still hard to beat.

During the last 10–12 years 3,000m. people from China and India have entered what we call the global economy. Currently, the economic power of China and India is growing at three to five times the gross domestic product (GDP) rate of Western states, which is the main reason for fast-growing demands for oil.[6] China was the world's second largest consumer of petroleum products in 2004, having surpassed Japan for the first time in 2003, with total demand of 6.5m. barrels per day (b/d). China's oil demand is projected by the US Energy Information Administration to reach 14.2m. b/d by 2025, with net imports of 10.9m. b/d.[7] China is currently seeking oil security through multiple channels, buying shares or making investments in various oil construction projects all over the world. In this atmosphere, competition for existing proven and prospective reserves is increasing sharply and dangerously.

In the century-and-a-half since Edwin L. Drake drilled the first modern oil well in Pennsylvania, the history of the oil industry has been a story of gigantic swings between times of over-production, when low prices and profits led oil producers to create ways to limit output and raise prices, and times when oil supplies were feared to be on the brink of exhaustion, initiating a world-wide search for new oil sources. At stake are thousands of millions of dollars in oil and natural gas revenues and the vast geopolitical and military advantages that fall to the power or powers that secure a dominant position in the oil regions. Two basic questions are key to understanding oil politics in the 21st century: who owns the remaining oil resources, and who will control the transportation of this oil to world markets? The answers to these questions will strongly influence how the world economy evolves in this century. In a world that runs on oil, the power that keeps the flow of oil under control has that key strategic authority.

---

[6] B. Bonner and A. Wiggin, *Empire of Debt*, New Jersey: Wiley, 2006, p. 16.

[7] China Country Analysis Brief, August 2005, Energy Information Administration, US Government, http://www.eia.doe.gov/emeu/cabs/china.html.

At the beginning of the new millennium, this cycle may now be approaching an end, simply because soon there may not be enough oil left. It appears that world oil supplies may truly be reaching the natural limits imposed on them by the laws of physics. With proven world oil reserves anticipated to last less than 40 years, the age of the modern oil industry may be coming to an end. There are already some indications that, in the years to come, the search for new sources of oil may be transformed into a quest for entirely new sources of energy. Oil politics is no longer just an industrial matter or a regional matter, but a world-wide security issue. Today, more than ever, oil politics is at the core of security and world politics. Many international conflicts in the world today are rooted in oil politics. That is why, in the first decade of the 21st century, oil politics represents world politics more than anything else.

As Good as Gold: Oil and the Global Political Economy

DARRELL WHITMAN

'The price or money-form of commodities is, like their form of value generally, a form quite distinct from their palpable bodily form; it is, therefore, a purely ideal or mental form.' Karl Marx, *Capital: 107.*

Perhaps nothing is more readily assumed and poorly understood as the value of money. While goods and services appear to increase and decrease in price, few attribute those changes to variations in the value of the currencies used to purchase them. Yet changes in currency values, rather than changes in the use value of a commodity or service, determine the price that is paid: a gallon (US gallon = approximately 3.8 litres) of petrol will propel a car for 'x' number of miles whether it is priced at 75 pence or 90 pence per litre, there will always be four eight ounce glasses in every quart of milk, whatever its price, and a 10-minute consultation with your doctor will yield the same advice regardless of the charge. Values do change for things over long periods of time as social and technological changes transform the demand for them, but as Karl Marx pointed out 140 years ago the price is, in fact, what you believe the value to be expressed in a particular currency.

What then is currency, and why does its value change? In its most basic form, currency is a medium of exchange through which transactions for goods or services are made possible. Currencies have been around for a very long time, but their form has changed according to the context in which transactions occur. When a transaction is completed between a willing seller and buyer, with both directly desiring the goods or services involved, it may require no medium of exchange because it is merely barter. However, more often, and particularly in modern market economies,[1] mediums of exchange are required because barter is inefficient. Thus, the context, or need for a medium of exchange, creates currency as a representation of a 'value' agreed between those involved in the exchange. The form of the currency is important only to the extent that its value is agreed.

Over time, many commodities have served as currencies, including gold and silver. They have been accepted as currencies because of their implied value and use over time. But other forms of commodity currency have also been used, such

---

[1] 'Modern market economy' as used here refers to the process of complex exchanges of goods and services 'for value'.

as wheat, nails and cowry shells, when gold and silver were unavailable, or when the scarcity[2] of these commodities, compared to the demand for them, made them highly desirable. The value of such currencies changes for several reasons: there is an overall decline in trading that requires a currency, the use value of the commodity currency declines causing a decline in its exchange value, or the availability of the commodity either increases or decreases, which then reduces the perception of its scarcity and thus its value and desirability as a medium of exchange.

In the current global trading market, the principal currency in use is the US dollar. This is a paper currency, rather than a commodity currency, which creates a different context for ascertaining its value. For reasons discussed below, the value of paper currency is much more sensitive to change because it is more highly dependent on perceptions about the various factors that contribute to its exchange value. Throughout most of financial history, paper currencies have generally had a very short life, or their value was formally or informally linked to the value of another commodity, such as gold or silver. The use of a paper currency that has no such link is very unusual, and in the case of the US dollar the delinking of this paper currency from an underlying commodity value has produced important changes in the global political economy. Whether or not this is sustainable, or for how long, is the subject of this discussion, which asks questions about the relationship between currency, oil and nation states in the global marketplace.

The 'Money Game' in the International Political Economy

The US dollar's ability to act as a medium of exchange in the global marketplace rests on two factors: 'liquidity', or the amount of dollars available, and 'reliability', or how much confidence market participants have in the durability of the value of the dollar. These factors have always been required of currencies, regardless of their form. In fact, the decline in a particular currency's ability to meet one of these requirements has always resulted first in a financial crisis in the market where it is employed, followed by a political crisis where the currency is exchanged. This is why markets and currencies are described as part of an inseparable *political economy*, and where they operate outside of purely national boundaries as an inseparable *international political economy*. The factors that influence how politics and economics interact can be very different, depending on the time or the place where they occur, because national politics differ, and these features are difficult but not impossible to replicate at the international level. But as the international economy has evolved, the lines between what is a national and international political economy have eroded, and the very concept of the value in currency has taken on a more global orientation.

---

[2] 'Scarcity' in this case refers to their desirability measured against the relative supply and demand of these commodities.

To understand the current state of currency in the international marketplace, we must begin by deconstructing the elements that link it to the states that issue it and the marketplace where it is used. These elements include looking closely at what constitutes a currency's value, and how perceptions of its value change with changes in the political environment where it is exchanged, and understanding how the relationship between states and markets developed as part of modern industrial capitalism. However, it should also be understood that there is no 'bright line' between these elements, and in fact they interact in interesting ways to shape and reshape states, currencies and markets.

At present, there is much debate about whether states construct and control international markets, or whether the global marketplace acts independently of states. This suggests that power in the international political economy is vested in either state governments, or in those who manage the marketplace. This debate is important because it represents two very different ways of seeing how the international political economy actually functions, and which side you take will say something about your assumptions regarding governments and markets. In this case, I am assuming that power is systemic rather than volitional, or in other words that governments shape and manage markets in a variety of ways that affects how they work, and that the system itself has been constructed over a very long period of time. But I also argue that precisely because of its deeply rooted history in a state-organized political economy that relies on markets, value of currency is now co-produced within a co-dependent relationship between governments and markets.

Currency, Trade and the State: a Brief History

Central authorities have been issuing currencies for millennia, sometimes as a way to finance state activities, but also as a symbolic representation of their power.[3] Most commonly, these were commodity currencies that were a convenient tool used to value an exchange. Historically, that meant that paper currency, which reputedly began in Japan in the 15th century, was invariably linked with some form of recognized commodity such as gold (Greenfield, 2001). In issuing paper currency, however governments lent currency their authority as guarantors of its value, thus making the government accountable for any problems that might arise concerning its value. Governments took this risk because in national trading systems, currency had the effect of expanding trade by making transactions easier to complete. This is where currency created a co-dependency between governments and markets: as trade expands, governments are rewarded with increased tax revenues that allowed them to adopt various programmes which enhance their popularity with citizens, and merchants accumulate more profits and thus more economic power in the marketplace. The problem comes when an economic or

---

[3] As Liah Greenfield points out, the ability to issue currency did not confer any special power to control its effects, with monetization of the Japanese and Chinese economies from the eighth until the thirteenth century resulting in serious challenges to the feudal order (Greenfield, 2001, 303–305].

political 'crisis' undermines faith in either currency or government, and reduces currency's ability to promote trade. This type of crisis can feed on itself, with growing uncertainty about a currency leading to reduced trade, which then undermines confidence in government. This is what happened in Germany in the 1920s when the value of the Mark declined so far that it literally wasn't worth the paper it was printed on.

The co-dependency of governments and markets also has reallocated power in important ways and particularly in the current era where paper currency has essentially 'freed' value from its old reliance on an underlying commodity. This has given rise to the now popular perception that the value of currency depends to a significant degree on the health and vitality of its home country's economy. More directly and mechanically, people in the international marketplace tend to prefer currencies that can easily and readily be 'invested' in an economic 'safe haven', which translates into a home country whose economy is sufficiently large and dynamic to assure that the demand for its currency will continue with enough strength to maintain the currency's value. Before Keynesian economics became fashionable in the 1930s, capitalist governments generally did little more than passively respond to changes in their domestic economies, believing that markets alone could effectively manage them. But this 'hands off' approach led to repeated and increasingly severe swings from rapid growth to equally rapid economic declines. Socialist economics, which developed with the Soviet Union in the 1920s, took the opposite view that governments should be the prime if not exclusive source of economic activity. That left open many questions about how to manage an economy, but it also insulated Socialist governments from the worst of the market swings, and especially the Great Depression in the 1930s. Trying to strike a balance between the two, Lord Keynes, a British economist, argued that in their own interest governments had to intervene in the economy to smooth out market-generated extremes.

Almost all modern governments now follow some form of Keynesian economics, primarily by engaging in 'pump priming', or increasing government spending in times of economic decline, and monetary management. But while these on the surface may appear to be separate, they are actually interdependent and co-produced by market economics. This is because government 'pump priming' can only be accomplished during periods of economic decline through deficit spending, or in effect borrowing against future revenues that will appear once the decline is reversed. President Roosevelt's government borrowed huge sums of money that were repaid only after the successful conclusion of the Second World War and the increase in revenues that followed from the economic boom of the 1950s. Governments borrow money by selling bonds, or promises to pay the amount plus interest at some future date. The US government does this through various kinds of 'Treasury' bonds that come in short-, medium-, and long-term maturities. These are sold to market investors, who in effect are betting on the short-, medium-, or long-term value of the dollar, and when confidence in the future value of the dollar is high, the interest on long-term Treasury bonds is low, compared to shorter-term rates. But when the longer term value of the dollar is less certain, interest on long-term bonds must rise to attract competitive investments. In this way, markets and governments are co-dependent and co-produce monetary policy in capitalist countries.

Not surprisingly, modern capitalist governments place great importance on the management of currency and trade. But all governments are not created from one mould, and their relationship to currency and trade varies. For example, as a percentage of its total economic activity—its gross domestic product, or GDP—the US dependence on international trade in goods and services is small relative to most European countries and countries with developing economies. Yet, the structure of international trade is critically important to the USA because of its dependency on imports of critical raw materials, particularly oil, and the role of the US dollar as an international reserve currency. This interwoven relationship been oil and currency has grown as modern economies increasingly become energy-dependent in what is now the 'carbon age', with the value of currency similarly becoming dependent on access to oil on economically favourable terms.

Classical Political Economy: 'Value' and Currency

The 'value' of currency has been a subject of keen interest in political economy since the time of John Locke, Adam Smith, David Ricardo, and Karl Marx, each of whom made a singular contribution to understanding of the relationship between currency and value, and markets and politics. In this pantheon of political-economic theorists, Locke represents the transition between feudal and capitalist organization, Smith articulated the basic operation of markets, Ricardo applied Smith to international economic relations, and Marx linked them together as a system of political economy. What joins these separate contributions is the classic definition of value, developed by John Locke. Locke reasoned that *value* was not conferred but produced through human labour that 'makes the far greater part of the value of things' (Locke, 1963: 42), and deduced from this that *value* existed in currency only as a necessary evil to 'protect value from spoilage' (Locke, 1963: 46).[4] Thus, in Lockean terms, currency could have value only in a transitory and instrumental sense that would always be connected in some form to the intrinsic value of some more corporeal thing, such as gold or silver.[5]

Like Locke, Adam Smith considered that economic matters were moral and ethical issues. However, unlike Locke, Smith accepted that economic systems were necessary if unnatural evils, and that states had a central role in creating and maintaining markets. The finer points of his thinking appear in *The Wealth of Nations*, where he argues for an unregulated domestic market but a state-regulated international market, and where he also offers the first definitive

---

[4] It was an assumption that the classical and the Marxist theorists who followed in large part borrowed and debated as the 'labour theory of value'. Thus, the implied link between intrinsic and represented value became subsumed in generally theorizing about money to and beyond the time when paper money became delinked with such guarantors as gold and other precious metals.

[5] As Locke observed, money was 'that little piece of yellow Metal' (Locke, 1963, 37).

discussion of the 'origin and use of money' as it now exists in modern capitalist economies. His analysis of market economics begins with the observation that, 'Every man thus lives by exchanging, or becomes in some measure a merchant, and the society itself grows to be what is properly a commercial society' (Smith, 1950: 24). He recognizes that currency is the means through which commercial activity acts, but abandons the idea that currency protects 'labor value' (Smith, 1950: 24–25).[6] Smith retains the idea of currency as a commodity but clearly links its value as borrowed from an intrinsic value, with precious metals having a superior claim because 'Metals can not only be kept with as little loss as any other commodity, scarce any thing being less perishable than they are, but they can likewise, without any loss, be divided into any number of parts ... ' (Smith, 1950: 25). Smith also acknowledged that metal money comes with certain 'inconveniences', most notably 'the trouble of weighting; and secondly, with that of assaying them' (Smith, 1950: 26), and that there is a distinct possibility of fraud. But here Smith introduces the state as the source of monetary security, suggesting that only the state can guarantee 'purity and weight', and thus guarantee the value of state-backed currency (Smith, 1950: 27). However, Smith's advocacy for state monetary management is not unlimited, and he gives his endorsement only as a practical matter, arguing that state monetary manage-ment is not to be wholly trusted (Smith, 1950).

Smith's approach to value did not translate well into the international market-place, where the value of labour itself varied considerably according to the circumstances of production, but he did recognize the increasing importance of international markets to economics (Smith, 1950). International commerce una-voidably involved international relations between governments, and while Smith laid out a detailed roadmap for state regulation of currency, to preserve trust in its value, he was equally suspicious of government economic regulation (Smith, 1950), and he continued to assume that currency could only function where it was anchored by some more fundamental value, such as gold or silver (Smith, 1950). A product of its time, *The Wealth of Nations* can be read as a manifesto of the middle-class merchant, which while resenting state interference with free trade also embraces state regulation as the only means through which markets can be protected from predatory capitalists.

David Ricardo's approach to currency and value can be viewed as an elabora-tion of Adam Smith, but applied to international markets. Like Smith, he began by applying Locke's labour theory of value to currency, and like Smith he sought to impose a definite and immutable definition of value on what was a dynamic system of market exchange. However, unlike Locke and Smith, Ricardo was a practitioner of economics, who was deeply involved in the day-to-day world of finance. He offered theory to practice because it served his practical interest in understanding how economic systems organized financial transactions and investments. For him, determining what gave currency *value* was a search for

---

[6] Ironically, Smith, the father of modern capitalist theory, exchanges Locke's moral construction of 'labour value' for what would later become Marx's theory of 'surplus value'.

security, and while he accepted the labour theory of value, he strongly supported links between paper currencies and commodities, such as gold and silver, as insurance against government mismanagement of its national currency.

Ricardo thought that the value of a currency could be measured by fixing it to a requisite quantity of labour, which was a gloss on Locke's old labour theory of value. But Ricardo quickly realized that states could alter this value by imposing some form of *seigniorage* or duty on currency, or limit its supply, and thereby frustrate the standard (Sraffa, 1951). Thus, Ricardo recognized what Smith had missed, and that was the ability of the state to manage currency not just for commercial interests, but for the interests of the state. This epiphany alarmed Ricardo, whose experience gave him little confidence in state currency management, and led him to insist that paper currency at all times must be fully convertible to some stable and independently valued commodity, preferably gold or silver (Sraffa, 1951).

Ricardo's ideas about currency did not solve the problem of value, but merely relocated it back to the underlying commodity. While there might be some agreement as to the value of gold or silver, fixing the value of state-issued paper currency to state-held gold and silver stocks allowed states to artificially manipulate the supply of paper money for their own purposes. As a strong market advocate, Ricardo found this unacceptable, particularly where it was viewed as the source of periodic economic crises. The solution he offered was to allow the free exchange of gold and silver and accept that its value would be set by market forces (Sraffa, 1951). This took control from the state and put it in the hands of the market, but it then exposed the value of paper money to considerable uncertainty as an exchange currency, which further complicated its value in international trading.

Whatever its limits, Ricardo's work was the beginning of modern studies in political economy. Where Smith had been preoccupied with national market capitalism, Ricardo represented the interests of international finance capital, setting up the classic tension within economics between markets and politics. As a financial capitalist, Ricardo approached monetary policy as a technical issue that could be addressed by managing currency to create an ever-increasing pool from which value could be drawn. He argued that variables in the value of an international currency would be corrected when international trade became asymmetrical—that is when trade between nations became specialized and particular goods or services produced by one state had no comparative value in another state. What Ricardo assumed was that technological changes that increased the value of labour would only have an effect internally and not externally, and that currency values would adjust according to the value of labour 'saved' by those technologies, something that economist Joseph Stigler would later dub 'the 93% labor theory of value' (Stigler, 1958).

While Ricardo's mathematics and theories are questionable, his arguments advanced the idea that the value of currency was the exclusive and primary territory of private banking. Reviewing the history of state-issued currencies, Ricardo observed that they frequently became the vehicle through which states shifted costs for state activities to the society as a whole. Acknowledging the public benefit that might follow, Ricardo none the less argued against state monetary management because 'it would be disadvantageous to commerce' (Sraffa, 1951: 363). These ideas became deeply embedded in 19th century economics and politics, which itself reflected the consolidation of mercantile capitalism into a global system under the flag of the British Empire. Their power was great enough to survive the enormous economic instability of the late 19th century, the decline of the British Empire, and the First World War. But they faltered as the Great Depression and the rise of Socialism challenged classical economics.

Karl Marx and Critical International Political Economy

A broad reading of Ricardo and his discussion of currency and banks demonstrates the degree to which he was preoccupied with value as a conservative concept—that is as a means though which the full integrity of debtor obligations could be enforced. In modern terms, he would be defined as be a fiscal conservative, prepared to protect the economic and political *status quo* at all costs. His insistence on the convertibility of currency to gold and/or silver, and on a wholly privatized banking system, proved catastrophic to a rapidly growing world marketplace. The critique of Locke, Smith, and Ricardo that changed classical economics into modern, state-supervised systems came from an alternative reading of Locke's labour theory of value and Ricardo's convertible currency by Karl Marx.

In his critique of Ricardo, Marx focuses on two qualities of currency that distinguished it from being a mere medium of exchange. First, he accepts that currency itself is a commodity with its own exchange value, which is determined in accordance with the circumstances of the market under which it is produced (Marx, 1971). Secondly, he distinguishes between metal as a commodity currency and paper currency, and argues that the value of paper currency is dictated not by its comparative labour value, but by the amount of currency in circulation (Marx, 1971). In this critique, Marx establishes that the value of money is a function of politics and not a mechanical result of either Smith's 'hidden hand' of the market, or Ricardo's benign management by finance capital. What Marx recognized is that markets are what they have always been—forums for exchange by willing buyers and sellers. But he adds that paper *currency*, in capitalist markets where competition for profit dictates relationships, becomes politically valued according to the relative political strength of those participating in that market. Here, the value of currency is managed by expanding or restricting its supply according to the interests of those with the ability to control the supply of paper money.

This seemingly simple but subtle observation allowed Marx to make a final argument, that as capitalism develops it requires credit as a means to pay for new investments, which in turn requires an expansion of paper money *as a function of credit* (Marx, 1971). Thus, the use of only paper money marks a stage in capitalist development where a currency's transaction value replaces its labour value and effectively *nationalizes* currency management. Extrapolating from Marx's view of money, it follows that in modern times the value of paper currency in international markets is similarly subject to credit requirements, and its management is *internationalized* to accommodate the needs of global investment capital. In this way, Marx anticipates the development of global state-centered public financial institutions, such as the World Bank and International Monetary Fund, the parallel development of global private financial institutions, such as global investment conglomerates, international banks, and the conterminous organization of global currency speculation and trading markets.

The purpose of this brief review of the historical development of the concept of value as it relates to currency is to underscore the importance of this concept to contemporary international financial and trading markets. With currency measured in the trillions of dollars now daily racing electronically around the globe through the *virtual* marketplace, much depends on the perception of its value. Even relatively small shifts in perception can quickly sink the value of a currency, as many discovered during the global currency meltdowns of the late 1990s. But if we no longer have the value of currencies pegged to commodities, much to the dismay of modern Ricardo enthusiasts and the delight of 'gold bugs', what does secure the value of our dollars, or in other terms, is there something there that is as good as gold in confidently fixing its value?

The Politics of Currency, States and Markets in a Global Economy

Arguments over whether the states control markets or markets dictate state economic policies often overlook the role that currency plays as a medium through which the politics of states and markets act. As the brief history outlined above demonstrates, a pathway has been constructed by currency between states and markets that has a politics of its own. This currency politics elaborated itself further as trade pushed beyond national borders, and now has carved out its own powerful marketplace. Currency, as will be argued here, has become not only the thread that binds together states and global markets, but the very measure of the politics of states and markets as it defines and redefines the issue of value.

Historically, the debate over the politics of states and markets has concerned the relative power of each to define the other. As we have seen, classical economics preferred the market to the state, whereas modern Keynesians have preferred the state to markets. Neo-classical political economists take the argument one step further by reasoning that markets act as forums for choice, and therefore markets act independently in response to the power of private enterprise (Gilpin, 2001). Critical political economists counter that it is the state that makes the market possible by providing political institutions that protect and enable it (Helleiner, 1994), and Marxists and neo-Marxists argue that states and markets are simply products of ideological constructions and interests (*see*, for example, Chase-Dunn 1997; and Cox 1997). But, what all of these debates tend to assume is that states and markets occupy independent political spheres (*see*, for example, Lindblom, 1977).

Debates over the role of currency in the international political economy tend to follow the contours of these larger debates, except that they also grant currency its own sphere of power and confine their analyses to how it is managed in reference to states and markets (*see*, for example, Frieden, 2000; and Cohen, 2000). Limiting the discussion of currency in this way deprives it of its utility in uncovering how wants and needs that are created outside of the marketplace are imported into it and restructure it by redefining value itself. It is here that states and markets also meet in a co-dependent relationship and attempt to secure for themselves the requisite legitimacy that they require for their self-preservation.

Dividing states and markets from one another overlooks their common creation as inseparable parts of the modern system of nation states created by the Peace of Westphalia in 1648 (Kindleberger, 2000). While this system made no direct provision for the management of an international economy, or for a currency to enable it, it created the national boundaries that made possible national currencies. As national economies internationalized, the Westphalian system defined the nature of the problem of currency by drawing the state itself into the process of guaranteeing currency stability at a risk to its national economy.[7] Thus, the structure and operation of the international economy becomes 'nationalized' by the way in which it redistributes value among sovereign states. This can be seen in the current global system of capitalist markets where national wealth, reflected in a growing GDP, is conditioned on access to both critical natural and financial resources. Yet, an economic system that requires growth also requires expanding markets, and where domestic markets have limited potential for growth, national economies must look outward to acquire a greater share of the global market. Thus, when states manage their currency to facilitate access to the global market, they are acting to support the profits of domestic participants in that market.

The principal method through which states act to promote or protect international trade has been through the managed use of currency exchange rates (Frieden, 2000). Classically, if a state wants to encourage exports, it reduces the value of its currency in relation to the currency of other states, and conversely if it wants to protect domestic production it increases the value of its currency. Traditional economic theory says that devaluing currency makes domestic goods less expensive in the international market, and that rational buyers will respond by increasing purchases. Similarly, increasing value makes imports more expensive and less competitive. It is a nice simple little theory, but it rarely works in the way imagined because it falsely represents the market as static and predictable, when in fact markets change in response to shifting valuations of goods, services *and* currencies.

This contradiction in the management of currencies by states for the purpose of protecting domestic markets highlights the persistent problem of how to combat competition among currencies in the global marketplace. Theoretical realists

---

[7] This is readily apparent from the economic choices made by Great Britain in the 19th century, when domestic markets remained opened to competition from the far reaches of the British Empire. (*See* Strange, 1971, 41–43].

argue that the problem can be resolved by the creation of an hegemonic power—a single dominant political entity that can dictate stability (Mundell, 1968).[8] Theoretical institutionalists, on the other hand, argue that states following their self-interest should act collectively to promote trade, which then will produce economic and political stability to the benefit of all (Polanyi, 1944).[9] However, both arguments assume that states have the power to instrumentally manage their economies and bring currency and markets under state control. Neither recognizes that currency and markets are insulated from absolute state control by their co-dependent relationship.

What is 'value for money' in the international marketplace can be resolved by asking, 'How does value determine money?' The thin paper and binary codes that now make up international marketplace currency suggests that mobility and liquidity—the ease with which money can be used—are values against which currency is measured. A currency's value can no longer be fixed against a commodity like gold or silver simply because they limit a currency's mobility and undermine its liquidity by setting limits on the volume and exchange of currency. This is the primary reason that the Nixon Administration buried the dollar-gold link in 1971, and why no modern government has seriously argued for its return. Yet, the international market place also demands some value for currency, simply to ensure that prices are not illusory. What constitutes the value of a currency, then, rests on what market participants believe it to be.

Currencies and Crises in a Global Capitalist Market

The problem of currency value has been the Achilles heel of the global capitalist market system since its inception. Even during the 'hegemonic' rule of the British pound during the 19th century, the global financial system experienced repeated crises induced by shifting perceptions of its value. The dominant economic and political position of the Empire offered a belief in the pound's stability, but as the Empire's powers declined so did confidence in its currency. This pattern repeatedly reappeared throughout the 20th century, and even after the construction of a new hegemonic power by the USA following the Second World War. It seems that the search for currency stability has been both endless and fraught with political and economic dangers.

At its height, Imperial Britain offered its pound as a symbol of its power and as a tool for international market transactions. As confidence in the Empire and its pound grew, non-British banks began to accumulate pounds to hold in 'reserve' to enable them to participate in global market transactions and to act as a guarantor of their own national currency. It is possible to measure the rise and fall of the British Empire through the rise and fall of the pound as a reserve currency held by non-British banks, and to trace the outline of power shifts in international

---

[8] Generally known as 'hegemonic stability theory', this in its essence is the argument of the current neo-conservatives in the USA.

[9] This is the basic underlying thesis upon which the European Union was created.

relations according to the rising tide of currency crises at the end of the 19th and beginning of the 20th century (Polanyi, 1941; Strange, 1971). In response to these crises, banks and economists followed Ricardo's reasoning and began to call for a return to a metal standard for currency.

For a time in the late 19th century, Britain cushioned its decline by shifting from an economy rooted in production and trade to one based on financial management.[10] If it had to increasingly share the global market with the rising industrial powers of Germany, Japan and the USA, it could continue to profit from market transactions that were tied to the pound, even if they didn't directly involve British imports and exports. Britain was able to gracefully maintain its service-based economic power up to the beginning of the First World War, but thereafter the great economic burden imposed by the War and the relative immunity of the USA and Japan from its destructive effects finally sank the pound in the 1920s (Lake, 2000). The pound's collapse, and the inability of the US dollar or the Japanese yen to assume its role as an international reserve currency, plunged international trade into a crisis that significantly contributed to the prolonged economic slump that became the Great Depression.

The 'crisis of global capitalism' that was the Great Depression led directly to two major reforms of the national and international capitalist economies: the abandonment of any attempts to maintain a formal metal standard for currency, and the assumption of control over national economies by states. The tacit maintenance of a gold standard for currency before the Depression was seen as one of the primary factors leading to the collapse of currencies during the crisis (Polanyi, 1941), and with paper currency tied to the value of gold a decline in demand for gold resulted in the disappearance of gold and silver coinage—they represented real value in the minds of traditional economists—and a contraction in the supply of paper money—if the value of gold reserves declined, so did the amount of currency that could be issued against that value. This quickly became a vicious circle, with disappearing gold deflating the value of paper currency, which in turn caused more gold to disappear. Clearly, no trading system could tolerate such circumstances.

The adoption of Keynesian economic theory during the 1930s meant that states would be free to print paper for political purposes, and thus side-step the market 'discipline' that had existed with a metal currency standard, leaving the value of currency wholly within the power of states. When the Allies triumphed in the Second World War, it was also seen as a triumph of Keynesianism, and the Bretton Woods international system of finance and trade that followed the war began with an institutional framework that assumed Keynesian economics, but with the USA as the hegemonic economic power that had replaced the old British one. This included centering the world's trading system on the US dollar as the

---

[10] The British global service economy in this period took the form of providing insurance, shipping and international banking, which had developed with its vigorous colonial rule and persisted primarily because of the residual sense of value that followed its customary use, and because the British ensured that contracting in its colonies continued to be done in pounds (Strange, 1971, 37).

principal international reserve currency. Expectations were that this system would avoid international financial instability through a form of international co-operative management (Eichengreen, 2000).[11] However, as events subsequently demonstrated, 'the fact [is] that the hegemon has been incapable of dictating the form of the monetary system ... [because it] was unable to eliminate the need to compromise with other countries in the design of the monetary system (Eichengreen, 2000: 229).

During the 20 years that it survived, the Bretton Woods system rebuilt the half of the world destroyed by the Second World War. But that very success also heralded its demise, because as that half was rebuilt it ignited a new competition within the international economy. While it reconstructed Europe and Japan, it also flooded the world with dollars that were theoretically supported by the great stores of gold that the USA had accumulated during and after the war. But as the dollars accumulated in foreign banks their actual value sank against gold, which everywhere beyond the USA was openly traded. The tension between the accumulating dollars and accelerating price of gold in dollars finally broke the system, and the USA abandoned Bretton Woods on 15 August 1971, admitting that it could no longer protect the dollar from market speculation (Helleiner, 1994).[12]

The immediate effect of the US withdrawal was to allow the USA to escape from the threatening overhang of dollars in world markets, and to demonstrate that global capital markets had assumed control over the value of currency (Gilpin, 2001). In the short term, the collapse of Bretton Woods had effectively devalued a considerable part of the US foreign debt. But in the longer term it provoked a series of currency crises that pushed the global economy into its worst recession since the Great Depression. Under these conditions, the USA appeared powerless to manage the value of the dollar based on its economic and political hegemony, which also had been in decline even before the collapse of Bretton Woods. Power had shifted away from the Keynesian state and toward the unregulated international marketplace, opening a new era for the global economy that became known as neo-liberalism (Helleiner, 1994).

As state control over the global financial system waned, the USA attempted to adapt by shifting its focus from hegemony over global trade and finance to one that depended more on capturing control over the currency market itself. As had the British Empire in the 19th century, the USA found itself unable to directly compete with the newly emerging industrial powers in Europe and the Far East. And as had the British Empire, the USA moved to recreate itself as a service

---

[11] Hegemonic stability theory, which was popularized by the Bretton Woods, minimized problems of inter-state co-operation by assuming that the 'comparative advantage' that it offered would reduce the incentive to compete. As one economic historian has observed, 'the evidence also underscores the fact that the hegemon has been incapable of dictating the form of the monetary system ... [because it] was unable to eliminate the need to compromise with other countries in the design of the monetary system (Eichengreen, 2000, 229).

[12] The first major crack in the Bretton Woods system appeared when the private capital markets severely discounted the value of the dollar against its official 'fixed' exchange rate.

economy that was increasingly dependent on banking, insurance and transportation. But where Britain had failed to protect the pound, the USA focused its attention on strategies to ensure that the dollar remained as the key international reserve currency. Whether that strategy will work, or whether it will fail, remains to be proved. The 21st century is historically different from the 19th century, in the way that production is organized and in the way that international power is distributed. As the remaining hyper-military power, the USA holds a position that was denied to Britain before it. But as the carbon age dictates new terms for national power, even this advantage may be more illusion than reality.

An Uncertain Future: Oil and Dollars in the Global Carbon Economy

In the brave new world of the global carbon economy, the value of currency is once again measured by a valued commodity—oil. It has been said that modern economies are addicted to oil, and that modern states are enslaved to its politics. But no self-respecting state can claim to be modern without it, and only a few have a secure source that can meet their current and expected needs. Oil and its derivatives, which include pharmaceuticals, fertilizers, plastics and synthetic fibres, are woven throughout modern life, not simply as fuels, but as essential components of modern societies. Thus, unlike gold and silver, oil has the added dimension of defining the system of production itself. This makes oil not just a fetish commodity—something that can be replaced as fashions change—but a key player in determining the vitality of national economies and governments, and in the construction of the value of national currencies.

What makes the future of currency in the carbon age uncertain is that there are no clear guide-lines for theorizing about a global economy that is critically dependent on a single, relatively scarce resource. This has generated considerable discussion and concern over a potential decline in net global production of oil, something that is commonly identified as 'peak oil' (*see*, for example, Roberts, 2004; and Deffeyes, 2005). Some argue that there is a technological 'fix' that can eventually cure the problem, but it remains to be seen how technology will address the variety of ways that petrochemicals have invaded our systems of production. While we all wait for Godot, we should recognize how oil and currency have become intertwined in the global financial system in ways that problematize national politics and international relations.

Technology and the Global Economy: New Rules for the Game

Power may be latent, but it must be used at some point or risk becoming a mere illusion. According to traditional theories of international political economy, the monetary system lies at the heart of the global economy (Spero and Hart, 2003), and state power can be measured by its ability to organize and direct international financial systems (Keohane and Nye, 1997) and control currency exchange rates (Frieden, 2000). The over-riding goal of this organization and management of the monetary system, however, is to ensure the efficient operation of a global marketplace that generates and protects capital. While such organization management might provide a structure for the market, it does not necessarily follow that by itself it can provide the power that states require to govern. This power, generally defined as the ability to affect the behaviour of others (Held, 1989: 62–64), has a much richer texture, and rests with the tools that can be used to influence behaviour (Castells, 1998). In some cases, the very tools used to manage the world's economy can also be the means for subverting the legitimacy of governments (Caufield, 1996).

The last half of the 20th century has witnessed profound technological changes that have greatly enhanced industrial efficiency and transformed transportation and communication systems. These changes, however, have been a two-edged sword for states and markets because while they have increased the reach and profitability of international financial markets, they also have redistributed power from states and international institutions to decentralized webs driven by individual action. In turn, this has redefined the form of currency and the distribution of information about its value. The most obvious source of these changes is telecommunications and the development of powerful computer programmes, which have compressed calculating and decision-making from the days and hours required in the past to the minutes and seconds that dominate the present. Having access to these tools is not merely an advantage, but the difference between being in or out of the marketplace, and the further miniaturization of these systems means that calculations and decisions can be accomplished without a phalanx of institutional support. But this increased access and speed has a dark side in that it distributes power away from centralized control and increases the potential for sudden and uncontrollable shifts in financial markets.[13] Each day, more than US $1,600,000m. in value pass through foreign-exchange markets, with most of it automatically transacted electronically by banks and businesses, and this brave new world is now open for business at your convenience globally, 24 hours a day, 365 days a year. As one writer has observed, 'Everything is in play ... Now, it's fear and greed that count.' (Newman, 1999).

Technology has also created new forms of money, currency and value. It began with credit cards, which eliminated the need to carry actual cash, and extended to the electronic accounting of assets and debits, which let you make your payments 'automatically' and almost unconsciously. Other 'paperless' currencies on the horizon may eliminate the need even for these.[14] These are sold as efficiencies that reduce the time and cost involved in conducting transactions. But they also change the appearance and reliability of the information that is processed, and the

---

[13] For example, the 1997–98 currency crisis that swept global financial markets and devastated numerous emerging economies was triggered by an earthquake in Japan, unsupervised currency trading by a 28-year-old derivates trader at a 233-year-old British bank, and the advent of computerized trading. When the dust settled, the bank had lost £1,300m. and was bankrupt, and the global financial markets had survived their worst crisis since the early 1930s ([bbc.co.uk, 2005; and Schwartz, 2001).

[14] Computer-to-computer transactions are now commonplace, including online transportation ticketing, online banking, cross-linked electronic data collection, virtual libraries and accounting, tax payments and the software management of personal finances.

sense of economics that is involved. As Catherine Caufield reminds us, these illusions mask harsh realities about the ruthless world of markets and finance that produce real world consequences (Caufield, 1996). This is particularly a problem for the notions of value and currency that lie at the heart of all modern economies, because as they become ever more abstracted from daily experience they generate and sustain a fog of data that obscures rather than clarifies the movements underneath. This give special meaning to the 'information age' as a time when the quality not just the quantity of knowledge dictates relationships of power (Thussu, 2001). Critical questions, such as the actual extent of oil reserves, are subject to manipulation by self-interested oil executives,[15] as are data generated by public and private financial institutions (Frank, 2001).

Beyond the Bipolar World: Unipolarity or Post-structural Politics?

The dismemberment of the Soviet Union introduced a unipolar configuration into the global financial system that has been difficult to digest. The old system had been built, at least in part, to reflect a bipolar world, with the USA supervising the global system of capital through Bretton Woods and the Soviet Union managing a system of state-to-state trading based on COMECON, the economic organization of Socialist states. While they appeared to be in conflict, they more often than not served to moderate the internal contradiction inherent in both systems by creating opportunities for each to balance the internal dynamics by trading between them.[16] When the Soviet Union collapsed, this opportunity for balance was lost. The years that immediately followed left the capitalist system exposed to its own contradictions, which quickly generated a series of monetary and financial crises that Paul Erdman described as a 'tug of war' between speculators that remains as a spectre haunting international currency markets (Erdman, 1997). The problem that these currency crises exposed was that states no longer had exclusive control over credit, knowledge, or the system of production (Strange, 1994).

The USA and its capitalist allies had initially gained by the deconstruction of the former socialist world because it created a huge demand for capital to reconstruct it. As demand for capital increased, it increased the demand for dollars, which through US efforts had remained as the essential global reserve currency. This greatly expanded the volume of dollars, creating an enormous pool that began to slosh around in national banks and treasuries. As had happened in the past following the oil price boom of the 1970s, US-based financial and trading institutions enjoyed a jump in profits even as the waves of currency began to destabilize global finance and trade, leading to sequenced national currency crises

---

[15] As some analysts allow, in spite of the official statements about oil reserves no one really knows because the data from key sites, such as Saudi Arabia, Russia, Iran and Libya, are regarded as national secrets (Duncan and Youngquist, 1998).

[16] As Charles Lindblom noted in 2001, 'Market ideologies have learned that there is little to fear from communism. They can come away from their ideological barricades and talk sense about the market and its problems. On their side, socialist ideologues have realized that aspiring for a better society is not enough. They have to face the complexities of constructing one.' (Lindblom, 2001, 3).

in the late 1990s. The psychological effect was to puncture the illusion of a promised global economic stability and US dollar hegemony, which was replaced by a recognition that the international political economy increasingly was less a system of institutions, and more an arrangement of symbols and ideas.[17]

'Peak Oil': A New Standard of 'Value' in a World of Carbon Economics

Diamonds and coal are both nearly pure carbon but their relative value varies according to our sense of need. In times of plenty, when essential physical needs are easily met, diamonds easily command a premium price because of their extraordinary durability, manufactured scarcity,[18] and aesthetics that have long made them desirable. Their value, however, declines rapidly in times of scarcity, when essential needs, such as heat, are difficult to meet. In these cases, fuels such as coal enjoy a relative higher value than diamonds, because you can burn coal but not diamonds. Thus, modern industrial societies place a premium price on oil—not just for use value, but for the perception that it is indispensable.

In the 19th century, the absolute volume of international trade was minuscule compared to that of the 21st century. Systems of production were similarly inefficient, and the range of products and services limited. Trading required considerably less transportation by volume, and was conducted mostly through massive trading cartels, such as the East India Company, the Dutch East India Company, and the Hudson Bay Company, that operated in colonial systems that were largely immune from market competition. In contrast, production and trade in the 21st century is both huge and energy-intensive, requiring vast amounts of petroleum with ever-increasing rates of production. In fact, current world demand for petroleum exceeds 75m. b/d, up from 63m. b/d in 1980, and growing at the rate of 1%–2% per year (US Energy Information Administration, 2003).[19] It has been estimated that world petroleum demand will grow to some 100m.–125m. b/d by 2025, with the majority of production coming from a handful of countries in the Middle East and the area around the Caspian Sea (US Energy Information Administration, 2004). The price of a barrel of oil in US dollars has grown tenfold in the last 30 years, from US $4.80 in 1973 to near and above US $50 in 2005 (US Energy Information Administration, 2005). These statistics represent the basis for the current debate that at some point demand for oil will exceed available supply.

The economics of oil are rather dense: oil is not simply oil, but grades of oil, some of which are easily accessible and cheap to extract, and other that are difficult to access and expensive to bring to the market. Light, sweet crude is the most desirable grade because it is the most easily refined, and this demand puts a

---

[17] As one postmodern political economist notes, 'In modern capitalist societies, money or species payments are instruments through which both subjectivities and places are dissolved rather than reinforced or formed.' (Shapiro, 1997, 318).

[18] DeBeers, the durable Dutch diamond cartel, has been able to retain its control of at least 70% of the world's diamond trade by hoarding diamond stocks and by cajoling and threatening world diamond producers to limit production.

[19] There are 55 gallons of crude oil per barrel.

premium on its price and a focus on its primary source, the Niger Delta in West Africa. Other grades of oil are thicker and more difficult and expensive to refine, with 'tar sands' sinking to the bottom of the list. 'Cheap' is also a relative term, as the price of accessing, drilling, pumping, transporting, marketing and refining oil includes political as well as technical factors. The oil of the Middle East has been historically cheap to drill, transport, market and refine, but the cost of accessing it now appears to include the price of a hostile Arab population. Oil production also comes with an environmental cost, and areas that are sensitive to environmental politics, such as the Arctic National Wildlife Refuge (ANWR), generally imply an added cost, if not in dollars then in political capital. The current market price for a 42-gallon barrel of crude oil thus varies according to these various factors, and with perceptions about its future availability.[20]

This makes the debate over 'peak oil' very political, and to the extent that it is believed, it raises expectations that in the long term oil prices will continue to rise in terms of absolute cost.[21] Those who argue that the peak is near foresee fundamental, if not catastrophic, changes in the world's political economy that will push human civilization back to 'Olduvai Gorge' (Duncan, 2000). However, even those who argue that the peak is somewhere in the future recognize that it will appear at some time, and most probably in the next 20–40 years (Wood, Long and Morehouse, 2004). However, the realities of 'peak oil' are less important than the perceptions it injects into the global capitalist market economy, because changes in information technology have transformed the global energy market from a simple supply and demand relationship to one based on speculation about supply and demand.[22] Here, predictions matter and major market participants respond to events, such as political instability and interruptions in supply, by dramatically discounting the value of the dollar against the value of oil (Porter, 2005), particularly when, as now, OPEC claims to have lost control over oil markets (Schoen, 2005).

What the debate over peak oil points to is the reality that national economies are hostage to oil, and that oil has become the new commodity measurement of value.[23] In these conditions, the ability of a state to 'hold' oil in reserve, by either actually possessing it or securing access to it, reflects the history of modern finance that conditioned the value of a national currency on the ability of a state to acquire and hoard gold and silver. It also resonates with the more contemporary view that a national economy, rather than metal reserves, is the ultimate guarantor of a nation's currency. But in both cases, it is oil that sets the value of currency.

---

[20] For example, the recent 'revaluation' of oil reserves by Shell Oil, one of the major oil companies, caused a flurry of oil price increases based on a shift in perception about total world oil reserves.

[21] Here, 'absolute cost' refers to the price discounted for currency changes.

[22] A revolution in oil marketing has been under way since the first phase of energy deregulation in 1978. In the current market, oil is sold not at a fixed price, but at a price set by energy 'futures and options' (US Energy Information Administration, 2005).

[23] This assumes that modern currency provides a secure value for transactions, rather than merely a convertible value.

Classic economics says that 'bad money drives out good': or that in a contest between unsecured paper currency and a commodity-based currency, the more valued commodity-based currency will be hoarded and tend to disappear. In times of currency crises, markets react to a declining currency value by exchanging it for something that is presumed to offer a more secure value, which can be another currency or some money instrument, a commodity, or land. When the US dollar was disconnected from gold in 1971, the value of gold rapidly increased, from US \$35 per ounce before the announcement to more than US \$800 per ounce eight years later in early 1979. It might be said that this was an example of speculators trading 'bad' US dollars for 'good' gold, a circumstance that fed on itself until speculators exhausted their reserves of dollars. For non-speculators, the consequence of this twentyfold increase in the dollar price of gold produced a period of hyperinflation, which in the USA reached 20% in the late 1970s. Although at present there is no formal relationship between the US dollar and oil, there is an informal one that has served to protect the value of the dollar and cushion oil price increases for the USA—the pricing of oil in dollars that creates an artificial demand for them.

As Good as Gold: Oil and the Value of Currency

An increasing number of political economists argue that an overall decline in state power is fundamentally changing the way in which the global economy functions (Strange, 1996; and Goodman and Pauly, 2000). Within this group, some argue that this decline is linked to economic competition between states (Cox, 1997), others argue that it reflects fundamental changes in the way that production and the markets are organized (Cerny, 2000), and some simply express an undifferentiated anxiety about it (Gilpin, 2001). The response of most mainstream political economists is that these changes merely represent a reorganization of the global market place which requires a corresponding redefinition of state management through the exercise of 'soft power', or the socio-political management of markets (Nye, 2004). But all seem to agree that the global political economy is experiencing considerable stress at the beginning of the 21st century, particularly with regard to global finance.

The arguments presented by mainstream political economists here are both old, in that they represent long-term conditions and trends dating back to the 19th century if not earlier, and new in that they anticipate new and fundamental shifts in the structure of production and finance in the global economy. At the centre of these changes is oil and the new carbon era, which is creating a new way of calculating financial value, not in terms of the human labour that classical economists saw as the ultimate measure of currency, but in terms of the mechanical energy that now drives modern systems of production. This 'energy theory of value' looks to energy as the fundamental source of personal and national wealth, and recognizes the central role that oil plays in greasing the wheels of modern production. In saying that, it argues that with oil as the valuing agent, a link has been formed between it and the dollar, and that this link is essential to the value of the dollar. As Ron Cooke recently argued, the effect of rising oil prices, which under a peak oil scenario will continue to rise and accelerate in real terms, will be to force the value of the dollar down, the rate of inflation up, and US foreign policy out in search of access to a secure supply of 'cheap oil' (Cooke, 2005).

Bibliography

bbc.co.uk. (2005) *Nick Leeson and Barings Bank*: http://www.bbc.co.uk/print/crime/caseclosed/nicklesson.shtml

Billingsley, Tara. Non-OPEC Fact Sheet. US Department of Energy, 2001: http://www.nigc/eia/nonopec.asp

Caravale, Giovanni A., and Tosato, Domenico A. *Ricardo and the Theory of Value,* London, Routledge and Kegan Paul, 1980.

Distribution and Growth. London, Routledge and Kegan Paul, 1980.

Castells, Manuel. *End of Millennium, Vol. III*. Malden, MA, Blackwell Publishers, 1998.

Caufield, Catherine. *Masters of Illusion*. New York, Henry Holt and Company, 1996.

Cerny, Philip G. 'Globalization and the Changing Logic of Collective Action', in Frieden, Jeffry A., and Lake, David A. (Eds), *International Political Economy*, 4th Edn, Boston, Bedford/St Martins, 2000, pp. 446–460.

Chase-Dunn. 'Interstate System and Capitalist World-Economy: One Logic or Two?', in Crane, George T., and Amawi, Abla (Eds) *The Theoretical Evolution of International Political Economy*, 2nd Edn, Oxford, Oxford University Press, 1997, pp. 144–157.

Cohen, Benjamin J. 'The Triad and the Unholy Trinity: Problems of International Monetary Cooperation', in Frieden, Jeffry A., and Lake, David A. (Eds), *International Political Economy*, 4th Edn, Boston, Bedford/St Martins, 2000, pp. 245–256.

Cooke, Ronald R. 'Will Higher Oil Prices Fuel Inflation?', published by *Future-Reality.Org*, 2005: http://www.energybulletin.net/5330.html

Cox, Robert. 'Global *Perestroika*' in Crane, George T., and Amawi, Abla (Eds), *The Theoretical Evolution of International Political Economy*, 2nd Edn, Oxford, Oxford University Press, 1997, pp. 158–172.

Deffeyes, Kenneth S. *Beyond Oil: the View from Hubbert's Peak*. New York, Hill and Wang, 2005.

Duncan, Richard C. *The Peak of World Oil Production and the Road to the Olduvai Gorge*. Seattle, Institute on Energy and Man, 2000.

Duncan, Richard C., and Youngquist, Walter. *The World Petroleum Life-Cycle*. Seattle, WA, Institute on Energy and Man, 1998.

Eichengreen, Barry. 'Hegemonic Stability Theories of the International Monetary System', in Frieden, Jeffry A., and Lake, David A. (Eds), *International Political Economy*, 4th Edn, Boston, Bedford/St Martins, 2000, pp. 220–244.

Energy Information Administration. *Monthly Energy Review*. Washington, DC, US Department of Energy, 2005.

Erdman, Paul. *Tug of War*. New York, St Martin's Griffin, 1996.

Esser, Charles. Non-OPEC Fact Sheet. US Department of Energy, 2004: http://www.eia.doe.gov/emeu/cabs/nonopec.html

Frank, Thomas. 'When Markets Rule Politics', in the *Financial Times* of London, 2001: http://www.commondreams.org/cgi-bin/print.cgi?file=/views01/0407-04.htm

Franklin, Benjamin. 'A Modest Inquiry into the Nature and Necessity of a Paper Currency', in *The Works of Benjamin Franklin*, Vol. II, Boston, Hillard, Gray and Company (1836).

Frieden, Jeffry. 'Exchange Rate Politics', in Frieden, Jeffry A., and Lake, David A. (Eds), *International Political Economy*, 4th Edn, Boston, Bedford/St Martins, 2000, pp. 257–269.

Friedman, Milton. *Market or plan? An exposition of the case for the market*. London, London Centre for Research into Communist Economies, 1984.

Gilpin, Robert. *Global Political Economy*. Princeton, NJ, Princeton University Press, 2001.

Glantz, Michael H., and Krenz, Jerrod H. 'Human components of the climate system', in Trenberth, Kevin E. (Ed.), *Climate System Modeling*, 1992, pp. 27–49.

Goodman, John B., and Pauly, Louis W., 'The Obsolescence of Capital Controls? Economic Management in an Age of Global Markets', in Frieden, Jeffry A., and Lake, David A. (Eds), *International Political Economy*, 4th Edn, Boston, Bedford/St Martins, 2000, pp. 280–297.

Gourevitch, Peter A. 'International Trade, Domestic Coalitions, and Liberty: Comparative Responses to the Crisis of 1873–1896', in Frieden, Jeffry A., and Lake, David A. (Eds), *International Political Economy*, 4th Edn, Boston, Bedford/St Martins, 2000, pp. 90–108.

Greenberg, Dolores. 'Energy, Power, and Perceptions of Social Change in the Early Nineteenth Century', in *American Historical Review*, Vol. 95, No. 3, 2000, pp. 693–715.

Greenfield, Liah. *The Spirit of Capitalism*. Cambridge, MA, Harvard University Press, 2001.

Held, David. *Political Theory and the Modern State*. Palo Alto, CA, Stanford University Press, 1989.

Helleiner, Eric. *States and the Reemergence of Global Finance*. Ithica, Cornell University Press, 1994. *The Making of National Money*. Ithica, Cornell University Press, 2003.

Henning, C. Randall. *Currencies and Politics in the United States, Germany, and Japan*. Washington, DC, Institute for International Economics, 1994.

Higgins, Matthew, and Klitgaard, Tomas. 'Reserve Accumulation: Implications for Global Capital Flows and Financial Markets', in *Current Issues in Economics and Finance*, Vol. 10, No. 10, 2004, pp. 1–9.

Hollander, Samuel. *The Economics of John Stuart Mill, Volume II Political Economy*. Toronto, University of Toronto Press, 1985.

Keohane, Robert O. *International Institutions and State Power: Essays in International Relations Theory*. Boulder, CO, Westview Press, 1989.

Keohane, Robert O., and Nye, Joseph S. 'Interdependence and World Politics', in Crane, George T., and Amawi, Abla, *The Theoretical Evolution of International Political Economy*, Oxford, Oxford University Press, 1997 pp. 122–132.

Kindleberger, Charles P. 'The Rise of Free Trade in Western Europe', in Frieden, Jeffry A., and Lake, David A. (Eds), *International Political Economy*, 4th Edn, Boston, Bedford/St Martins, 2000, pp. 73–89.

Krasner, Stephen D. 'State Power and the Structure of International Trade', in Frieden, Jeffry A., and Lake, David A. (Eds), *International Political Economy*, 4th Edn, Boston, Bedford/St Martins, 2000, pp. 19–36.

Lake, David A. 'British and American Hegemony Compared: Lessons for the Current Era of Decline', in Frieden, Jeffry A., and Lake, David A. (Eds), *International Political Economy*, 4th Edn, Boston, Bedford/St Martins, 2000, pp. 127–139.

Lindblom, Charles E. *Politics and Markets*. New York, Basic Books, Inc, 1977. *The Market System*. New Haven, Yale University Press, 2001.

Locke, John. *Two Treatises of Government*, Revised Edn, Cambridge, Cambridge University Press, 1963.

Mandel, Ernest. *The Formation of the Economic Thought of Karl Marx*. London, Monthly Review Press, 1971.

Marx, Karl. (1971) *A Contribution to the Critique of Political Economy*. London: Lawrence & Wishart, 1971.

Marx, Karl (Ben Fowkes, trans.). *Capital : A Critique of Political Economy, Vol. 1*. New York, Penguin Classics, 1992.

Mundell, Robert. *International Economics*. New York, Macmillan, 1968.

Newman, Peter C. 'Fear and Greed Rule in the Age of E-Cash', in *Maclean's*, Vol. 112, No. 14, 1999.

Nye, Joseph S., Jr. *Soft Power*. New York, Public Affairs, 2004.

Organization of Petroleum Exporting Countries. *The Petroleum Industry*. 2005: http://www.opec.library/FAQ/Petrol Industry.htm

Perkins, John. *Confessions of an Economic Hit Man*. San Francisco, Berrett Koehler, 2004.

Polanyi, Karl. *The Great Transformation*. Boston, Beacon Press, 2001.

Porter, Adam. 'Superspike report raises questions', in *Al Jazeera.net*, 2 April 2005.

Roberts, Paul. *The End of Oil*. Boston, Houghton Mifflin Company, 2004.

Schoen, John W. 'OPEC says it has lost control of oil prices', in *MSNBC*, 3/16/ 2005: http://msnbc.msn.com/id/7190109

Schwartz, Herman M. 'The East is in the Red: From Economic Miracle to Economic Crisis In East and Southeast Asia', in *New Zealand Journal of Asian Studies*, Vol. 3, No. 2, 2001, pp. 198–205.

Schwartz, Pedro. *The Euro as Politics*. London, The Institute of Economic Affairs, 2004.

Sen, Amartya. *Poverty and Famines: An Essay on Entitlement and Deprivation.* Oxford, Oxford University Press, 1984.

Shapiro, Michael J. 'Sovereignty and Exchange in the Orders of Modernity', in Crane, George T., and Amawi, Abla (Eds), *The Theoretical Evolution of International Political Economy*, 2nd Edn, Oxford, Oxford University Press, 1997, pp. 309–325.

Shubik, Martin. *The Theory of Money and Financial Institutions, Vols I & II.* Cambridge, MA, The MIT Press, 1999.

Singer, Hans W., and Ansari, Javeda A. *Rich and Poor Countries*, 4th Edn, London, Unwin Hyman, 1988.

Smith, Adam (Edwin Cannan, Ed.). *An Inquiry into the Nature and Causes of the Wealth of Nations*. London, Methuen and Co. Ltd, 1950.

Spero, Joan E., and Hart, Jeffrey A. *The Politics of International Economic Relations*, 6th Edn, Belmont, CA, Wadsworth/Thomson, 2003.

Sraffa, Piero (Ed.). *The Works and Correspondence of David Ricardo.* Cambridge, Cambridge University Press, 1951.

Sreenivasan, Gopal. *The Limits of Lockean Rights in Property.* New York, Oxford University Press, 1995.

Stigler, George J. 'Ricardo and the 93 Per Cent Labor Theory of Value', in *American Economic Review*, Vol. 76, 1958.

Strange, Susan. *Sterling and British Policy*. London, Oxford University Press, 1971.

States and Markets. London, Pinter, 1994.

The Retreat of the State: the Diffusion of Power in the World Economy. Cambridge, Cambridge University Press, 1996.

Thussu, Daya Kishan. *International Communication: Continuity and Change.* London, Arnold Publishers, 2001.

United State Energy Information Administration. *World Petroleum Consumption (Btu), 1980–Present.* Washington, DC, US Department of Energy, 2003.

United States Energy Information Administration. *International Energy Outlook.* Washington, DC, US Department of Energy, 2004.

United States Energy Information Administration. *Future and Options Markets Changed Energy Marketing.* Washington, DC, US Department of Energy, 2005: http://www.eia.doe.gov/emeu/25opec/sld017.htm

Wood, John H., Long, Gary R., and Morehouse, David F. 'Long-Term World Oil Supply Scenarios'. Energy Information Agency Bulletin, Washington, DC, US Department of Energy, 2004.

'Oil could spike to $105, Goldman Sachs says' in *Reuters*, 3.31.2005: http://moneycentral.msn.com/content/invest/extra/P113712.asp

'2 Big Appetites Take Seats at the Oil Table', in *The New York Times*, 2/18/2005, Vol. 154, No. 53129.

'Gold Standard' in *Wikipedia*, 2005: http://en.wikipedia.org/wiki/Gold_standard

Geopolitics of Oil and Pipelines in the (Eurasian) Heartland[1]

EMRE ISERI

Introduction

The main assumption of this essay is that geopolitics (the geographical distribution of political and military power) still matters, contrary to arguments that offer geo-economics (the geographical distribution of wealth) as the only game left in town. Geopolitics is one of the most important elements that influence a state's foreign policy behaviour. For instance, the presence of natural frontiers, as in the case of the USA, an insular power, may overwhelmingly affect policy-makers' foreign policy choices. Hence, it is supposed that classical geopolitical theory of the Heartland could give us an insight into the present strategic rivalry in the region. Moreover, it is held that oil and pipelines have been playing major roles in these strategic rivalries. Thus, political control of oil-rich territories and their transportation routes through pipelines are considered as strategic assets. Simply, this study addresses the issue of the geopolitical dimensions of oil and pipelines in the present strategic rivalries in the Heartland.

Central Asia or the Heartland, to use Sir Halford Mackinder's term, has long been the playground for geopolitical rivalries. This region's strategic location and proximity to great powers on the Eurasian landmass have been the main factors that foster these rivalries. Apart from its strategic location, wide, rich oil resources in the Caspian Sea basin part of the Heartland have also cultivated these strategic contentions to a great extent. During the First and Second World Wars, oil played a major strategic role. Until the dissolution of the Union of Soviet Socialist Republics (USSR) in 1991, this region had been closed to external interference. Since that time, the huge oil resources of the region have opened to external powers' influence. Thus, the oil factor has stimulated strategic rivalries in the Heartland once again in the post-Cold War period.

The USA, major European powers, Russia, Japan, and China, together with transnational corporations, have been in quest of alliances, concessions, and possible pipeline routes in the region. Iran, which is considered to be a member of the 'axis of evil' by US foreign policy-makers, is also a major power in the region. It should be noted that the US interest in the region is mainly political, rather than economic. The USA has been importing its energy needs mainly from the Persian (Arabian) Gulf region, which is under its auspices to a great extent, particularly in the aftermath of the war in Iraq in 2003.

[1] The author would like to thank Dr Drosily Hamourtziadou for her edits and comments on the draft.

In order to understand its interest in the Heartland, the USA's grand strategy in the post-Cold War period should be acknowledged. Throughout the Cold War, the USA had controlled Western capitalist countries through a protectorate system. Through that system, those countries were dependent on the protectorate system of the USA to a great extent, both politically and economically. With the end of the Cold War, Western countries' dependency on the protectorate system of the USA has declined. Therefore, those countries' potential to form regional alliances with Russia and rising China, thus restricting global US hegemony, has emerged. Clearly, such alliances would undermine US leadership in the post-Cold War period. Thus, the US protectorate system of the Cold War days should be restructured in order to sustain Western countries' dependency in the post-Cold War order. Moreover, states that have challenged US leadership, such as Iran, should be isolated. Hence, it has become evident that the USA must enhance its sphere of influence in the land-locked Heartland. Again, as an insular power, this time it is the USA which must prevent consolidation of power in the Heartland.

In the early 20th century, Sir Halford Mackinder maintained that control of the Heartland could lead to a global empire. If well served by industry and modern means of communication, a land power controlling the Heartland could exploit the region's natural resources. Therefore, it would overcome the insular sea powers. Today, overland transport increasingly connects economies and energy supplies within the region. Thus, it is argued that the insular sea power of the USA fulfilled the requirement of preventing major land powers—Russia, China, the European Union (EU) and Iran—from unifying their economies and energy supplies. This is vital for US policy-makers' restructuring of the protectorate system of the Cold War period to fit post-Cold War realities.

In this context, oil is not merely a commodity traded on international markets. Control over oil-rich territories and their transportation routes is a strategic asset. The Caspian Sea basin, with its huge reserves of oil, its land-locked location and strategic position, emerges as a key arena for a future strategic rivalry. As each power has its own preferences regarding how the oil should be transported, there arises the question of pipeline routes. What is at stake is not only oil revenues, but also, and more importantly, securing and maintaining influence in the Eurasian Heartland, whereby the pipeline network is one of the key geopolitical assets.

The Baku-Tbilisi-Ceyhan (BTC) pipeline project is a product of these geopolitical calculations of US policy-makers. The USA has given its full support to the actualization of the BTC oil pipeline project, despite its low feasibility and the lobbying activities of oil companies favouring a possible Iranian route. BTC, together with its sister, the Baku-Tbilisi-Erzurum (BTE) gas pipeline project, would not only serve to diversify land-locked energy resources in the region and isolate the 'axis-of-evil' country Iran, but would also lessen the dependency of the EU on Russia and Iran. Moreover, pipeline routes other than Russian routes would diminish the newly independent countries' dependency on Russia. It should be noted that pipeline construction provides several economic and political benefits, such as transit fees, access to oil, and political leverage over the flow of oil. Therefore, it would be plausible to argue that pipeline routes determine which countries' dependency on Russia would decrease and which countries' dependency on the US protectorate system would increase. This is simply the case for newly independent Azerbaijan and Georgia. Moreover, BTC would also bolster NATO ally Turkey's economy and serve as a plus on its accession process to the EU. In the light of these arguments, it would be plausible to contend that BTC would underpin US political influence in the Caspian part of the Heartland.

Eurasian Heartland

Heartland Theory is probably the most well-known geopolitical model that stresses the ascendancy of land-based power over sea-based power. Sir Halford Mackinder, who was one of the most prominent geographers of his era, first articulated this theory as '*The Geographic Pivot of History*' in 1904 and later, in 1919, redefined it in a paper entitled *Democratic Ideals and Reality*, in which pivotal area became the Heartland. According to Mackinder, the pivotal area, or the Heartland, is Central Asia, from where horsemen dominated Asia and Europe.

While developing his ideas, Mackinder's main concern was to warn the declining sea-based power of Great Britain, which had been the dominant power since the age of maritime discoveries in the 15th century, about the possibility of a land-based power that could control the Eurasian landmass between Germany and central Siberia and lead to world hegemony. If well served by industry and modern means of communication, a land power controlling the Heartland could exploit the region's rich natural resources. 'Mackinder suggested that either a Russo-German alliance or a Sino-Japanese empire (which conquered Russian territory) could contend for world hegemony. In either case, oceanic frontage would be added to the resources of the great continent, thereby creating the geopolitical conditions necessary for producing a great power that was supreme both on land and at sea.'[2]

During this time, Tsarist Russia, as the geographic pivot of the Eurasian Heartland, was on the verge of completing the Trans-Siberia railroad. Mackinder, who perceived world history through the prism of a struggle between sea man and land man, claimed that centrally positioned land man, Tsarist Russia, gained the upper hand in the Eurasian Heartland. Mackinder assumed that the railroad would significantly increase the mobility of a centrally positioned land power by using interior lines in Eurasia. Thus, the land power would project its power more rapidly to the Eurasian island (East Europe), whereby it would gain the capability of controlling the global agenda. He expressed his ideas in these words: 'Who rules East Europe commands the Heartland: Who rules the Heartland commands the World-Island (Europe, Arab Peninsula, Africa, South and East Asia), Who rules the World-Island commands the World.'[3]

---

[2] Francis P. Sempa, *Geopolitics: From the Cold War to the 21ˢᵗ Century*, Transaction Publishers: New Brunswick, 2002, p. 12.

[3] Halford Mackinder, *Democratic Ideals and Reality*, Constable and Company: London, 1919, p. 113.

Following Tsarist Russia's collapse in 1917, as a result of the Russian Revolution, Mackinder warned Great Britain about the possible threat of Bolshevik alliances with democracies and backed anti-Bolshevik strategy. According to Mackinder, the West should have fostered the independence of Central European countries, such as Ukraine, together with Armenia, Azerbaijan and Georgia, in order to prevent the Bolsheviks from consolidating their power in the Eurasian Heartland.

'During the 1920s and 1930s, unfortunately, Mackinder's ideas had little influence in Britain or the United States. That was not the case, however, in Germany where Mackinder's global view attracted the attention and praise of Karl Haushofer and his associates at Munich's Institute of Geopolitics.'[4] Although it is dubious to what extent Haushofer's ideas influenced Hitler's global strategy, 'the Nazi-Soviet Pact of August 1939, the beginning of the Second World War and Germany's subsequent invasion of the Soviet Union drew attention in the United States to Mackinder's work'.[5] The Heartland Theory provided the intellectual ground for the US Cold War foreign policy. Nicholas Spykman was among the most influential American political scientists in the 1940s. Spykman's Rimlands thesis was developed on the basis of Mackinder's Heartland concept. In contrast to Mackinder's emphasis on the Eurasian Heartland, Spykman offered the Rimlands of Eurasia—that is, Western Europe, the Pacific Rim and the Middle East. According to him, whoever controlled these regions would contain any emerging Heartland power. 'Spykman was not author of containment policy, that is credited to George Kennan, but Spykman's book, based on the Heartland thesis, helped prepare the US public for a post-war world in which the Soviet Union would be restrained on the flanks.'[6] Therefore, Mackinder's ideas had provided certain guide-lines for US policy-makers during the Cold War period.

'From a geopolitical perspective the twentieth century with the First and Second World Wars, and the Cold War, was a struggle to prevent Mackinder's prediction coming true.'[7] The imprint of Mackinder on US foreign policy has also continued in the aftermath of the demise of the geopolitical pivot, the USSR. 'Mackinder's ideas influenced the post-Cold War thesis – developed by prominent American political scientist Zbigniew Brzezinski – which called for the maintenance of "geopolitical pluralism" in the post-Soviet space. This concept has served as the corner-stone of both the Clinton and Bush administration's policies towards the newly independent states of Central Eurasia.'[8]

---

[4] Sempa, p. 17.

[5] Ibid., p.18.

[6] Brian W. Blouet, 'Halford Mackinder and the Pivotal Heartland', in Brian W. Blouet (Ed.), *Global Geostrategy: Mackinder and the defence of the West*, Frank Cass Publishers: London, 2005, p. 6.

[7] James Kurth, 'The Decline and Fall of Almost Everything', *Foreign Affairs*, Vol. 72: 2, 1993, p. 159.

[8] Igor Torbakov, 'Reexamining Old Concepts About The Caucasus and Central Asia', 02.04.2004 in http://www.eurasianet.org/departments/insight/articles/eav020404a.shtml, retrieved on 28.02.2006.

US Grand Strategy

Throughout the Cold War, the USA had controlled Western countries through a protectorate system. Through that system, these countries were dependent on the protectorate system of the USA, both politically and economically. In the realities of Cold War days, the reason for their dependency was simple: the USSR and communism. Their liberal democratic way of life, based on market economies, had led Western countries to become dependent on that system. Although it was regarded as a multilateral system on the basis of international organizations, such as NATO, it was mainly based on US unilateral power.

> 'In the official ideology of the protectorate system, that system was a means to the end of containing the Soviet threat. But objectively means and ends could be viewed also in reverse direction. The containment of the Soviet Union could thus also be the means to the end of maintaining US political dominance over the rest of the capitals core.'[9]

This protectorate system evidently became crucial in the 1970s and early 1980s. During that time period, the influence of the US economy on other capitalist countries was in decline mainly because of the costs of the Viet Nam War, the subsequent oil crisis and the increased competitiveness of Japan and Europe. 'The Reagan administration sought to use its power over the protectorate system to restructure socio-economic relations in favour of American capitalism.'[10] However, the fall of the USSR left this restructuring undertaken by the Reagan Administration unfinished in Western Europe, mainly because its dependency on the protectorate system of the USA diminished. Western Europe established the EU as a regional block and enlarged it towards the East by including former socialist Central and Eastern European Countries (CEECs). More importantly, Europeans created their own currency, the euro, as an alternative to the dollar in international markets in 2002. This currency has the potential to diminish the dominance of the dollar as the world's reserve currency. As discussed below, sustaining the denomination of petroleum trade in dollars rather than euros is playing a vital role for US policy-makers.

During this time, Russia has also been turning to the market economic system, like other former socialist states, while looking for ways to reinforce relations with the EU. From the perspective of Washington, a primary Russian-European linkage on the basis of energy supplies away from the US protectorate system should be avoided. On the other hand, in East Asia, Japan and South Korea's dependency on the US protectorate system remained strong because of the rise of China and rogue state North Korea (Democratic People's Republic of Korea). In the long term, however, even there there existed the possibility of a break in that protectorate system. China's turn to the capitalist market economy made it an attractive field for capital that could foster its military build-up and redouble its

---

[9] Peter Gowan, 'The New American Century?', in Ken Coates (Ed.), *The Spokesman: The New American Century*, Spokesman Publisher: Nottingham, 2002, p. 10.

[10] Ibid., p. 10.

military threat. A deepened Sino-Russian regional formation could also be expected in the future. 'The nightmare scenario for conservative analysts in Washington is a Sino-Russian alliance aimed at undermining American interests in the region.'[11] The Shanghai Co-operation Organization (SCO) and its military operations had traces of this possibility. It should also be noted that Iran was to become a member of this organization in the summer of 2006. 'Although Russia is a charter member of the SCO and has supported its expansion, China has been the driving force ... and while the role is formally defined in political and economic terms, it may soon add a military dimension.'[12] China, Russia and also forthcoming SCO member Iran have been sceptical about US interference in the region with war-on-terror rhetoric. They perceive US dominance in their respective regions as constraining and even deleterious to their own strategic ambitions. Rather than being a blessing, a great power located in the Heartland would feel insecure rather than secure because of its central position. Hence, it is understandable that the increasing US presence in the region may have disturbed them. This has led them to look for ways to strengthen their military ties among themselves. As an insular country in East Asia, Japan has been in search of a regional network and strong institutional establishments. It is alarmed by the rising power of China and anxious about the effectiveness of security guarantees from the USA.

Another point that should be underlined is that, for other countries, the political capture of the Caspian region and its potential resources would probably lessen their dependence on US-controlled Persian (Arabian) Gulf oil. Clearly, this would give them more space to manoeuvre out of the protectorate system of the USA. Therefore, the importance of Caspian oil and its transportation are mainly political issues rather than economic ones, in the eyes of the USA.

In the light of these arguments, it is evident that the US protectorate system of the Cold War period should be restructured in accordance with the realities of the post-Cold War period, but how? US policy-makers have responded to this situation by extending the US hegemonic system towards the East, the Eurasian Heartland. This formed the basis of US grand strategy in the post-Cold War period.

'US Grand Strategy had the task of achieving nothing less than the shaping of new political and economic arrangements and linkages across the whole of Eurasia. The goal was to ensure that every single major political centre in Eurasia understood that its relationship with the United States was more important than its relationship with any other political centre in Eurasia. If that could be achieved, each such centre would be attached separately by a spoke to the American hub: primacy would be secured.'[13]

---

[11] Michael Klare, *Blood and Oil: How America's Thirst for Petrol is Killing Us,* London: Penguin Books, 2004, p. 172.

[12] Ibid., p. 175.

[13] Gowan, p. 13.

Therefore, it would be plausible to argue that, again, an insular power, the USA, had the duty to prevent the land-based powers from unifying their economies and energy supplies in order to restructure its protectorate system to fit post-Cold War realities. For our purposes, we stress the energy aspect of US strategy in the Eurasian Heartland by relying on Caspian oil and its transportation through pipelines.

Caspian Oil and Pipelines

'...Oil and gas are not just commodities traded on international markets. Control over territory and its resources are strategic assets.'[14] This is particularly the case for the Caspian region, which is located at the centre of the Eurasian Heartland whose rich oil resources made it a playground for strategic rivalries throughout the 20th century.

> 'The Oil from this region played a major strategic role during the First and Second World Wars. Protecting oil fields of the Caspian was an Allied priority in the First World War. During the Second World War, oil from the Caspian Sea basin was an essential target of Hitler's expansionist policies. Following the 1939 German-Soviet Pact, Soviet oil from the Caspian Sea basin accounted for a third of Germany's imports. Hitler's attempt to secure the oil wells of the Caspian collapsed in the face of the fierce resistance of the Red Army.'[15]

Until the dissolution of the USSR in 1991, this region had been closed to external interference. Since then, the huge natural resources of the region have been opened to foreign powers' influence, whereby it became the focal point of strategic rivalries once again. Rich energy resources stimulated these strategic contentions. 'The Caspian Sea basin, with its huge reserves of oil and natural gas and its strategic position, is a key arena of rivalry between the United States, major European powers, Russia, Japan, and China. All of the major powers, along with transnational corporations, have been seeking alliances, concessions, and possible pipeline routes in the region.'[16]

For our purposes, the geopolitical interest of the USA in the Caspian region should be underscored. The USA, which controls Persian (Arabian) Gulf oil to a great extent, is not dependent on oil from the Caspian region. Hence, it could be argued that US interest in the Caspian region and its oil resources went beyond merely economic considerations. Actually, it was part of a US grand strategy of restructuring its protectorate system and sustaining its hegemonic position in the

---

[14] Mehdi Parvizi Amineh and Henk Houweling, 'Caspian Energy: Oil and Gas Resources and the Global Market' in Mehdi Parvizi and Henk Houweling (Eds), *Central Eurasia in Global Politics: Conflict, Security and Development*, Koninklijike Brill: Leiden, 2004, p. 82.

[15] Bulent Gokay, 'The Most Dangerous Game in the World: Oil, War and US Global Hegemony', *Alternatives: Turkish Journal of International Relations*, Vol. 1, No. 2, Summer 2002, p. 55.

[16] Vassilis K. Fouskas & Bulent Gokay, *The New American Imperialism: Bush's War on Terror and Blood for Oil*, Connecticut: Praeger Security International, 2005, p. 156.

post-Cold War period. The US policy-making élite have realized that controlling the transportation of Caspian oil will strongly buttress the success of restructuring the US protectorate system. By controlling the transportation of Caspian oil, one of the main channels of unification, energy supplies, the USA contends that potential power consolidations outside the US protectorate system would decline in the Heartland.

'The leaders of Azerbaijan, Kazakhstan and Turkmenistan view the development of their hydrocarbon resources as a cornerstone to their economic prosperity.'[17] However, these littoral states are land-locked. In other words, they cannot use tankers to ship their oil resources. Therefore, they are required to transport their oil through pipelines, which would cross multiple international boundaries. 'Thus, the issue of potential routes through neighbouring countries has become a priority for both regional and international powers, as well as for oil companies.'[18] It should be noted that pipeline construction provides several economic and political benefits, such as transit fees, access to the oil and political leverage over the flow of oil. 'Thus, the process of choosing and constructing pipeline routes is complicated and requires delicate negotiations with many parties. Until recently, the existing pipelines in the Caspian region were designed to link the former Soviet Union internally and were routes through Russia. Most of the Caspian's oil and gas shipments terminated in the Russian Black Sea port of Novorosiisk. This existing network, however, does not correspond to the new economic and political dynamics since the early 1990s.'[19] In that context, there emerged many pipeline projects. It should be acknowledged that 'politics, not economics, will dominate future decisions about pipelines and major investment projects.'[20] US policy-makers have played a significant role in deciding which projects should be realized.

Russia and Iran are the two main regional rivals to the USA. According to US policy-making élites, these countries have the potential to obstruct the USA's grand strategy of extending its protectorate system to the Eurasian Heartland. Russia and Iran's geographical location in the region reveals the strategic considerations of the pipeline battle in the Eurasian Heartland. One of the points that should be mentioned about Russia is that it considers the newly independent countries as its natural sphere of influence. In order to alleviate Russia's influence in the region, US administrators have supported the process of state-building within each of these countries and bolstered their economic and political interdependence through the 'global polarity' concept of Brzezinski. It should be

---

[17] Gawdat Bahgat, 'Pipeline Diplomacy: The Geopolitics of the Caspian Sea Region', *International Studies Perspectives*, Vol. 3, 2002, p. 322.

[18] Ibid., p. 322.

[19] Bahgat, p. 322.

[20] Stephen J. Blank, 'The United States: Washington's New Frontier in the Transcaspian', in Michael P. Croissant and Bülent Aras (Eds), *Oil and Geopolitics in the Caspian Sea Region*, Greenwood Press, 2000, p. 249.

noted that this was what Mackinder was talking about when he promoted anti-Bolshevik strategy in the early 1920s.

Diversification of oil supplies becomes important in that respect. Thus, the US policy-making élites have supported pipeline routes through the newly independent countries. For instance, the USA has given its full-support to the realization of the BTC oil pipeline project, despite its low feasibility and the lobbying activities of oil companies favouring a possible Iranian route. 'The establishment of the BTC pipeline and its transport corridor allows the newly independent states of the greater Caspian region to decrease their dependence on Moscow and make cooperation with the United States their new security orientation.'[21] Therefore, the BTC pipeline provided the proper environment for the USA to extend its protectorate system to pipeline countries. When we consider projects linking the BTC to Kazakhstan, which has the richest natural resources in the region, the BTC's significance for the USA must be acknowledged. It should also be noted that this process not only leads the USA to have more say in the supply of oil, but also provides fertile ground for corporations of US origin to make investments with high returns. Thus, the USA would establish new spheres of influence in the region. In summary, 'the goal of winning the pipeline battle was not for the oil or gas, but to maintain (in the case of Russia) or attain (in the case of United States and Iran) significant presence in the region. At the crossroads of two continents, the Caspian region is worth geo-strategic prize.'[22]

Another point that should be raised about the BTC is that the USA could diminish regional powers' dependency on Russia and Iran by controlling the oil flow to the Caspian basin through that pipeline. For instance, the EU's heavy energy dependency on Russia is not in the USA's best interest. Clearly, the BTC would function to decrease the EU's energy dependency on Russia. Moreover, the BTC would also enable NATO ally Turkey to strengthen its economy and serve as a plus in the process of Turkey's accession to the EU. Hence, Turkey's importance would increase in the eyes of EU policy-making élites and its accession would be more desirable for them. It should be noted that the BTE gas pipeline, which extends from the Shakh-Deniz natural gas field in the Azeri Caspian Sea region through Georgia to Turkey, would reach 100m. cu m of gas. It is expected that gas will be supplied to Turkey by late 2006. Clearly, both the BTC and the BTE pipelines would underpin Turkey's energy hub character in the region.

Finally, it should be noted that littoral states of the Caspian basin, except Iran, are non-OPEC countries. 'Caspian oil is non-OPEC oil, meaning that supplies from this region are less likely affected by the price and supply policies applied by the oil-exporting cartel.'[23] By considering Saudi Arabia's prominent position in

---

[21] Brenda Shaffer, 'From Pipedream to Pipeline: A Caspian Success Story', *Current History: A Journal of Contemporary World Affairs*, 104, No. 684 (October 2005), p. 343 in http://bcsia.ksg.harvard.edu/BCSIA_content/documents/ShafferCurrentHistoryOct2005.pdf, retrieved on 29.12.2005.

[22] Brenda Shaffer, 'US Policy in the South Caucasus in the Second George W. Bush Administration', in Nursin Atesoglu Guney and Fuat Aksu (Eds), *The Prospects for Cooperation and Stability in the Caucasus*, Foundation For Middle East and Balkan Studies (OBİV), 2005, p. 58.

[23] Fouskas and Gokay, p. 151.

OPEC and its royal family's special relationship with the USA, non-OPEC Caspian oil should also be exported in US terms. Clearly, it is in the best interest of the USA to sustain marketing of Caspian oil to world energy markets in dollars.

The dominance of the dollar as the world's reserve currency is one of the main elements of US economic power. 'The dominance of the dollar is not simply the result of the size of the US economy. It is also and importantly the result of two other things: politics and finance ... A state that controls the sources of world oil politically can ensure that oil is priced and largely paid for in its currency-in this case, in dollars-and thus can defend its international dominance.'[24] There had been no alternative to the dollar until the emergence of the euro as a potential rival reserve currency in late 1999. 'Today, the euro accounts for one-quarter of the global market.'[25] Moreover, there is a growing tendency by OPEC countries such as Iran and Venezuela to denominate petroleum trade in euros. 'Since the oil trade is a central factor underpinning the dollar's hegemony, all these are potentially very significant threats to the strength of the US economy in particular, and US global hegemony in general.'[26] Thus, the USA is required to extend its influence on the oil-rich states of the Caspian region by preventing them from pricing their oil in euros rather than dollars.

Conclusion

Much has changed since Sir Halford Mackinder wrote '*The Geographic Pivot of History*' in 1904. However, his assertion regarding the Eurasian Heartland remains relevant. Once again an insular power, the USA, has the duty to prevent the consolidation of land powers in the region. This obligation emerges from its intention to adapt the Cold War protectorate hub-spoke system to the realities of the post-Cold War period in which it has lost its leverage over Western European countries. Expanding this protectorate system to the Eurasian Heartland established the basis of the US post-Cold War grand strategy. The US policy-making élite has realized that controlling the transportation of Caspian oil will strongly buttress the success of restructuring the protectorate system. By controlling the transportation of Caspian oil, one of the main channels of unification, energy supplies, potential power consolidations out of the US protectorate system would decline in the Heartland. The US endeavour for the realization of the BTC pipeline is part of the grand strategy to sustain its protectorate system in the Heartland. Execution of this grand strategy has been accelerated in the aftermath of the events of 9/11. The USA, with the rhetoric of the war on terror, has established a military presence in the Eurasian Heartland. It is obvious that this presence would enhance its ability to determine pipeline routes through the territory of its allies in the region. It should be emphasized that the main

---

[24] Peter Gowanb, 'US Hegemony Today', in John Bellamy Foster and Robert W. McChesney (Eds), *Pax Americana: Exposing the American Empire*, Pluto Press, 2004, p. 67.

[25] Tommaso Paddoa-Schioppa, European Central Bank, November 22, 2002, http://www.ecb.int.

[26] Fouskas and Gokay, p. 25.

difference between the war in Iraq and the BTC is related to means. In Iraq, the extension of influence required military operations, but in the case of the BTC fostering the route through Azerbaijan, Georgia and Turkey has so far been sufficient. Despite its low feasibility in comparison to a transportation route through Iran, the BTC is a product of the USA's strategic calculations. Thus, it would be plausible to argue that US interest in the Heartland and its preferences for transportation routes are fundamentally political. It should also be remembered that, consistent with Brzezinski's 'global plurality' concept, the BTC would promote the independence of former socialist Azerbaijan and Georgia from Russia and locate them in the orbit of the USA.

It seems that in the foreseeable future no serious challenge to the US strategy of restructuring the hub-spoke protectorate system will emerge in the post-Cold War global system. Although we can talk about reluctance to help the USA pursue its foreign policy objectives, it is hard to discern any serious initiative to constrain its freedom of action. The old cry of *Yankee, Go Home* is absent in Europe and Asia. Simultaneously, the principal adversaries of the USA are not the major powers but isolated and impoverished states.

Nevertheless, the sustainability of the USA's unilateralist style of foreign policy is dubious in the post-Cold War order. On the one hand, it would be too costly for the USA to pursue its grand strategy without allies. The USA's unilateralist manner has led Cold War allies, except for the United Kingdom, to be reluctant to support its policies, as in the case of the war in Iraq. On the other hand, this proactive foreign policy-making could drive other great powers to unite on the Eurasian landmass against the USA. Particularly in the aftermath of the US-led war in Iraq, relations with the EU have been tense. Furthermore, China, Russia and Iran are sceptical about the US presence in the Heartland. Despite several shortcomings in its potential to become a military bloc, the SCO does have the potential to transform itself into a kind of counter-balancing regional unit. It seems that Iran, deemed a member of the 'axis of evil' by the USA, will also become a member of this organization. For our purposes, these countries' co-operation in energy supply should be highlighted. By placing its economic and political interests directly opposite to those of the USA, China has been developing trade relations with Iran. This is particularly the case in the energy sector. Probably, it will not be long before Iran becomes China's largest source of imported oil. In addition to Iran, China is enhancing its energy dialogue with oil-rich Kazakhstan. China has commenced building the major Kazakh-China oil pipeline, which will be functional in 2007. It could be argued that this oil pipeline will undermine the geopolitical significance of the US-backed BTC oil pipeline. Despite projects to link Kazakhstan's oil to the BTC, China has already gained the lion's share of these resources. It looks like 'sleeping China', to use Napoléon Bonaparte's term, has also woken up in terms of securing its energy supplies. In summary, it seems that the political control of oil resources and their flow will not be an easy task for the US superpower in the Heartland.

Oil and Power in the Caspian Sea Region: Supermajor Oil Companies and Geopolitics

E. K. MOFFORD

Introduction

'When everyone else is dead the Great Game *is finished. Not before.'*[1]

> *Who rules East Europe commands the Heartland*
> *Who rules the Heartland commands the World Island*
> *Who rules the World Island commands the World*

Sir Halford Mackinder[2]

Since the time before Tsarist Russia, the Caspian Sea region has been known to have an abundance of natural resources that would prove to be of extreme use. Some estimates put the reserves of oil at up to 200,000m. barrels, while others have assessed them at only 70,000m.–160,000m. barrels.[3] It is also anticipated that Caspian oil will reach about 7% of the world market. Caspian oil is more important than ever as a new source of oil and gas, for the world now consumes approximately four times more oil than is discovered.[4] It is clear why the foremost nations of the world would want to be a part of the new generation of oil production.

The 'Great Game' for Central Asia, a term coined by Rudyard Kipling in his novel *Kim,* foresaw the struggle for geopolitical dominance in the region—the *Great Game*. It was originally viewed as the quest of the 19th century great empires of British India and Imperial Russia and their vying for superiority and authority along the mountainous border region of the Eurasian 'Heartland', which separated their spheres of influence. This *Great Game* was played out over the passes and in the valleys of Central Asia. The link between the imperialist nature of Victorian Britain and autocratic Tsarist Russia is central to the actual events of that time and to contemporary events.

Azerbaijan is considered to be the epicentre for Caspian oil. When Marco Polo ventured east to explore the exotic 'Orient' on his Silk Road journey, he stumbled

---

[1] Kipling, Rudyard. *Kim,* p. 288.

[2] Mackinder, Sir Halford. *Democratic Ideals and Reality,* 1919.

[3] www.eia.gov.

[4] www.peakoil.com/sample

upon the 'land of fire'[5], now called Azerbaijan, a land with pools of oil which can be scooped up with rags. In the late 19th century, Baku was the world's leading exporter of crude oil, out-exporting the US Pennsylvanian oil rush headed by the oil monopolist and pioneer John D. Rockefeller! With foreign investment being maximized at this time by famous families such as the Norwegian Nobel brothers and the Rothschilds of France, the Caspian Sea region was rich in prospects for new development in the oil industry.

The irony of the Caspian region is that despite its holding, potentially, billions of dollars' worth of natural resources, they remained virtually unexploited and unexplored until the beginning of the last century. The political history of the Caspian Sea region from the time of Tsarist Russia is rich and complicated; privatization to nationalization back to privatization makes for a complex subject. It was in 1905 when the Nobel brothers of Norway came to the region and began to survey the land and assess its opportunities that true foreign investment in the Caspian Region commenced. However, with the onset of the Cold War in 1945, the region went into dormancy and retreated from the international market. It was not until the post-Soviet era, after 1991, that markets were opened to outside investors, such as the supermajor oil companies which came in to start imple-menting a major investment programme to manage and extract value for the oil market. The first multinational entity in this process was the Azerbaijan Interna-tional Operating Company (AIOC),[6] which was formed in 1993 as a direct partnership between Azerbaijan and the oil companies to implement a future of foreign oil investment.

The supermajors were first in line, together with the state-sponsored oil companies, to start the exploration for and exportation of Caspian oil. Due to the fact that these Commonwealth of Independent States (CIS) countries were newly-formed independent states (all except Russia and Iran), governmental stability was and remains a question of concern. The problem with investor security is still a major concern that affects oil companies' investments in the region. Whether it is economic security or physical security, the sustainability of the oil companies' billions of dollars' worth of assets in the region must be secured, by the individual nation state or by non-governmental organizations, such as the oil companies. However, security aspects are not the main concern of this paper.

The primary focus of this essay is to investigate the impact of the supermajor oil companies in the 'New Great Game' of Caspian regional geopolitics. It should be understood that the real question is, who is controlling the politics of oil in the region? Is it the oil companies or the regional nation states? As a springboard to the core question, we will turn the focus to the basis of Sir Halford Mackinder.

---

[5] Etymology of the name Azerbaijan is 'land of fire'

[6] Investors in the AIOC are as follows: BP (34.14%), Unocal (10.05%), Inpex of Japan (which in 2003 bought LUK Oil's 10% share for $1,354m.), Socar (10%), Statoil (8.56%), ExxonMobil (8%), TPAO (6.75%), Pennzoil (4.82%), Itochu (3.92%), DeltaHess Khazar (2.08%) and DeltaHess ACG (1.68%): www.allbusiness.com.

Mackinder theorized that whoever controlled Eurasia, controlled the world. Therefore, I am asking: who controls Eurasia? Is it the regional nation states? In this essay I hope to analyse the region as a whole; investigating exploration practices, production processes, transport issues and, finally, the oil market in which Caspian oil is processed. Also included is the role of the multinational oil companies, which will be analysed with the aim of showing who is involved in the geopolitics of Caspian oil, and, basically, who is 'running the show'.

Mackinder's 'Heartland Theory' is one that is widely accepted and acknowledged as the basis of modern (i.e. with reference to the last 100 years) geopolitics. Whether it was British post-First World War policy or the US policy of containment,[7] the Heartland Theory has been present internationally since its development in 1919. The theory is based on the idea that Central Asia or the Heartland is the key strategic link between the East and West. In practice, the push for control of the area has been seen as the West (Britain and the USA) trying to contain Soviet Russia during the Cold War. Although the Cold War is over, post-communist Russia is still seen as a competitor to the West, together with the littoral states of the South Caspian, such as Iran and the Middle Eastern nation states.

There are five littoral Caspian states that will be included for the purposes of this essay in the oil exploration and exploitation of the region. They are: Kazakhstan, Russia, Azerbaijan, Turkmenistan and Iran. In some academic research, Uzbekistan and Georgia are also included. However, for my purposes, they will not be considered. The five littoral states are considered to be the actual Caspian states, for they all border the Caspian Sea. Uzbekistan, although a hydrocarbon-rich state in its own right, does not border the sea and will therefore not be considered here. Georgia is also acknowledged as a strategically important country for transportation incentives and for its access to the Black Sea and the newly commissioned Baku-Tbilisi-Ceyhan (BTC) oil pipeline, which runs from Baku through Georgia to Turkey and will be discussed later in this essay.

Historically, in the development of Caspian oil, Baku, the capital of Azerbaijan, has been the centre of the oil trade. Baku is considered to be the 'Houston of the East', with Houston being the US base of ChevronTexaco, ExxonMobil and BP America. It was in 1859 that the first oil refinery was built in Surakhany, Azerbaijan. Starting from there, an industrial revolution took place in the region. It was in 1878 that the first oil pipeline was inaugurated in Russia to link the oilfields at Balakhany to the refineries built in Baku.[8] From the end of the imperialist stage of Russian control of the lower Caspian basin, throughout the Soviet era to contemporary times, Caspian oil development has steadily grown,

---

[7] American Containment theory created in 1953 after the release of the *Long Telegram* outlines a policy of containment toward the Russians and their communist allies, thus beginning the Cold War. Heartland Theory is seen throughout the basis of this document. *See* NSC-68 (http://www.fas.org/irp/offdocs/nsc-68.htm) for further reading.

[8] For more information, see Adeebtar, T., *Geopolitical Dimensions of the Main Export Pipeline in the Caspian Region,* Tehran, IIES, 2005; Gokay, B. (Ed.), *The Politics of Caspian Oil,* Basingstoke, Palgrave, 2001; Dekmejian, R. H., and Simonian, H. H., *Troubled Waters. The Geopolitics of the Caspian Region,* London, I. B. Tauris, 2001.

and in 1994 exploded into a booming industry that is currently reshaping the future of the world's petroleum industry.

Regional Statistics

It is estimated that the reserves of the Caspian Sea region comprise some 200m.–276m. barrels of oil and about 16,300,000m. cu m of natural gas. At the current time proven reserves of oil amount to 17,000m.–22,000m. barrels. In Kazakhstan alone, earning potential for oil and gas development is estimated at around US $700,000m. over the next 40 years. This implies that there are some 6,000m.–9,000m. barrels of oil in Kazakhstan. Other estimates have assessed the resource at 9,000m.–17,000m. barrels: a total potential of around 101,000m. barrels of oil. In Azerbaijan, reserves have been estimated at 3,000m.—5,000m. barrels of oil. Other sources have assessed Azerbaijan's reserves at 7,000m.–12,500m. barrels, excluding the potential assets of 44,500m. barrels. Iran is known to have reserves that total some 90,000m. barrels, about 9% of the world's total. Out of this 90,000m., however, only 15,000m. are in the Caspian Sea portion of Iran's holdings. Turkmenistan has estimated proven reserves of 1,700m. barrels and potential reserves of 38,000m. barrels. Russia has proven reserves in the Caspian area of about 3,000m. barrels.

World Comparisons

Although estimates vary greatly, the Caspian's holdings can be compared to those of Iraq at the high end and/or the equivalent of those of the North Sea. It is predicted that by 2010 the Caspian alone could be producing between 2.4m.–5.9m. barrels per day (b/d). This would exceed Venezuela's *annual* output! At present, the world's daily demand for oil totals approximately 82.2m. barrels! Demand is growing at its fastest pace for 24 years, at around 1.73m. b/d (or by 1.8% annually), with additional pressure developing from expanding Chinese and Indian demand. In 2005, OPEC raised its output to 29.04m. b/d. As the Caspian is a non-OPEC region, its contribution to the world oil market, both at present and in the future, is clear.

The main question for geopolitical analysis is, why is the oil majors' presence in the Caspian region so significant? The answer to this is neither simple nor clean-cut. However, a suggested reply is that because of the latest stage of globalization the world is in, it can be seen that the global political economy has shifted from a state centric-based economy to a non-governmental organiza-tion-dominated system. The global economy has been dominated by oil interests since the Second World War. However, the role of the multinational oil companies in the international political economy is new and has recently attained more prominence than ever before.

The new term for the largest of the multinational oil companies is *supermajors*, the 'lords of black gold' in my own terminology. The supermajors dominate the Caspian Sea region. Without the recent influx of investment from them, the

Caspian oil industry would not have flourished as it has. Using the supermajors as a prime example of how multinational organizations are taking over or dominating global politics, I will illustrate how this has so far been an extremely advantageous movement, and a profitable shift for the regional actors and the companies involved. However, first we must ask, why are the oil majors in the Caspian?

If the Caspian is seen as the next Middle East, it is only logical for businesses to seek potential economic windfalls from it. The rush to invest in the Caspian has been nicknamed 'The New Great Game', a fight for regional supremacy by the world's superpowers. The West, China, Japan, India and Russia are an overwhelming presence as regional actors with investment opportunities. Western oil companies present in the Caspian may be regarded as direct representatives of their Western states. Only seven multinationals are considered to be supermajors and all seven are present in the Caspian Sea region. These supermajors or 'lords of black gold' are:

BP (formerly British Petroleum)	British
Chevron Texaco (Unocal)	US
Conoco-Phillips	US
ENI	Italian
ExxonMobil	US
Royal Dutch Shell	Dutch
TotalFinaElf	French/Italian

Investment by these companies has been quite high. Since 1993, numerous Production Sharing Agreements (PSAs) have been concluded. These PSAs have included one in 1994 which the industry refers to as the 'Contract of the Century'. This was a deal between foreign oil companies and Azerbaijan to develop the AIOC. BP primarily operates this company. However, of the seven supermajors, BP stands out as the foremost contributor to the region. Total investment in the region by the supermajors so far is around US $20,000m. This money has gone into exploration, exploitation, the construction of oilfields and pipelines, and directly into communities and society.

In Kazakhstan, Chevron is the primary supermajor present. In 1993, Chevron signed a PSA worth US $20,000m. to develop the Tengiz oilfield. In the same year, foreign oil companies funded extensive offshore seismic surveys in the Kazakh region of the North Caspian Sea. After years of negotiations, a PSA between Kazakhstan and Chevron to develop the offshore area of the North Caspian was concluded in 1997. In Turkmenistan, owing to political risks and restraints, very little foreign oil company investment has been made; however, it is known that ExxonMobil and Shell have offices in the capital. Owing to Western sanctions no US oil companies have operations in Iran. However, Shell has been negotiating a pipeline deal with the Iranian government, for Iran is seen as a main transit centre of the future.

In the region, it is recognized that Azerbaijan is the centre of foreign investment in the Caspian. A major pipeline has recently been brought into production, running from Baku, Azerbaijan, to Tbilisi in Georgia and onwards to the Ceyhan terminals in southern Turkey on the Mediterranean. It is referred to simply as the BTC pipeline. The main stakeholder in and operator of the BTC pipeline is BP. The BTC pipeline is considered to be the main export pipeline for the Caspian Sea at this time. In Azerbaijan alone, more than 23 PSAs have been concluded for exploration and exploitation since 1993. Much investment and development is needed in the region for regeneration due to the limited and primitive Soviet maintenance practices and failure to update technology and equipment. Nevertheless, production in Azerbaijan in 2005 is estimated to be running at 400,000 b/d, is forecast to rise to around 700,000 b/d in 2007, and, finally, to reach its peak of 1m. b/d in 2010.[9] The estimated profit for Azerbaijan alone is expected to be more than US $81,000m. over the next 30 years, with an additional US $300m. in signing bonuses. However, as BP official Eric Mofford has said, 'People need to understand there is an associated risk of doing business in these neglected regions, they are old and need a lot updating and regeneration.'[10] The regeneration mentioned above, in order to profit from the investment, is needed to update what remains of the old Soviet oil derricks that litter the shores of the Caspian Sea.

On that subject, Russia has massive earning potential and a huge presence in the region off the North-West Caspian. BP, Exxon, Shell and Chevron are all known to have invested here; however, at this time and stage knowledge is limited regarding the size and extent of their investments. It has, however, been documented that Shell is the only Western oil company to venture into Iran to have talks about future projects and development in the country.

In the geopolitical spectrum, the USA and most Western countries are looking for an alternative to dependence on Middle Eastern oil. The oil in the Caspian region is considered to be good quality, sweet crude. Regional demand for oil is relatively low and therefore the majority of the oil produced can be exported. The oil market in the Caspian is new and open compared to that of the Middle East, leaving more mobility for investment for foreign oil companies. With the new pipelines being built, connecting the West with the East, the Caspian is centrally located, which makes transportation issues minimal and prospects high. With Asian countries such as China and India experiencing increased energy demand, Caspian oil is a gateway opportunity for regional investment and imports. The US Central Intelligence Agency estimates that China and India will be seeking to import around 120m. b/d of oil in the next 30 years.

---

[9] Note: these pumping estimates are barrels all taken from the ACG field that is around 190 km off shore from Baku.

[10] Quote from an interview with Eric Mofford of BP Sunbury via telephone in May 2006.

Exploration and Production Within the Caspian Littoral States

The potential reserves of oil in the Caspian Sea region are estimated to be around 270,000m. barrels[11] and those of natural gas at some 16,300,000m. cu m,[12] which will sustain the investment that is being committed. Statistics like this place the reserves of the Caspian region as the world's second largest in gross terms after those of the Persian (Arabian) Gulf. Taken as a whole, the Caspian region is being thought of as the new Kuwait. In addition to the quantity of the reserves, the type of oil is also advantageous: it is light, sweet crude. This type of oil is easier to produce and refine, making it cheaper and more accessible.

In Azerbaijan there are an estimated 3,000m.–5,000m. barrels of proven reserves. As mentioned above, many PSAs have been signed and operations implemented to establish exploration and production schemes. Since 1993, when the 'Contract of the Century' was concluded, Azerbaijan's oil industry has become the focus of Caspian development and exploration. Just as Houston is the location of the head offices of BP America, Exxon and Chevron, and the Offshore Technical Conference, Baku is the home of the AIOC, BP's Caspian headquarters and the annual Caspian Oil and Gas Oil Show and Convention. The supermajor oil companies (among others present in Azerbaijan) are BP, Royal Dutch Shell, Exxon-Mobil, TotalFinaElf, Chevron Texaco and Conoco-Phillips. Although most of the supermajors are present, BP is regarded as the foremost foreign oil company (FOC) in the country, with the most holdings and responsibility. The reason it has attained this status is because it is the main operator of both the AIOC and the BTC company.

Chevron has estimated the 'earning potential' in Kazakhstan at around US $700,000m. from offshore oil- and gas fields alone over the next 40 years. The other supermajor oil companies present in Kazakhstan are BP, ExxonMobil, Royal Dutch Shell, TotalFinaElf and the primary investor, Chevron Texaco. In 1993, Chevron signed a PSA with Kazakhstan worth US $20,000m. to develop the Tengiz oilfield. The potential oil reserves here have been estimated at 6,000m.–9,000m. barrels. The expansion of this field alone has been immense, creating an entirely new earnings bracket for the companies involved in the Tengiz development.

Turkmenistan is the third Caspian state that is known to have immense potential for oil and gas exploration and production. However, owing to strict governmental control, Western oil firms have hesitated to initiate businesses in Turkmenistan. Turkmenistan's production has been estimated at around 162,500 b/d. In January 2004, Turkmenneftgaz (Turkmen National Oil Company) produced 486,300 metric tons of crude oil, which represents a 5% increase compared with the same month of the previous year. In addition to this, production and exports of petrochemicals increased by 54% in 2004 compared with 2003.[13] Supermajor oil companies that have invested in Turkmenistan are

---

[11] www.eia.com

[12] www.eia.com

[13] News Central Asia, News: Gas and Oil Production Increases in Turkmenistan (http://www.newscentralasia.com/modules.php? name=News&file=article&sid=526

Mobil, now ExxonMobil, and Royal Dutch/Shell, which is known to have offices there.

Iran, the fourth littoral Caspian state, is one that has little Western investment in its oil industry. Owing to the economic sanctions imposed on Iran by the USA, no US oil companies have been allowed to invest in the highly volatile anti-Western state. The US Iran-Libya Sanctions Act of 1996 limits all investment by US companies in these two countries to a maximum of US $20m. annually.[14] Iran is known to have oil reserves that total around 90,000m. barrels, about 9% of the estimated world total. Of the Iranian total, about 15,000m. barrels are located in the Caspian Sea region.

In view of the sanctions, and also because of intimidation by and the influence of Western nations seeking to obstruct investment in Iran, supermajors tend not to invest in Iran, with the exception of one well-known case: a pipeline deal concluded by Royal Dutch/Shell. The main role for Iran in the Caspian Sea oil industry is (viewed as) that of its main transit centre. With access to the Persian (Arabian) Gulf and the Arabian Sea, and as the gateway to the East and the West, Iran is strategically significant.

Russia is the fifth Caspian state that contributes to the oil business in the region. Exports from energy resources account for 40% of Russian exports and contribute 14% of the country's gross domestic product (GDP).[15] Of the 48,600m. barrels of proven reserves of oil Russia possesses, about 10,000m. are located in the North Caspian Russian region. This essay will examine political dealings between the nations in more depth. However, one main aspect of geopolitical manoeuvres will involve the relationship between Russia, the oil companies and the anonymous ethnic republics that lie within the Caspian borders: the republics of Dagestan and Kalmykia. The primary question being asked here is, what is the strategy or approach of the oil companies throughout negotiations and deals with political institutions in the region? BP has large holdings in Russia, but they are held in the name of BP-TNK. ExxonMobil, Royal Dutch/Shell and Chevron Texaco are also major stakeholders.

Production Sharing Agreements (PSAs)

The first of the post-Soviet PSAs was the Chevron Texaco-Kazakhstan PSA signed in 1993 to fund extensive offshore seismic surveys of the Kazakh Caspian offshore region. Additionally, a US $20,000m. joint venture to develop the Tengiz oilfield in the Kazakh region of the Caspian was included in this PSA. The second PSA was concluded between Chevron Texaco and Kazakhstan in 1997 to develop the offshore area of the North Caspian. This PSA has been particularly controversial for Russia, which has not been enthusiastic about non-Russian participation in the Caspian, especially in Kazakh-Russian waters.

---

[14] Caspian Basin Alert: an overview of the Oil Industry in the Caspian Basin (www.uwec.edu/grossmzc/caspianoil.html)

[15] Ibid.

On 17 November 1997 a PSA was signed with a number of Western oil companies (including the supermajors BP, Royal Dutch/Shell, Mobil—now ExxonMobil—and Total—now TotalFinaElf), which allowed for further exploration and production in an offshore area of Kazakhstan in the North Caspian Sea region. This PSA was developed from Chevron's 1993 PSA, under which the supermajors agreed to fund extensive seismic work in the Kazakh region of the Caspian, which was completed in 1997, leading to this timely PSA.

Within Azerbaijan alone some 23 PSAs have been signed since 1993. Most of these 23 PSAs are headed or funded by the Western supermajor oil companies. The largest of oil exploration fields is the Azeri-Chirag-Guneshli (ACG) field. It has been in existence since the Soviet era, however, and has suffered from neglect, lack of (Soviet) investment and inadequate export capacity. The ACG field alone is home to an estimated 5,400m. barrels of oil.[16] Direct investment in the ACG field is estimated at around US $10,000m., of which US $2,900m. is being utilized for the construction of the BTC pipeline to connect ACG oil exports to the West. In 2005, around 400,000 b/d of oil was produced, and this total has been forecast to increase to 800,000 b/d in 2007, and to reach peak capacity of 1m. b/d in 2010.[17]

The 'Contract of the Century'

'The signing of 'The Contract of the Century' on September 20, 1994 marks the beginning of independent Azerbaijan's new oil strategy and doctrine.'[18]
– Heydar Aliyev, Immortalized President of the Azerbaijan Republic

On 20 September 1994, the 'Contract of the Century' was signed and the AIOC was formed. The AIOC has 10 main participants: BP[19] (34.136%), Unocal[20] (10.2814%), SOCAR[21] (10%), INPEX[22] (10%), Statoil[23] (8.5633%), Exxon-Mobil[24] (8.006%), TPAO[25] (6.75%), Devon Energy[26] (5.6262%), Itochu[27] (3.9205%), and Delta Hess[28] (2.7213%). This collaborative corporation was formed with the intention that it should be the link between business and politics. Under the former Azeri President Heydar Aliyev, the AIOC forged the way

---

[16] Caspian ACG: (www.caspiandevelopmentandexport.com/ASP/ACG.asp)

[17] Ibid.

[18] Quote from Heydar Aliyev, President of the Azerbaijan Republic, in *The Contract of the Century*.

[19] British-based.

[20] US-owned.

[21] Azerbaijan state oil company.

[22] Japanese-owned.

[23] Norwegian-owned.

[24] US-owned.

[25] Turkish State Oil Company.

[26] Formerly Pennzoil, a Royal Dutch/Shell Company.

[27] Japanese-owned.

[28] US-Saudi Arabian owned.

forward for the development, exploration and production of the ACG oilfields.[29] Although this production company was strictly for Azeri oil production, the 'Contract of the Century' is also considered to include the agreements made in Kazakhstan as well. The estimated profit of this deal for Azerbaijan alone is expected to be more than US $81,000m. over the next 30 years, with an additional US $300m. in signing bonuses.[30]

However, although this contract was welcomed by Azerbaijan and the Western states, not all of the Caspian littoral states were pleased. The new Russian Federation, for instance, was highly displeased with it and has stated that the signing of the contract was illegal under international law. The Russian foreign minister, Grigory Karasin, was quoted as saying, 'unilateral actions, especially on resources and the Caspian Sea contradict international law and risk damaging the ecological system of the sea'.[31] Citing former Soviet treaties between the Soviet Union and Iran of 1921 and 1941, however, the Russian point of view was considered out of date and not applicable due to the fact that all treaties made under Soviet rule were now void. Nevertheless, still insisting that Azerbaijan and the participating Western States were acting illegally, Russia's position was that their contracts were to be considered illegitimate. In addition to Russian complaints, Iran has also put forth additional objections about Western influence in the Caspian region, especially with regard to benefits from the region's natural resource exports and its development. At this time, Russia and Iran were regarded as allies pursuing the same agenda and their own plans for the development of the Caspian Sea resources.

Transportation

Strategically, transportation in the Caspian Sea region is a fundamental issue. Since the Sea itself is land-locked, the only options are pipelines, sea tankers, trains or trucks. Economically speaking, the nations and the companies involved in the region's oil business want the solution that is logistically the most economically viable and profitable. Today, with modern technology, pipelines seem to be the answer. With the introduction of the BTC pipeline, new lines of transport have been opened and access to the West granted. One million barrels of oil per day will be safely delivered through the BTC pipeline to the Turkish Mediterranean port of Ceyhan for export to Europe, the USA and beyond.

The Baku-Tbilisi-Ceyhan Oil Pipeline (BTC) and the BTC Company

The Baku-Tbilisi-Ceyhan oil pipeline is the southern route to be followed by the proposed Caspian export pipelines. Considered to be the main export route, the BTC pipeline runs to the Mediterranean from the Baku oil terminals. The BTC

---

[29] www.caspianenergy.com, Contract of the Century is 10.

[30] Sagheb, Nassar, and Javadi, Masoud, *Azerbaijan's 'Contract of the Century'*. Azerbaijan International, Winter 1994 (2.4): www.azer.com.

[31] Russian Foreign Minister Grigory Karasin, in *Azerbaijan's 'Contract of the Century'*, Azerbaijan International, p. 4.

pipeline is run and operated by a consortium of multinational oil companies that are responsible for the financing and general operating and production of the pipeline: the BTC Company.[32] BP has been named as the main operator of this company and is responsible for the facilitation of all of its operations.

Notably, on 18 November 1999, and again, on 21 June 2000, the parliaments of Azerbaijan, Georgia and Turkey signed and ratified the Intergovernmental Agreement (IGA) pledging full support and co-operation for the future development of the BTC oil pipeline.[33] The BTC Company has been stated to exist to help protect the countries involved. The main objective is security, both physical and financial. The IGA is a guarantee by the BTC Company that the host nations will be the first priority in assurance of security for their people, economy and environment. Further declarations by the BTC Company and their financiers indicate that they have dedicated themselves to the proper function of the pipeline, and to ensuring that security, whether economic, physical or financial, is guaranteed.

Northern, Southern and the Eastern Pipeline Routes
In addition to the main export route that is the BTC pipeline, there are currently two smaller northern pipeline systems and proposals for an additional two more pipelines, one of which would run south to the Persian (Arabian) Gulf and the other east to China, via Pakistan or Afghanistan. It is important to mention that the Caspian oil rush is not only part of the Western quest; the East Asian market is a new market that is making strong attempts to be included in the Caspian's future exportation and wealth.

Iran in the Caspian Oil Game
Iran is viewed through the international geopolitical lens as an unstable arena. What is threatening the international world is not the country's fiercely held Islamic ideals or its quasi-dictatorial political system, but rather its inability to compromise with the West's democratic ideals and reluctance to address the issue of neutralizing its nuclear material holdings and testing. Iran claims that its nuclear 'testing' is purely for peaceful purposes. However, the West views the matter differently.

Iran's deputy petroleum minister Mahmood Khaghani, in a speech to the 2005 Caspian Oil and Gas Conference in Baku, Azerbaijan, set out the country's plans and intentions for oil production in the Caspian and the international market. In this speech, Khaghani presented Iran as promoting 'peace and stability within OPEC, E.C.O., Caspian and the Black Sea Region ... no one will benefit from world conflict and turmoil'.[34] Furthermore, the primary purpose of Khaghani's

---

[32] Companies that are shareholders in the BTC Company: BP, Unocal, Delta Hess, Lukoil, US TFE, Aglip, Itochu, INPEX, Conoco-Phillips, Statoil, TPAO and SOCAR.

[33] The Baku-Tbilisi-Ceyhan Pipeline Company, BTC Human Rights Undertaking, Document Link: (www.caspiandevelopmentandexport.com)

[34] Khaghani, Mahmood, Director General for Caspian Sea Oil and Affairs, Deputy Petroleum Minister for Caspian Sea Affairs of the Islamic Republic of Iran, Ministry of Petroleum. Speech at the 12th Annual International Caspian Oil and Gas Conference, Baku, Azerbaijan, 8–9 June 2005.

rhetoric was to state that Iran is not evil, as the West claims it is, but, rather, a catalyst in securing world energy despite 'insecurity that is occurring in the oil rich Middle East'.

Proposals were offered to make Iran a major export route for the Caspian oil riches. Iran would not compete with the BTC pipeline, but would develop a system to complement it. The BTC supplies the West, whereas a pipeline through Iran could supply the East. This is a very plausible opportunity that would create an entirely new eastern market that is more accessible, not to mention a cheaper method for accessing parts of the Eastern corridor, such as India, China and the Far East.

Conclusion

In conclusion, how does the increasing world reliance on oil affect the value of the Caspian region's natural resources? The answer to this is dramatically complex; it affects the Caspian in a sizeable and very significant way. In a recent article published in *The Economist* it was stated that Saudi Arabia is considered the 'Central bank of oil'.[35] If Saudi Arabia is the central bank of oil, then what is the Caspian region to the Saudis? It could be argued that the Caspian region is a threat, a competitor that threatens to discredit Saudi Arabia's reputation and sole control over the world's oil supplies. The fact that the price of oil is currently so high—as of 6 July 2005 it had reached a peak price of US $60.00 per barrel—has led to dissatisfaction among the world's energy consumers, who want to know why it is so high. As stated in *The Economist*, 'Oil companies do not set oil prices, OPEC essentially does . . .'. Therefore, if OPEC continues to allow oil prices to rise so high, consuming countries will turn to non-OPEC sources, such as the Caspian region, to fulfil their needs. This is excellent news for the Caspian region: there will be increased investment in the region because of its status as a non-OPEC producer.

Moreover, the Caspian Sea region could prove vital in delaying the prospect of Peak Oil. What is Peak Oil? According to the Peak Oil institute, Peak Oil is a theory which states 'that any finite resource, (including oil), will have a beginning, middle, and an end of production, and at some point it will reach a level of maximum output' (*see* Figure 1).[36] Once oil peaks, production will normally decline by 2%–3% annually. On the other hand, demand for oil is constantly rising, by 2%–3% per year. This will result in a 4% shortfall just one year after the peak is reached, rising to a 15%–20% gap over the next five to 10 years.

With oil prices at US $70 per barrel and rising, one has to question how far it will go. Has the peak been reached? Or will it come shortly? As the originator of the term 'peak oil', Marion King Hubbert of Shell correctly predicted that US oil production would peak in 1970. Since the first 'oil shock' in 1973, the USA has been transformed from a creditor into a debtor nation. Moreover, if this was true for the USA, when will it become true for the rest of the world? Some other

---

[35] *Oil in Troubled Waters. The Economist*, 28 April 2005.

[36] Peak Oil news and messageboards at www.peakoil.com

Figure 1

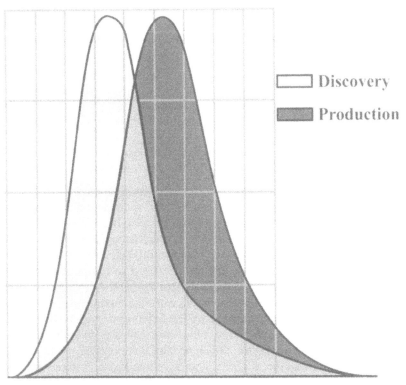

 Discovery

 Production

Reference: www.peakoil.com

countries whose production has already peaked are the United Kingdom, Norway, China, Mexico, Venezuela, Indonesia, Russia, Syria, Libya, Nigeria, Qatar— there are many more. Having a relatively new resource like the Caspian Sea region leads to speculation that it could delay the ultimate 'peak oil' for at least another decade or so.

The 'lords of black gold' and the world have focused their attention on the Caspian region since the end of Soviet control in the region in 1991. This is an up-and-coming energy market in the complexity of the 21st century's geopolitical energy arena. To provide a sustainable supply of oil and gas for the future, an alternative to oil from the unstable Middle East is a major, if not the most urgent, issue in today's global security agenda. In asserting that oil companies are now direct representatives of their host nations, it can only be said that their presence in the Caspian region shows the direct influence of how important energy policies are to Western and now Far Eastern industrialized nations alike.

Oil in Flames: 'Production Sharing Agreements' (PSAs) and the Issue of 'Petroleum Nationalism' in Iraq

Introduction: pre-2003 Expectations and Current Realities in Iraq

An important programmatic element in the pre-2003 US scheme of things concerning Iraq was associated with petroleum economics and calculations. The analysis went as follows: Iraq had 115,000m. barrels of proven reserves of oil, amounting to 11% of the world's total. Yet, there has been little exploration since the nationalization of the industry in 1972, whereas the current oilfields are 'badly under-utilized because of deteriorating equipment'.[1] The Energy Information Administration of the US Department of Energy (EIA-DoE) has been adamant that Iraqi oil reserves may well total over 400,000m. barrels, surpassing even those of Saudi Arabia (currently listed as first with 260,000m. barrels). Moreover, Iraqi oil is of high quality because it contains attractive chemicals, and has a high carbon content, lightness and low sulphur content that make it suitable for refining into high-value products.[2] Last but not least, the DoE argued that Iraq's oil production costs are the lowest in the world. Iraq has shallow wells and enormous fields with a high flow rate. US oil companies estimated that they could produce Iraqi oil for less than US $1.50 per barrel, including all costs incurred. By way of comparison, a barrel of oil costs about US $5 to produce in Malaysia and Oman, in Mexico and Russia US $6–$8 per barrel, whereas in offshore production, with the use of platforms and deep wells (North Sea, Canada, Alaska), prices can rise above US $20 per barrel.[3]

Lawrence Kumins of the Congressional Research Service has advised US authorities along the same lines. In a report written in September 2003 and updated in April 2005, he saw a wide range of possibilities in the structure of

---

[1] Neil King, Jr, et al., 'Iraq war would alter the economies of oil and politics of OPEC', *The Wall Street Journal Europe*, 19 September 2002, A10.

[2] Energy Information Administration, 'Iraq: Country analysis brief', June 2002, http://www.eia.doe.gov/emeu/cabs/iraq.html, and James A. Paul, 'Oil in Iraq: the heart of the crisis', Global Policy Forum, December 2002, http://www.globalpolicy.org/security/oil/2002/12heart.htm (both sites accessed on 17 December 2005)

[3] Paul, ibid.

possible future Iraqi oil export revenues, and argued that they can be presented as follows:

Range of possible future Iraqi annual oil export revenues

Exports (m.b/d)	Rev. @ $30/bbl	Rev. @ $40/bbl	Rev.@ $50/bbl
1.5	$11	$15	$18
2.55	$27	$37	$46
3.0	$33	$44	$55
3.5	$38	$51	$64

The two reports of September 2003 and April 2005 are almost the same, particularly in terms of their calculations and projections, the only substantial difference being the note of pessimism and caution Kumins added to his second report: 'While the potential to earn substantial export revenues is real, big revenue increases might be hard to achieve'.[4]

Why was—and is—the USA so anxious to return oil production to pre-war levels so quickly? The answer is rather simple: to finance the reconstruction and occupation costs, plus the profit-making capabilities of foreign companies operating through Production Sharing Agreements (PSAs—see below).[5] These processes, in turn, will pump petrodollars into the global equity and bond markets led by the American Treasury. Overall, the philosophy was and remains that there is enough oil in Iraq to support the reconstruction of the country, the wages and the operations of the US occupation army, plus the profit-making requirements of private companies and operators. The social, political and geopolitical reality of the new Iraq, however, is running counter to the expectations and wishes of US assessors in Baghdad and Washington, DC. The key aim of this essay is to explore the reasons behind the mismatch between US expectations about Iraqi oil before the invasion of spring 2003 and Iraq's current situation by way of focusing on the issue of 'petroleum nationalism'.

My claim is that the main obstacle thwarting the USA's oil politics in Iraq is a peculiar type of nationalism developed by ethnic and religious groups in Iraq, all of which see control of oil resources as a means to sovereign statehood and/or regional independence. The USA's invasion and occupation of Iraq has exacerbated pre-existing tensions between the rival ethnic and religious groupings and movements. The socio-political dynamics of those movements have been crystallized in the new controversial Constitution of the country, which I shall be

---

[4] Lawrence Kumins, 'Iraq oil: Reserves, production and potential revenues', CRS Report for Congress, The Library of Congress, Order Code RS21626, 29 September 2003 and 13 April 2005, 6.

[5] See, *inter alia*, Michael Klare, 'More blood, less oil', *TomDispatch*, 21 September 2005, http://www.globalpolicy.org/security/oil/2005/0921moreblood.htm (accessed on 14 December 2005)

examining in some detail. For the purposes of this introduction, let us set out the main issues upon which I will be focusing.

The classic case of 'petroleum nationalism' is that of the Kurds in the north. The Kurds are aiming at controlling the oil wells of Kirkuk and Mosul, thus establishing a state out of the oil revenues. The Shi'a have similar aspirations for the south, although their claim at times extends to Iraq as a whole, since they constitute the majority of the population. Sunni 'petroleum nationalism' can be described as a nationalism of deprivation, inasmuch as they have lost all of the power and privileges they enjoyed under the Baathists. Only after the election of 15 December 2005 did the US occupation authorities begin to address Sunni 'petroleum nationalism', by trying to integrate Sunni and even former Baathists into the governing structures of the new Iraq. In this context, it is no accident that there have been proposals on the part of the US Embassy in Baghdad in favour of revising the Constitution.

We shall become aware that the main patterns of the resistance have been and are formed around this issue, that is the way in which the Constitution reflects the nationalistic and sectional demands of the various ethnic/religious groups over the governance of oil.

For its part, US oil politics and strategic aims in Iraq remain the same: to increase production and output levels to the degree of covering occupation costs and generating extra profits. Most recently, the specific means which Western oil assessors envisaged to achieve this aim has been the proposal to introduce Production Sharing Agreements (PSAs) between oil companies and the Iraqi government. We shall examine the nature of these agreements in detail, trying to show that, if implemented, they will accentuate tensions in Iraq, corroborating sectarian violence and 'petroleum nationalism'.

Last but not least, I should point out that 'petroleum nationalism' should be distinguished from the classic Arab nationalism developed during the Cold War. Arab nationalism was about public control of hydrocarbon resources and key chokepoints (e.g. the Suez Canal) in the structured system of Middle Eastern states. 'Petroleum nationalism', instead, is *a means* to statehood, with the legal and economic status of oil resources to be resolved once a proper state sovereign structure is in place.

Resistance, the Constitution and the Iranian Factor

The swift development and endurance of the resistance, 'the speed with which it took off', Patrick Cockburn argued in *New Left Review*, has not received due attention. The USA started 'to suffer casualties as early as June 2003' and this resulted in the postponement of the elections for the following year.[6]

These remarks carry weight, for they point to the legitimate speculation that plans for resisting the occupying forces had been in store before the US-UK invasion of March 2003. In addition, they suggest that the Baathists, pushed now

---

[6] Patrick Cockburn in his interview with *New Left Review*, No. 36, Nov.–Dec. 2005, 35–67.

out of power, began organizing the resistance with means and techniques acquired from the Iraqi state they ruled for decades. US and British forces are now facing departmentalized, but well-organized and considered strikes that paralyse key economic sectors and institutions and certainly obstruct reconstruction and political processes. All in all, both the USA and the United Kingdom miscalculated the tenacity, persistence and organizational skills of the insurgents, mainly, but not exclusively, recruited from amongst the Sunnis and the Baathists, certain Shi'a factions and also fundamentalists and anti-imperialists from other states.

The Western media are giving the wrong impression that insurgents and suicide bombers target only civilians. Although this is happening—Iraq is going through a period of civil war—this is wrong as an overall concluding remark. *What dominates the acts of the insurgents is strategic sabotage on Iraq's oil infrastructure.* According to the Institute for the Analysis of Global Security, insurgents conducted 282 major attacks on Iraq's oil and gas pipelines, oil installations, terminals and personnel from 12 June 2003 to 24 October 2005.[7] According to the Department of Energy of the USA and former Iraqi oil minister Ghadban, the total of attacks on oil infrastructure during the same period was 642, at a cost of US $10,000m.[8] As well as increasing overall social insecurity, this disrupted production, modernization projects, hence oil extraction, refinement and exports.

Iraq is crisscrossed by more than 6,400 km of oil and gas pipelines, which are difficult to protect. Iraq's oil industry is a shambles. As we saw earlier, fuel shortages, rationing and long queues at petrol stations are becoming endemic. In order to increase the level of security across the country, the USA has contracted private companies with very low-cost personnel recruited from Africa and Latin America. One such company is Erinys, contracted by the Pentagon for US $40m. a year, an additional expense for the occupation to succeed.[9] Another, even more expensive attempt, was the establishment of a highly trained Task Force Shield, composed of US commandos, to guard the sensitive Kirkuk-Ceyhan oil pipeline. But current production of oil in Iraq remains well below pre-war levels, at 1.9m. barrels per day (b/d), and the resulting modest income is scarcely sufficient to allow such a luxury.

The fighting on the ground is crystallized in the new emerging institutions of the country, both by what is included in them *and* by what has, rather mindlessly, been brushed aside. In this context, the Iraqi Constitution is important and we shall pay attention to that document in order to clarify some of its crucial provisions, thus understanding better the resistance, the political and ideological

---

[7] IAGS, Iraq Pipeline Watch, http://www.iags.org/iraqpipelinewatch.htm (accessed 5 December 2005).

[8] Energy Information Administration (June 2005), http://www.eia.doe.gov/emeu/cabs/iraq.html (accessed 14 December 2005)

[9] In Greek mythology, the Erinys were three goddesses, attendants of Hades and Persephone, who guarded the Underworld. What a name to choose for a contermporary mercenary company! Their headquarters are in Johannesburg and Dubai.

tensions and the civil conflict that characterize present-day Iraqi society, under-mining the US programme.

Article 1 of the Constitution defines the Republic of Iraq as 'an independent, sovereign nation', whereas the governing system is 'democratic, federal and representative (parliamentarian)'.[10] Islam is considered as the official religion of the state and as its basic source for legislation, whereas Arabic and Kurdish are stipulated as being Iraq's two official languages. However, all Iraqis have the right to educate their children in whatever minority language they wish (Assyrian, Turkmen, etc.). Article 7 brings up a point of tension: 'Entities or trends that advocate, instigate or propagate racism, terrorism, 'takfir' (declaring someone an infidel), sectarian cleansing, are banned, especially the Saddamist Baath Party in Iraq and its symbols under any name'.[11] The Baath Party with its Sunni com-ponents, having been in power for decades and having an established middle class inside and outside the state apparatus, is now being told that it cannot be repre-sented in Iraq's new institutions. This in itself created a governing/institutional vacuum that had to be filled, whereas the exclusion of Baathists was bound to generate further violence, thus undermining the political process per se.

Article 29, clause 4 stipulates that 'the State guarantees social and health insurance', but as we have tried to show above, no such objective can be achieved without putting an end to corruption and invalidating the Law that gives the right to private companies to have PSAs. Article 35 rather lacks seriousness. It says that 'no-one may be detained or investigated unless by judicial decision, and that all forms of torture, mental or physical, and inhuman treatment are forbidden', but what springs to mind while reading this is the social and prison conditions under US occupation, particularly the case of Abu Ghraib prison. Acts by US occupa-tion forces are silently exempted from Article 35 and the Iraqi Constitution as a whole, for who can bring to justice the guarantors of the new Iraqi Constitution? This is another point that irritates the Iraqis, pushing them to join the resistance movement.

From our perspective, Chapters 3, 4 and 5 of the Constitution are the most important, for they deal with the structure of federal authorities and their competencies/powers, as well as with the management of the oil industry. The institutional architecture reflected in those chapters has ambiguous federal ele-ments. The legislative authority is made up of two bodies, the Council of Representatives (Parliament) and the Council of Union (dealing with the regions). The federal executive authority consists of the President and the Cabinet. The President is elected by the parliament by a two-thirds' majority for a term limited to four years. The President charges the leader of the majority party/coalition with forming a cabinet and confirming his intention to become Prime Minister. In the judiciary branch, the key institution is the Supreme Federal Court, made up of judges who are experts in *shari'a* (Islamic law).

---

[10] *Text of the Draft Constitution*, translated from the Arabic by The Associated Press, http://www.iraqigovernment.org/constituion_en.htm, 1 (accessed 16 December 2005); henceforth: *Constitution*.
[11] Ibid., 2.

According to the Constitution, the federal authority is supposed to be solely responsible for the country's foreign and defence policy, financial and customs policy, issuing currency and organizing issues of nationality and naturalization. As for the oil question, Article 109's vague formulation that 'oil and gas is the property of all the Iraqi people in all regions and provinces' is superseded by the following Article 110, which stipulates: 'The federal government will administer oil and gas extracted from current fields in cooperation with the governments of the producing regions and provinces on condition that the revenues will be distributed fairly in a manner compatible with the demographical distribution all over the country.'[12] It also says that law should privilege regions and areas that were previously treated unfairly by the former regime, a clear reference to the Kurds in the north and the Shi'a in the south. And Article 111, the most controversial of all, states that 'all that is not written in the exclusive powers of the federal authorities is in the authority of the regions'. Moreover, in case of conflict 'between the federal government and the regions, the priority will be given to the region's law'.[13] The governments of the regions, the Constitution goes on to stipulate, have the right to practise legislative, executive and judicial powers, 'except in what is listed as exclusive powers of the federal authorities'. Moreover, Article 116, clause 2, reconfirming the controversial provision of Article 111, states that the regional government has also the right to amend the federal law in case of conflict between regional and central governments in matters that *do not pertain to the exclusive powers of the federal authorities.*[14] We are given a further qualification in Article 128, clause 1, which reads as a co-federal, rather than federal, stipulation: 'The revenues of the region are made up of its designated share from the State budget and from the region's local resources.'[15] It transpires, therefore, that the issue of energy management is not an exclusive matter of the central government and that it swings more on the side of the regions.

On the issue of energy resources, a matter of life and death for Iraq that represents 95% of its revenues, the Constitution, at best, is vague and, at worst, is more co-federal than federal. It will not be an exaggeration to argue that, as regards the governing and institutional technicalities of the new Iraqi polity, the Constitution is federal, but as regards the governance of energy it is rather clearly co-federal. All in all, given the crucial importance of oil and gas and other minerals for Iraq, the Constitution is a patchwork that undermines the political cohesion of the country, encouraging pre-existing centripetal tendencies to grow. These tendencies are found at the heart of the new Iraqi polity: the Constitution

---

[12] Ibid., 18.

[13] Ibid., 19.

[14] This is further corroborated by Article 136, clause 4: 'No amendment is allowed that lessens the powers of the regions that are not among the exclusive powers of the federal authority, except with the agreement of the legislative council of the concerned region and the consent of a majority of its population in a general referendum', ibid., 22.

[15] Ibid., 21.

and the actual relationship of forces, which under the aegis of the USA, have given shape to it.

As we saw earlier, the occupation authorities, in collaboration with specific Shi'a, Kurdish and Sunni parties and groupings, drafted the following political schedule: due chiefly to reasons that had to do with the unexpected resistance movement, Iraq had to be governed for a year by the Coalition Provisional Authority (CPA); then, on 28 June 2004, CPA transferred authority to an interim Iraqi government under Iyad Allawi, a secular Shi'a and 'a long time CIA asset'.[16] Elections were held on 30 January 2005 when it became clear that Shi'a and Kurdish factions were rapidly moving into the new Iraqi polity to fill the power vacuum. The Sunnis did not participate in this election. It took more than three months for the new government to be formed (3 May 2005) under Ibrahim Jaafari, also a secular Shi'a. The main task of the coalition composed of Kurdish and Shi'a parties was to draft a Constitution (discussed above) by October and then organize an election, which was held on 15 December 2005.

Many analysts that adopt the main tenets of our perspective on Iraq, US foreign policy and the Middle East, think of the new Iraqi government as a puppet in the hands of the USA, manipulated at will. In a way, this is understandable, because the USA is the occupying power of the country. However, I would argue that the issue is far more complicated.

First of all, the USA can only set the legal and political framework within which domestic forces can operate in order to achieve the objectives described above. Domestic forces that fall outside the perimeter of the constraints set by the USA receive *dictatorial* treatment. Such forces are the various groups of insurgents. But even this sketch is very much of an 'ideal type'. In essence, the situation on the ground is very chaotic throughout the country, and Iraqi police, security forces and US marines are acting in a dictatorial, indiscriminate and violent manner. Overall, however, the USA does not wish there to be disorder in Iraq, hence its political strategy to initiate political and institutional processes, trying to create the impression that domestic forces are democratically in charge of the post-Saddam Iraq and that its intention is to withdraw its troops from the country once the security problem has been solved.

Second, the new Iraqi polity is cut across by inexorable ethnic, religious and class tensions, which the USA seems to be unable to manipulate and direct. The overthrow of the Baathist bureaucratic cast brought at the same time a significant destruction of Iraq's middle classes. Now there is a ferocious struggle by Kurdish and Shi'a factions not only because they want to rise to the class status of the Baathist/Sunni within the branches of the central state creating their own power base, but also because they want to direct developments towards complete regional autonomy/independence for their respective, oil-rich regions: the south for the Shi'a and the north east for the Kurds. The Shi'a, in addition, being the

---

[16] James Cogan, 'After the Iraq election: Washington steps in to shape the next government', *WSWS*, 21 December 2005, http://www.wsws.org/articles/2005/dec2005/iraq-d21.shtml (accessed 21 December 2005).

majority ethnic group in Iraq, view themselves as representing the whole of Iraq, thus laying claims to governing the entire country from Baghdad, as well as controlling the southern regions for themselves. In this context, the Sunni felt completely marginalized. Thus, 'The priority', *The Economist* advised after the election of 15 December 2005, 'is to involve in government those Sunnis who have been undermining it.'[17] But there is more to the affair than meets the eye.

The area around Baghdad, where the bulk of the Sunnis are living, is very poor in mineral/energy resources. Most of the oilfields are concentrated in Shi'a (Basra) and Kurdish (Kirkuk) areas. The constitutional and political arrangements so far deprive the Sunnis of any meaningful presence or return to positions of power within and outside the state. As we saw earlier, the Constitution's provisions are structured in such a way as to reflect the regional and class interests of the Shi'a and the Kurds, leaving the Sunnis out in the cold. This is more than conspicuous in all of its provisions related to the governance and regional allocation of oil resources. In this respect, a new observable class reality seems to be emerging at the heart of the new Iraqi polity, which has to do with a new type of 'petroleum nationalism'. The Kurdish élites, wanting to build an independent Kurdistan in the north east, need control over the oilfields of Kirkuk and Mosul in order to finance their emerging state out of oil revenues. This Turkey opposes ferociously, lest the Kurds one day envisage a greater Kurdistan including the 20m. Kurds of Turkey, but the USA does not seem, as yet, to have found a comprehensive formula that can accommodate both sides. The USA, however, has unofficially brought Turkey into negotiations with Sunni Iraqi factions, in their attempt to pacify those factions and convince them to join the new executive.[18]

For their part, however, the Kurds have already started signing oil contracts with private companies, disregarding the central authorities in Baghdad.[19] The Shi'a have the numbers—they represent more than 60% of the Iraqi population—the Constitution and their strong link with Iran on their side. Their own 'petroleum nationalism' is consubstantial with their upward social mobility in positions of central and regional power. The backbone of the Shi'a United Iraqi Alliance (UIA) is the Supreme Council for the Islamic Revolution in Iraq (SCIRI), which has close contacts with Iran. Its leaders and followers refused to fight against Iran in the 1980–88 Iran–Iraq War. Interior minister Bayan Jabr until the election of 15 December 2005 was a SCIRI member and most of the Shi'a 'death squads' and militia are directly organized by specific branches of the interior ministry. On 2 August 2005, Steven Vincent, an American journalist, was

---

[17] Unsigned, 'The wrong lot won, dammit', *The Economist*, 7 January 2005, 51.

[18] See Bulent Aras, 'Turkey's options', http://www.bitterlemons-international.org/inside.php?id=507 (accessed 21 March 2006).

[19] In November 2005 an oil exploration deal was signed between the Kurdish-controlled region of Iraq and the Norwegian oil company DNO; see Borzou Daragahi, 'Kurdish oil deal shocks Iraq's political leaders', *Los Angeles Times*, 1 December 2005, http://www.globalpolicy.org/security/oil/2005/0928heritageoil.htm. In September 2005 the Kurds had signed a Memorandum of Understanding (MOU) with Heritage Oil Corporation (HOC), which also caused uproar among the Sunnis.

kidnapped and murdered, because he had exposed Shi'a 'death squads'. Grand Ayatollah al-Sistani and various SCIRI leaders meet Iranian officials and discuss with them 'border security, cooperation on oil projects' and intelligence and other matters.[20]

Soon after the election of 15 December 2005, the Sunnis accused the Shi'a of storming polling stations and terrorizing Sunni voters.[21] Thus, the Sunni 'petroleum nationalism' is but a nationalism of deprivation: located in the centre of the country where no major oilfields exist, and with their rights undermined by the Constitution, the Sunnis feel squeezed out of politics and power arrangements. This induces them to join the insurgents and fight on three fronts: the Shi'a, the Kurds and the Americans.

Our analyses so far indicate that every ethnic and religious group in Iraq today has something to fight for, with the Sunni having to fight almost for everything as they have lost everything. In addition, our analyses suggest that the real winners of the US invasion and occupation of Iraq are the Kurds, but mostly the Shi'a, and through them, Iran. Thus, it transpires that the USA has recently begun to change its policy towards the Shi'a. US Ambassador to Iraq, Zalmay Khalilzad, hinted that the next head of the interior ministry 'should be trusted by all communities and not come from elements of the population that have militias'.[22] *The Economist*, as we saw earlier, seems to advise along the same lines. The official results of the election of 15 December 2005, announced nearly 40 days later (20 January 2006), gave the Shi'a coalition 130 out of 275 seats in the parliament, which means that the Shi'a need partners to govern.[23] The Kurdish Alliance took 53 seats, whereas the largest Sunni party, the Iraqi Accordance Front, won 44 seats and another Sunni party, made up of former Baathists, won 11. Ayad Allawi's party took 25 seats, whereas Ahmed Chalabi's Iraqi National Congress, Washington's favourite to lead the new Iraq, failed to win a seat. The Shi'a and Kurdish parties now hold 40 fewer seats between them than they held in the old parliament. The result, albeit a truncated one, represents a victory for the Shi'a and the Kurds and a further blow for the US-backed candidates, Chalabi and Allawi. The Sunnis—although by no means all of them—want now to be part of the game, as they realize that the Shi'a do need partners to govern and the Kurds are not forthcoming. Thus, Khalilzad, facing political chaos coupled with further attacks on both Shi'a and Sunni holy sites, in March 2006 invented a 19-member 'National Security Council' (NSC), composed of nine Shi'a, four Kurds, four Sunni and two 'secular' politicians, with Ahmad Chalabi, whose party won no seats, being one of them. This increases rather than decreases the difficulties

---

[20] Geoffrey Kemp, 'Iran and Iraq: the Shia connection, soft power and the nuclear factor', United States Institute of Peace, http://www.usip.org/pubs/specialreports/sr156.html (accessed 11 January 2006).

[21] *The Economist* concedes that 'serious offences almost certainly occurred, but probably not on a scale large enough to shift [the election outcome] more than a handful of seats', in 'The wrong lot ...', op.cit., 50.

[22] Quoted in Cogan, 3.

[23] See, Robert F. Worth and John O'Neil, 'Iraq's Shiites fall short of majority', *International Herald Tribune*, 21–22 January 2006, 1, 4.

facing the USA in Iraq. This NSC Iraqi-style has been given quasi-dictatorial powers, including the right to amend the Constitution.

The new election results are unable to affect the existing institutional crystal-lizations of power in Iraq without a further increase in violence. Soon after the election, Khalilzad wrote that the Constitution is now 'likely to be amended' in order to broaden support.[24] This was immediately denounced by Abdul Aziz al-Hakim, the leader of SCIRI, who ruled out any constitutional changes. Thus, in the event that the USA attempts to enforce constitutional changes in order to meet Sunni demands, it will threaten the alienation of the Shi'a. In fact, the Shi'a are difficult to remove peacefully from key positions of social and institutional power without interference from Iran. As we shall see below, every single option, or a combination of them, laying before the USA today is extraordinarily difficult and painful.

Corruption and Production Sharing Agreements (PSAs)

There are a number of other reasons contributing to the undoing of any move on the part of the USA to implement its pre-war oil programme. To begin with, corruption and mismanagement have become almost endemic, not only in the US-backed governments but also in US private companies managing some of Iraq's key oil projects and infrastructure.[25]

The situation in the Iraqi oil ministry is typical in demonstrating the overall crisis of the new Iraqi polity and US occupation policies. Since the invasion and until 2 January 2006, two people have been rotating in the position of Minister of Oil: Ibraihim al-Uloum, a US-trained petroleum engineer, and Thamir Ghadban, a UK-trained geologist and petroleum engineer. They both seemed to share, at least in public, the same expectations as the USA: 'daily crude production has risen to half a million barrels a day, enough to satisfy most of Iraq's domestic needs', Ghadban told a journalist from *The New Yorker*, John Cassidy, back in July 2003.[26] Uloum resigned on 2 January 2006, having been in office for only seven months (since May 2005). His resignation was triggered by an IMF-imposed rise in fuel prices, in order to compensate for a plan to cancel up to 80% of Iraq's US $120,000m. debt to creditor nations.[27] Uloum did not disagree with the IMF imposition, but he argued that the reform process should take place in stages in order to absorb wide popular protest against it. He also accused the government of wishing to pocket most of the income from the increased fuel price, as the cash was to go not to the creditor (mostly European) nations, but to corrupt factions in the government. Iraqi authorities are already facing a cash crunch, 'as funds from

---

[24] Ibid., 4.

[25] See in particular, John Sloboda et al., Oxford Research Group, *Iraqi Liberation? Towards an Integrated Strategy* (Oxford: ORG, December 2005).

[26] John Cassidy, 'Beneath the sand', *The New Yorker*, 14–21 July 2003, 71.

[27] See, Peter Symonds, 'Iraqi oil minister resigns amid protests and economic chaos', *WSWS*, 9 January 2006, http://www.wsws.org/articles/2006/jan2006/iraq-j09.shtml (accessed 9 January 2006).

a $4 billion stash of frozen Iraqi assets are gradually depleted and $2.5 billion in reconstruction funds appropriated by Congress run out'.[28] The crisis over the price of oil is coupled with serious fuel shortages, rationing and long queues at petrol stations.[29] According to Issam al-Chalabi, a former Iraqi Oil Minister (1987–90), 'since June 2003, Iraq has been importing gasoline, gas oil, LPG and kerosene, costing now over $300m a month. Iraq must have spent over 46bn so far', al-Chalabi argued in his October 2005 speech, 'and imports are expected to continue for another three years at least. There also have been claims of corrupt deals involving this trade.'[30] In this context, black market and corruption practices are flourishing: 'Just how much oil has been lost to corruption or black-market transaction is impossible to determine', says Michael Klare, 'but experts believe the amounts are substantial.' He goes on to quote Muhammad al-Abudi, the oil ministry's director-general of drilling: 'The robberies and thefts that are taking place on a daily basis and on all levels ... are committed by low-level government employees and also by high officials in leadership positions in the Iraqi state.'[31] Admittedly, all these are developments that are running counter to fulfilling the expectations of the USA and Ghadban's wishes, as he expressed them in *The New Yorker* in July 2003.

The situation is not better in the private sector, particularly in the oil industry. There are two aspects to that problem. The first is the issue of mismanagement and corruption. The second is that of Production Sharing Agreements (PSAs), which bring huge benefits to private companies and oil operators, but very little to the new Iraqi polity and its raw redistribution mechanisms.

Even before the USA invaded Iraq, the Bush Administration awarded a controversial no-bid contract to Kellogg Brown & Root (KBR). This is a Houston-based firm and a subsidiary of Halliburton, the oil-services giant, whose former managing director was the current US Vice-President, Dick Cheney. KBR's contractual obligation was to repair and modernize key Iraqi oil infrastructure and wells, pipelines and water treatment plants. According to T. Christian Miller of *Los Angeles Times*, the US government gave KBR up to US $332m. to repair and modernize: (a) the Qarmat Ali water treatment plant, a massive pumping complex that injects water into Iraq's southern oilfields to aid oil extraction; (b) the al-Fathah pipelines, a project to rebuild a pipeline network in northern Iraq; (c) the southern oil wells repair project, aiming at boosting production at dozens of Iraqi oil wells. In the first two cases, KBR failed to deliver satisfactory services. The third project was cancelled by KBR itself, which accused the US government of

---

[28] Warren Vieth and Alissa J. Rubin, 'Iraq pipelines easy targets for a saboteur', 14 December 2005 http://www.commondreams.org/headlines03/0625-06.htm (accessed 16 December 2005).

[29] On the issue of shortage of oil and other raw materials in Iraq, see Brian Conley, 'Iraq: So much oil, and so little', *IPSNews*, 14 December 2004, http://www.ipsnews.net/news.asp?idnews=31239 (accessed 16 December 2005).

[30] Issam al-Chalabi, 'What is happening to Iraqi oil?', *Middle East Economic Survey*, 10 October 2005, http://www.globalpolicy.org/security/oil/2005/1010iraqioil.htm (accessed 13 December 2005). This is a paper al-Chalabi presented to a conference held in London on 20–22 September 2005.

[31] Klare, 'More blood, less oil'.

failing to protect it from possible lawsuits.[32] As if this was not enough, Iraqi executives, under pressure from their superiors to maximize production, tend to employ faulty pumping methods, thus damaging underground reservoirs. This can happen when water aid fails to facilitate oil extraction, whereas the system keeps being switched on trying to pump oil. Time and again, this all can hardly contribute to an implementation of the US programme.

The other aspect related to Iraq's energy resources is the legal regime of their exploitation. Here, our focus is *oil companies* and not *service companies*, such as KBR. The former are dealing directly with oil exploitation and speculative contracts, which gives them the opportunity to make super-profits, whereas the latter are usually service operators, receiving a fixed fee on predictable contracts. Before the war, the 'internationalization' of the Iraqi oil and gas industry was a matter of implementing 'concession'-type contracts (see below), negotiated with oil companies mainly from China (China National Petroleum Corporation), France (TotalFinaElf), Russia (Lukoil) and Italy (Agip). After the war, the CPA appointed 'former senior executives from oil companies' to review Iraq's oil policy and set up a comprehensive framework composed of new guide-lines.[33] The CPA appointed Phillip Carroll, a former executive of Shell, Garry Vogler, of ExxonMobil, as well as assessors from the US Department of Energy and the Australian government. The table was turned upside down: excluded before the war, Anglo-Saxon oil companies now began vying for access to Iraq's oil wealth. For this purpose, they appointed lobbyists, recruited assessors, organized conferences and geology seminars; all in all, they began doing everything they could in order to win favourable treatment from the CPA and, later, from Iraqi governments. As regards the pre-war contracts, they have either been invalidated or are in abeyance, whereas oil companies in general are encouraged to sign Memorandums of Understanding (MOU) with whichever Iraqi authorities are in charge.[34] It should also be noted that Canadian (OGI Group), Italian (Agip/ENI), Russian (Soyuzneftegaz, Tatneft), Turkish (Avrasya Technology Engineering) and other companies have already signed contracts or expressed interest in developing certain Iraqi oilfields.

Iraq has about 80 known oilfields. However, only 17 of them are currently producing, with difficulty, oil. The policy under development by the Iraqi government, under the direct influence of US occupation forces and corporate interests, is that all the 'dormant' oilfields will be exploited by private companies on the basis of PSAs. The October 2005 Constitution is vague about this, but parallel to the Constitution a Petroleum Law had been drafted, to be implemented after the election of 15 December 2005.[35]

---

[32] T. Christian Miller, 'Missteps hamper Iraqi oil recovery', *Los Angeles Times*, 26 September 2005, http://www.globalpolicy.org/security/issues/iraq/reconstruct/2005/0926oilrecovery.htm (accessed 18 December 2005).

[33] We are relying here on the perceptive report produced by 'Platform', *Crude Designs; the Rip-off of Iraq's Oil Wealth* (London, Seacourt Press, November 2005), p. 17; henceforth: *Crude Designs*.

[34] Energy Information Administration, DOE, 'Iraq: Country analysis brief', June 2005, op. cit.

[35] Unsigned, 'Iraq Constitution lays ground for oilfield sell-off', *Carbon Web*, 1 October 2005, http://www.globalpolicy.org/security/oil/20055555/1001laysground.htm (accessed 20 December 2005).

This means two very important things. First, that nearly 65% of Iraq's known oil reserves will be controlled by private interests, as Iraq's 17 fields currently in production represent only 40m. of the country's overall 115,000m. barrels of known reserves.[36] Second, it means that the legal binding structure based on PSAs will bring enormous benefits to private companies and the USA's dollar-based strategy for energy policy, but a great loss of revenue to the new Iraqi state and, as a consequence, to its welfare policies. To understand this better, we need to shed some light on how a PSA contract works.

In general, oil- and gas-producing states have three legal ways to run their energy and mineral businesses. The first is that of a *nationalized industry*, where the state is in control of the entire revenue resulting from energy. The extent to which foreign companies are involved is determined by the state: they can be hired, for example, to 'carry out certain services under contract (technical service contract)'.[37] This has been the case with Iraq since 1972. In the wider Middle Eastern and Cold War context, the classic paradigm is that of Egyptian President, Gamal Abdel Nasser, who regarded the nationalization of Middle Eastern oil industries and Egypt's key strategic chokepoint, the Suez Canal, as the flagship of Arab national pride. *What can be called 'petroleum nationalism' is precisely the phenomenon of asserting state sovereignty and power over neo-imperial interests via blocking off access to strategic resources and chokepoints.* Another paradigm of nationalized oil industries is that of Saudi Arabia, which nevertheless has been regulated by other policy arrangements since the 1970s, favourable to the USA, and with the Saudi regime under the determining presence of the US army, stationed there since 1990.[38]

An alternative to nationalization is the so-called *concession model*, at times known as 'the tax and royalty system', which has been so perceptively analysed most recently by Bernard Mommer in his *Global Oil and the Nation State.*[39] Put very simply, this is a system in which the private company receives a licence from the state to extract, sell, refine and transport oil. In return, the company pays the state taxes and royalties.

A PSA contract is a third form of policy, with a rather complex legal structure/ contract between a national oil company—in Iraq's case the Iraqi National Oil Company (INOC)—and private investors/companies.[40] In a PSA, the private company finances the entire cycle of investment (exploration, drilling, infra-structure, etc.), with the entire proportion of the first oil produced going to the company in order to recover the costs incurred in the investment cycle. After that, profits are divided between the national company and the private company in

---

[36] *Crude Designs*, 19.

[37] Ibid., 11.

[38] See in particular, Said K. Aburish, *The House of Saud* (London, Bloomsbury, 2005).

[39] Bernard Mommer, *Global Oil and the Nation State* (Oxford, OUP, 2002). Mommer's account is one of the most significant contributions to our understanding of the private governance of mineral resources; see our review of Mommer in *The Political Quarterly*, v. 74, n. 4, Oct.–Dec. 2003.

[40] The classic work on PSAs is that by Daniel Johnston, *International Petroleum Fiscal Systems and Production Sharing Contracts* (Oklahoma, Pennwell, 1994).

agreed proportions. The aforementioned report, *Crude Designs,* produced by 'Platform', has estimated that with a full implementation of PSAs in just 12 of Iraq's underdeveloped fields, private companies will reap profits of between US $74,000m. and US $194,000m. in terms of 2006 dollars over a 30-year period, compared to keeping oil development under state control.[41] 'Platform' stated that this estimate is conservative because it is projected on the basis of an oil price of US $40 per barrel (the current price at the time of writing, February 2006, is around US $70 per barrel). We have no reason to believe that these estimates are wrong or misleading. In fact, what they mean is that the new Iraqi polity, being built under the direct influence and control of US occupation forces, will be deprived of substantial sums of revenue from oil, which would have otherwise enabled it to initiate a number of welfare reforms in education, health and pensions. Given that oil accounts for 95% of Iraq's government revenues, the negative impact of PSAs on the state's budgetary policies is more than obvious.

PSAs are not appropriate for countries with large oil reserves, because the complicated legal structure of the agreement concedes the largest chunk from the oil revenue to private companies. Venezuela had some PSAs, but this policy has now been substantially reversed under the strong 'petroleum nationalism' of Hugo Chávez Frías. Russia has also some PSAs valid today, which had been signed during the exhilarating period of 'shock therapy' reforms of the 1990s under Yeltsin, but they proved to be controversial and their renewal is doubtful. Indonesia's legal oil regime is based on PSAs, but Indonesia is not an important producer of oil and its fields are small with low production. All in all, PSAs are likely to accentuate the existing tensions between US occupation forces and the Iraqis, pushing more and more Iraqis to embrace the resistance, thus creating another insuperable obstacle to the implementation of the US programme.

Concluding Remarks

The failure of Anglo-Saxon powers in Iraq is colossal. The key programmatic goal regarding oil set before the invasion has not been accomplished and the situation on the ground remains highly volatile and precarious. In this respect, two issues stand out: first, the failure to provide a fair constitutional settlement representing the interests of all religious and ethnic groups has been more than pronounced. The USA has made the mistake of dismantling the Baathist apparatus *in toto*, destroying the Sunni middle classes, thus giving pro-Iran fundamentalist elements the opportunity to dominate the state machine. This is the context in which the issue of 'petroleum nationalism' in Iraq can be analysed and understood. 'Petroleum nationalism' is the result of sanctions and the imposition of 'no-fly zones' on Iraq since 1991, and it has been exacerbated since the USA's invasion and occupation of the country. Both major ethnic/religious groups, the Kurds and the Shi'a, managed to insert in the new Constitution their nationalistic claim on oil resources, which are concentrated in the northern Kurdish areas and

---

[41] *Crude Designs,* 20 ff.

the southern Shi'a zones. The Sunni have resisted this arrangement ferociously, as there is not much oil left for them to administer in the area around Baghdad. Thus, Sunni 'petroleum nationalism' and acts of violence are driven by the syndrome of deprivation.

Second, the so-called PSAs cannot turn the tide for the USA: they will contribute to the fulfilment of the USA's pre-war oil programme. Moreover, if adopted as the key contractual form between the government and oil companies, they will increase the economic burden on the Iraqi people, while depriving the Iraqi state of the revenue it needs to build a decent social and welfare infra-structure. This, in turn, will augment people's dissatisfaction and push more Iraqis towards insurgency, thus creating further problems for the US and UK occupation forces. It seems that we are still very far from a democratic and peaceful new Iraq.

Oil and Islam—Economic Distress and Political Opposition

ØYSTEIN NORENG

Introduction

The purpose of this essay is to contribute to the understanding of the quickly changing politics of the Gulf countries in light of sudden economic and social changes mainly due to the influx of high, but unstable oil revenues since the early 1970s, and against a historical and cultural background largely influenced by Islam. Contrary to a widespread opinion in the West, the root of the problem is not in Islam, but in the failure of oil-based economic and social policies (Askari, 2004).

The term Islamism is in this connection defined as the use of references to Islam and its basic sources for specific political purposes (Burgat, 1995a). Another usual denomination is Islamic fundamentalism (Hobsbawm, 1994). This essentially is a mass mobilization of people against unpopular and unaccountable governments (Vogt, 1992). The main objective is to alter or overthrow the present social and political order. The further aim is to establish a new social order based on alleged Koranic theological and juridical principles, which emphasize a proper personal conduct and social justice. In the mean time, the Islamist movements in the Middle East and North Africa serve as an alibi for repressive and often inefficient regimes (Naim, 1996). The immediate outcome is a political stalemate, but as an expression of broad social forces, the Islamist movements cannot be fought by repression alone, or repression may be counterproductive.

In the West, Islamist movements are often portrayed in their most extreme and violent form (Luders, 1995). The diversity of the movements and the bulk of non-violent Islamists receive little attention (Burgat, 1995b). By highlighting the extreme and violent forms of Islamism, the West tends to overlook the more profound historical issues, economic problems and social forces (Waterbury, 1994). In the West, there is little understanding of why the Islamist movements appear in the Muslim world. Consequently, there is also a general lack of comprehension of the sudden changes imposed on Muslim societies by the rise and fall of oil revenues. More seriously, there is hardly any understanding in the West of how the present social problems of the Middle East and North Africa have their causes in political conditions and mismanagement rather than in a lack of resources.

The hypothesis is that rising economic and social inequalities, based on the mismanagement of oil revenues, can be criticized as transgressing against basic political and religious principles of Islam. The second proposition is that historically, absolutist rule has also prevented the merchant class from gaining political power, contrary to the West European experience.

A third proposition is that the petroleum policies and economic policies based on petroleum revenues since the early 1970s in the Middle Eastern and North African countries today are easy targets of Islamic criticism. It is questionable whether Islam originally has some distinctive principles for organizing economic life, which are of present relevance. This does not prevent contemporary Islamic scholars from developing distinctive economic ideas. Some of these principles are relevant to economic policy in a modern society. They include the sanctity of private property, the prohibition of charging interest, the need to share risk, the prerogative to redistribute income as well as the prohibition of waste and idleness. These economic principles are also relevant to petroleum policy decisions. Interest considerations influence the rate of depletion of a finite resource. The Islamist charges are briefly that the economic policies based on petroleum revenues serve the narrow and short-term interests of a technocratic class based in the public sector. Consequently, they allegedly infringe upon the principles attributed to Islam. The critique is briefly that the ruling class is pumping out a finite resource too quickly and that the revenues serve a limited number of people. The revenues to a considerable extent finance the wasteful consumption of a Westernized civilian and military ruling class. In an Islamist perspective, abstaining from interest calculations, oil policies could give a higher priority to keeping more oil in the ground.

A fourth proposition is that the growth of the oil industry and of a large public sector based on oil revenues has infringed upon the interests of the merchant class. They have changed the relationship between the private and the public sectors. The arrival of the oil industry and subsequently large oil revenues fostered a new technocratic class, which is military personnel and civil servants occupying the public sector. They have marginalized the private sector and the merchant class. Large oil revenues enabled the governments to finance an extensive welfare state, legitimizing the rule of the technocratic and military class, in spite of the absence of democratic institutions. Therefore, the large oil revenues of the 1970s and early 1980s have strengthened a modern version of the absolutist state. It is generally based on the armed forces. A practical result has been a surge in military expenditure. This was also in the interest of the Western oil-importing countries that through arms exports could partly offset the financial burden of oil imports. With declining oil revenues, the conflict between civilian and military priorities intensifies.

A fifth proposition is that the decline in oil revenues since the mid-1980s has undermined the welfare state, with rapidly rising unemployment largely affecting an urbanized and educated young generation. The population pressure intensifies intergenerational conflict, over distribution as over values. There is a pressing need for income redistribution, but the absence of democratic institutions fosters violent conflict. Indeed, the problem of accommodating social and generational change and of redistributing income worsens through the absence of representative political institutions. Political power in the Middle Eastern and North African societies belongs to extensive royal families, military personnel and leading civil servants. There is hardly any participation by industrial or agricultural workers or even the merchant class. Autocratic governments with varying degrees of repression have traditionally gained legitimacy by offering services without taxing the population. Oil revenues financed public expenditure. An important purpose of expenditure was to selectively buy the favours of key segments of the population. Declining oil revenues have led to cuts in public services and fewer resources to buy favours and hence to a gradual loss of political legitimacy. At the same time, the modern absolutist rulers, often in military garb, cling to power. Hence they prevent the evolution of economic and political structures. With declining oil revenues and a growing population, the conflict between civilian and military priorities intensifies. The development of the Muslim societies generally would require that merchants replace soldiers as the politically dominant element, as happened in Europe in the past. There are, however, strong obstacles to such a change.

A sixth proposition is that the absence of liberal institutions and the prohibition of any independent political life outside the state make the mosque the only channel for political opposition. Under the pressure of deteriorating social conditions, the mosque is promising income redistribution, employment and improved public services by taxing the wealthy and by curbing conspicuous consumption. The social critique, which targets the established rulers and the new technocratic class in the Middle Eastern and North African societies, therefore acquires a religious accent. It fights social inequality and injustice as an evil. Islamism thus appears as the opposition to the Westernized technocratic ruling class, whether civilian or military, with the merchant class in critical cases joining this opposition. The social crisis enhances opposition to Western cultural influence. Marxism, which historically had a strong position in secular Iraq and Syria, is today a spent force. In this ideological void, religion lends itself to political use.

The seventh and final proposition is that eventual Islamist governments in Arab oil-exporting countries could have strong effects on economic policies in general and oil policy in particular. Insofar as a rapid rate of depletion accompanies a wasteful use of the oil revenues, an Islamist government would find reasons to reduce output. The military priority of the past 20 years has a high cost when measured in oil exports. Insofar as military expenditure is an indicator of wasteful consumption, prohibited by Islam, the alternative could have been to leave more oil in the ground. The effect on the oil market would have been strong. Indeed, without the military burden, essentially motivated by fears of conflicts with other Muslim countries as well as aggression and occupation by oil-importing powers, the Middle Eastern and North African oil exporters would have been far less strained financially. Consequently, they would have enjoyed more freedom in petroleum policies. Ideally, an Islamist government would synchronize the depletion of oil reserves with investing the revenues in new productive assets in order to maintain and expand the income base. In practice, this is difficult when population grows quickly and no other sources of income are available.

In the 1970s and early 1980s, the Middle East and North Africa appeared as economic and social successes, with rising incomes and social conditions improving. In the 1990s, with some exceptions, the region appeared as a resounding economic and social failure, with per capita income falling and social conditions deteriorating. Since 2000, there has been, again, a marked improvement, as high oil revenues finance more generous social policies. The situation is tenuous, dependent upon precarious oil revenues. There are too few jobs for the increasing young population, so that unemployment is rising quickly. Inadequate investment in education means that the growing young population often does not have the qualifications even if jobs were available (UNDP 2003). The alternative is to use oil revenues to subsidize employment. The Middle East and North Africa make up the only one of the world's major regions unable to feed its population, meaning that food supplies and nutritional standards depend on oil revenues; therefore they are under a stronger economic threat than elsewhere, with onerous political implications.

Petroleum and Religion

Religion and petroleum may seem unrelated issues, one spiritual, the other material, but there is an interactive relationship: religion influences the normative basis of economic activity, such as the extraction of petroleum and the use of the ensuing revenues; and the extraction of petroleum and the use of revenues shape societies and international relations, which are liable to cause tensions and conflicts that are part of the social and political basis of religious practice. Religion provides a normative basis which also encompasses economic activity, and in return economic activity has effects that at times infringe upon the principles of religion (Mills and Presley, 1999). In renaissance Europe, the Catholic Church prohibited charging interest for credit, so there was dispute between the banking business and the ecclesiastical authorities, which in the end were forced to yield, but not without strife that included the Reformation.

This is, briefly, why religion matters to oil, and vice versa. It is hardly possible to analyse the development of the international oil market since 1945 without an understanding of the internal and external tensions that affect the Middle East, but it is hardly possible to understand the Middle East without a comprehension of Islam. Likewise, it is difficult to analyse the evolution of capitalism in Europe in the Renaissance without a reference to the Catholic Church. Islam is essential not only to understanding the oil-exporting countries of the Middle East and North Africa, but also to appreciating the economic, social and political context in which the petroleum industries of these countries operate and the predominant principles for economic performance in these societies, as well as the inherited cultural and social setting in which the economic changes take place. Islam is a practical religion, with specific rules for daily life, also for conducting business, distinguishing ethically clean behaviour, *halal*, from ethically unclean behaviour, *haram* (Rodinson, 1966). Islam explicitly respects private property, but prohibits usury or wasting resources as long as people are in need, commanding the redistribution of wealth.

Islam, therefore, practically matters for oil policies in the Middle East and North Africa. The prohibition of interest calculation could influence the rate of depletion of a finite resource, with a preference for keeping more oil in the ground. Forbidding waste could limit the spending of oil revenues, and consequently the need to pump out oil. The imperative of redistributing wealth can mean that the state shall control the oil money (Rutledge, 2005). The tenets are pertinent to intergenerational equity, social equity and economic organization.

Such tenets are not unique to Islam; they have counterparts in many non-Muslim oil-exporting countries, from Mexico and Venezuela to Norway and Russia, but in the Islamic tradition they also have a spiritual foundation (Lamchichi, 2001). In the Western world, the national control of natural resources, depleting oil reserves slowly, not wasting oil revenues and using them to secure equality, are usually claims put forth by the secular left; in the Muslim world, such claims are also based on religious tradition and authority (Sivan, 1985). This indicates the potential of Islam to politically channel social discontent, but for Islam to radically engender social change in Muslim societies may require a transformation of religious practices (Chebel, 2002). From this perspective, the present social and political predicament of the Muslim world may offer Islam a historical chance to renew itself (Pott, 2001).

Islam has been and is a crucial force shaping the Middle Eastern and North African societies; it is also a product of the region (Lindholm, 2002). Many attitudes and practices which today are considered Islamic are often older, originating in the region and justified by its habitat (Fatany, 2004). The merchant and Bedouin legacies are important in this respect. A great religion can also be seen as a political project aiming to shape society, which is crucial to the historical consciousness of Muslim societies (Rodinson, 1993). Islam's overall political and economic principles are sufficiently vague to survive as a reference through the ages, and they lend themselves to different and often opposing interpretations, but there is a distinctive common trunk: Islam does not recognize any separation of the worldly and the godly (Mahfoud, 1994).

Through the ages, Islam's judicial, political and economic agenda has been developed and supplemented by the learned, the *ulama*, a combination of lawyers and theologians who have served as judges, administrators, teachers and religious advisers (Lapidus, 1975). Even if they have had at times a considerable degree of independence, they have usually been employed by the state, so that the development of Islamic law and the Islamic political and economic agenda has historically not taken place without regard for the interests of the state. The exception is the Shi'a tradition, prevalent in Iran and parts of Iraq, Lebanon and Syria, where the clergy has an independent income base.

Integrating the worldly and the godly from the outset distinguished Islam from Christianity, embodying the political project to reconcile and unite various clans and tribes and different social classes through a monotheistic religion, combined with a rudimentary welfare state. An important objective was to establish an institutional order for the emerging Arab merchant class, securing the support of the Bedouins. The merchant class often had large profits from long-distance trade, but the trading routes in most cases went through Bedouin territory; they had military superiority and control of the trading routes (Andersen et al., 1993). The traditional social base of the Muslim state has been the merchant class, traders in the bazaar. They represent the continuous and stable element in Middle Eastern and North African societies. The Prophet, Muhammad, was born into an urban merchant family.

By its origins and subsequent development, Islam appears as an urban religion (Planbol, 1994). Islam in many ways appears as the ideological superstructure of the merchant class, which is the reason for the close link between the bazaar and the mosque and the fundamental respect of Islam for private property and honest, personal enrichment (Rodinson, 1966). It has sufficient flexibility to take the Bedouin interests and points of view into account and make them submit to the authority of the new state (Planbol, 1994). The counterpart was a system of welfare and transfers from the wealthy to the poor, including the Bedouins, who were both conservative and egalitarian (Ruthven, 1991). The need to respect salient Bedouin traditions can perhaps explain Islam's references to group loyalty and puritan ways of life. As a consequence, Islam from the beginning also had a social promise. From this perspective, Muhammad was not only a prophet, but also a statesman (Hartmann, 1992). The project was not only to propagate a new faith, but also to establish a new state with a specific social and political order.

Historically, the most comprehensive codification of Islamic law took place in the early Abbasid Empire in the late eighth and early ninth century AD. The new Abbasid regime needed to legitimize its rule. At this time the religious scholars also acquired social and administrative positions, underlining the character of Islam as a continuous process, where the interpretation of the sacred texts serves a political purpose, most often to legitimize the power in place. In times of turmoil and the breakdown of power structures, Islam can also be invoked against the powers in place, with the reinterpretation of the sacred texts legitimizing disobedience to authority. An important historical example is the crisis of Caliphal authority in the Abbasid Empire in the early ninth century (Lapidus, 1975).

In modern times, the reinterpretation of the sacred texts for the purpose of opposing authority has been recurrent in Egypt since the 1920s, and more recently in other countries, including Iran (Pott, 2001). This development expresses the instability and turmoil of Muslim societies, caught between secularizing governments and rising social tensions. Since the mid-1980s, the Middle East and North Africa have witnessed an increasing ideological confrontation with religious references, reflecting an economic and social crisis and the gradual erosion of the legitimacy of the rulers in the aftermath of declining oil revenues. The battle for the interpretation of the sacred texts is also a battle for political power (Kepel, 2004). The audience is now an increasingly urbanized and educated population, distinguished by youth and high unemployment, in societies profoundly marked by the uneven flows of oil revenues since the early 1970s.

The Islamist charges are, briefly, that the economic policies based on petroleum revenues serve the narrow and short-term interests of a technocratic class based in the public sector. Hence, they allegedly infringe upon the principles attributed to Islam. The critique is briefly that the ruling class is pumping out a finite resource too quickly and that the revenues serve a limited number of people. The revenues to a considerable extent finance the wasteful consumption of a Westernized civilian and military ruling class. In an Islamist perspective, abstaining from interest calculations, oil policies could give a higher priority to keeping more oil in the ground.

Population Growth and Economic Instability

In the Middle East (and North Africa), economic, social and political development in the 20th century has been dominated by oil, regardless of the country in question. Huge oil reserves at low cost have attracted the attention of the great powers to the region since before the First World War and provided the basis for a specific form of development based on oil revenues, the rentier state, which until today remains predominant in the region. From the early 1970s to the mid-1980s, the Middle East was considered the economically most promising part of the world, in spite of its numerous political tensions and open conflicts. With oil income, the oil-exporting countries of the region had made an economic quantum leap. In some salient cases they went from dire poverty to extreme wealth within a decade. Their economic growth rates were exceptional and their relative position in the world improved remarkably.

Around 1980, Kuwait's per capita gross national product (GNP) was higher than that of most European countries. By that measure, Iraq and Saudi Arabia were at the level of Central Europe. The Middle East had become an important market for goods and services. The region also had the economic resources to be a politically significant part of the world community. The general impression was that the oil wealth was reasonably well managed and that the oil-exporting countries of the region were making a transition into modern economies. The wise use of an important natural resource apparently could propel a group of countries into the modern world. They also gave the impression of having a sophisticated and visionary leadership combining wisdom and power (Roberts, 1995).

The oil price rises of the 1970s made everyone in the oil-exporting countries of the Middle East richer, but some citizens became much richer than others. The mechanisms of particular enrichment were many. In some countries, there was little or no distinction between the coffers of the state and those of the royal family, so the rulers, their families and favourites were the first to benefit. Leading officials in government and the national oil company could amass vast fortunes through a mixture of private and official interests. Businesses dealing with the government and the oil industry could also profit disproportionately, as could some lucky landowners. In the aftermath of the first oil price rise came the beginning of ostentatious wealth and conspicuous consumption. This inspired grandiose and megalomaniac development plans, as for example in Iran. By the

1970s it was evident that the distribution of wealth and income was becoming less equal. However, this was relatively easy to bear, because even the poorest parts of the population also enjoyed rapidly improving living conditions. The exception was Iran, where the rapidly rising income inequality in the mid-1970s proved to be an important factor behind the revolution.

The immediate effect of the second oil price rise of 1979–80 was to flood the Arab oil exporters of the Middle East with easy money. This money was even less equally distributed—but that did not matter much politically. Most inhabitants experienced rising prosperity. For a few years, these countries experienced an acute embarrassment of riches. This came to an end when they had to cut oil export volumes to defend the price of oil before it fell and export volumes were still fairly low. The contraction that began at various points in the early 1980s, depending upon how much money had been saved during the boom years, was not equally distributed. Budget cuts hit the poor much more than the rich. By around 1980 the distribution of wealth and income had become more unequal in most Arab oil-exporting countries, and during the late 1980s and early 1990s income distribution became even more skewed. The poor were getting both more numerous, and more impoverished. The rich refused to relinquish their money and privileges—and they had the means to defend their interests.

By the late 1990s, evidently the Middle East had slipped behind and is continuing to do so, although high oil prices since 2000 have provided ample revenues. The need to create jobs is still urgent. Youth unemployment is in many cases between 30%–50%. The need to replace foreign workers with locals, such as exists in Saudi Arabia, raises difficult issues of labour productivity and income distribution. Iraq has historically been the exception, as a welfare state with relatively good social conditions. This is no longer the case, because of the Saddam Hussein regime, the war against Iran, the Gulf conflict, the subsequent embargo, the war and occupation by the USA and allies such as Denmark, Honduras, Poland and the United Kingdom. Average income is high by Western standards only in Kuwait, Qatar and the United Arab Emirates. Countries such as Oman and Saudi Arabia have an average income level below that of poorer West European countries, such as Greece and Portugal. Among citizens, income distribution is less unequal than among the working population, which includes a large number of foreign workers.

In other Middle Eastern oil-exporting countries, essentially Iran and Iraq, average income levels are much lower. The majority of the population has difficult living conditions by European or North American standards. The oil price decline of 1986 led to a serious drop in oil revenues for most oil-exporting countries and a subsequent and lasting deterioration of social conditions. Low oil prices in 1997–99 had a similar effect. Insofar as oil revenues are increasing less quickly than population and other sources of income are not sufficiently developed, the Middle Eastern oil-exporting countries are heading for economic decline. They are in a race against time to develop and diversify their economies (Fargues, 1994). In the mean time they are caught in a squeeze between high population growth and a critical dependence on oil revenues (Humphreys, 2001).

In oil-exporting Middle Eastern countries, social services for the bulk of the population have improved since the early 1970s, but they have mostly benefited the already privileged parts of the population, the people from whom the rulers wanted political support. Declining oil revenues since the 1980s should have caused a reduction in these transfers and special services, but most governments have not dared to follow such a policy, fearing opposition from resourceful groups. Instead, the budget cuts have hit hardest those groups that were already the most under-privileged. This has been accompanied by a vast array of subsidies and transfers to the private sector. Recent attempts at reintroducing taxes and withdrawing subsidies and transfers to the privileged have caused effective protests from the groups concerned. In Saudi Arabia, it has been politically difficult to cut the military budget, although the country evidently possesses more military hardware than it can use. Some key people receive commissions from arms purchases. Because of the political dependence of the regime on these groups, the proposed measures have been withdrawn. Persistent quarrels over the budget in the Kuwaiti parliament are but one example. Consequently, the new austerity has hit hardest those groups that have been the least privileged, as they are considered less dangerous by the regime. An example is the decline of health service and education quality in Saudi Arabia.

In 1972, before the first major oil price rise, the six leading oil exporters on the Gulf—Iran, Iraq, Kuwait, Qatar, Saudi Arabia and the Emirates—had an estimated total population of about 51m. (UN Statistics Database). By 2006, this figure had more than doubled to about 135m., with an average annual growth rate of 2.9%.

Gulf region population 1972–2006

1000	1972	1980	1998	2006F	Average annual growth rates 1972–2006
Iran	30,541	39,330	64,718	70,163	2.5%
Iraq	10,819	14,093	27,529	31,296	3.2%
Kuwait	1,137	1,007	1,474	2,789	2.7%
Qatar	203	171	565	862	4.3%
Saudi Arabia	7,959	7,251	20,216	25,242	3.5%
UAE	747	530	2,855	4,798	5.6%
Total	51,405	62,382	117,357	135,150	2.9%

Source: United Nations Statistics Database

Their total oil output increased from about 17.5m. barrels per day (b/d) in 1972 to about 21.5m. b/d in 2006. This modest total oil increase in spite of substantial rises in the oil output of Saudi Arabia and the United Arab Emirates, can be explained by lower volumes for Iran and Kuwait in 2006 than in 1972.

Gulf region oil extraction 1972–2006

Annual averages 1,000 b/d	1972	1980	1998	2006 Jan.–May
Iran	5,023	1,662	3,634	4,050
Iraq	1,466	2,514	2,150	1,800
Kuwait	3,283	1,656	2,085	2,600
Qatar	482	472	696	830
Saudi Arabia	6,016	9,900	8,389	9,500
UAE	1,203	1,709	2,345	2,600
Total	17,473	17,913	19,299	21,380

Source: US Department of Energy, Energy Information Administration Database

Consequently, average per capita oil output has been almost halved, from 0.34 barrels per person per day in 1972 to 0.16 barrels per person per day by 2006. In all countries included here, the decline in oil output per capita is substantial when 2006 figures are compared to those of 1972, but in the case of Iran not when compared to 1980 figures, due to the output reduction during the revolutionary turmoil and the war launched by Iraq.

Gulf region per capita daily oil output 1972–2006

Annual averages b/d	1972	1980	1998	2006 Jan.–May
Iran	0.16	0.04	0.06	0.06
Iraq	0.14	0.18	0.08	0.06
Kuwait	2.89	1.64	1.41	0.93
Qatar	2.37	2.76	1.23	0.96
Saudi Arabia	0.76	1.37	0.41	0.38
UAE	1.61	3.22	0.82	0.54
Total	0.34	0.29	0.16	0.16

Source: Author's calculations based on preceding tables

To some extent, the declining or stagnant oil output per capita has been offset by rising oil prices. The Energy Information Administration of the United States

Department of Energy has calculated oil export revenues since 1972 in constant 2005 prices for the countries concerned. For the countries included, the combined oil revenues, in constant values, jumped seven times from 1972 to 1980; subsequently they fell again by 8% until 1998, when they were just 50% above the 1972 level; since then they have risen three-and-a-half times, so that by 2006 they are expected to reach 90% of the record 1980 level. The variations are relatively less dramatic for Iran, due to the low 1980 volumes discussed above.

Gulf region oil export revenues 1972–2006 constant 2005 prices

Million 2005 US dollars	1972	1980	1998	2006F
Iran	15,300	26,800	11,200	49,200
Iraq	5,400	55,300	7,700	24,500
Kuwait	10,300	38,400	9,100	43,300
Qatar	1,700	11,000	3,900	22,900
Saudi Arabia	17,200	213,600	36,900	159,100
UAE	3,900	38,500	11,500	52,100
Total	53,800	383,600	80,300	351,100

Source: US Department of Energy, Energy Information Administration Database

For the six countries combined, per capita oil export revenues increased six-fold from 1972 to 1980, after which they by 1998 had declined to a level barely two-thirds of that of 1972; by 2006 they are estimated to be about 40% of their 1980 level. Only in Iran are 2006 per capita oil export revenues estimated to be above their 1980 level when measured in constant prices.

Gulf region oil export revenues per capita 1972–2006 constant 2005 prices

2005 US dollars	1972	1980	1998	2006F
Iran	501	681	173	701
Iraq	499	3,924	280	783
Kuwait	9,062	38,133	6,174	15,525
Qatar	8,363	64,327	6,904	26,560
Saudi Arabia	2,161	29,458	1,825	6,303
UAE	5,223	72,642	4,028	10,858
Total	1,047	6,149	684	2,598

Source: Author's calculations based on preceding tables

The vision of the Middle East progressing has faded, gradually emerging as a mirage. Part of the reason can be found in the international conflicts plaguing the region, for example over Palestine, Lebanon, Iraq, Iran, Yemen and Kuwait. The reason is also political leadership. Autocratic leaders have used conflicts with neighbours to entrench their power and to refuse or delay reforms.

In many Middle Eastern and North African countries the military and internal security forces seem to have priority over civilian tasks. In brief, arms purchases in many cases seem to have a stronger budgetary position than do food imports. Even if oil revenues in the fairly recent past provided tremendous wealth, there is no hope that oil alone can secure future prosperity. The oil exporters of the Middle East and North Africa evidently have not managed the transition into more diversified economics, supplementing oil and gas with other sources of income. As public funds based on oil run out, governments are unable to attract or stimulate private investment. Hence they seem to be running into ever more serious economic difficulties, with steadily more severe social strains and potentially ominous political repercussions.

Indeed, the countdown to the post-oil era is being forced upon the Middle Eastern and North African oil exporters, but so far the governments seem unable or unwilling to adapt. The question is, how could this unfortunate development have taken place? Did it occur in spite of an exceptional endowment in petroleum resources or because of the resource endowment? Whatever the case, the outcome is increasing political unrest, with religious references. In this context, these movements will be denominated as Islamist. In this perspective, Islamism represents the use of religious references to legitimize political grievances as a moral right. Following this perspective, there are no definite political institutions or economic or social policies prescribed by Islam, but the interpretations and uses of Islam should be analysed with reference to their proper historical, economic and social context. The background for the recent surge in Islamism in the Middle East and North Africa is certainly not only to be found in economic and social problems. It also represents a manifestation of cultural and national identity in opposition to the West, the former colonial or semi-colonial masters. Serious economic problems and the degradation of the social situation do, however, provide additional strength for the Islamist surge. These issues are related to the oil experience, but they have been largely ignored in the West.

Economic monoculture has made the Middle Eastern oil exporters highly vulnerable to the cycles of a single commodity market. Periodically high revenues have not led to any diversification of the economic base, except in small rentier economies such as Kuwait and the United Arab Emirates, where a substantial part of the economic surplus has financed foreign investment. For this reason, discontinuities are the trademark of the economic development of the Middle Eastern oil exporters. Breaking out of this pattern is a political rather than an economic problem. It will require changes in power structures rather than incremental resources.

In recent years, the economic and political system has been under stress in practically all oil-exporting countries of the Middle East. Since the mid-1980s,

85

low oil prices have forced severe cuts in public budgets. One example is Saudi Arabia in 1994 and 1995 and again in 1998. Budget constraints have led to transfer cuts and declining living standards for large parts of the population. They also diminish the bargaining power of the established rulers. In many cases economic growth rates have been lower than population growth rates, so that average incomes have fallen. Unemployment has risen, especially among youth, as governments no longer have resources both to educate and to employ young people. During the 1970s and 1980s expenditure on education had increased drastically in all oil-exporting countries. Today, the result is a large number of young people who often cannot find work commensurate with their qualifications (Ende, 1991). This has become an increasingly acute problem in Saudi Arabia, whose young people often have high expectations, as well as in Iran.

In practically all oil-exporting countries, budget cuts are painful, but have not been sufficient to reduce deficits, especially since the governments have not dared tax income and property. Hence, the economic leverage of governments declines sharply in times of social and political unrest.

All Middle Eastern oil-exporting countries have become increasingly dependent on oil revenues as population grows and the development of other sources of income is lagging. The low oil prices of 1998 revealed economic and political vulnerabilities that could be potentially fatal to the regimes in place, unless they should manage political change. Budget and trade deficits suddenly reached unsustainable levels. The high oil prices in 1999–2000 have markedly improved budget and trade balances, but these mask structural problems due to economic monoculture, high-risk exposure to oil prices, together with population growth. Against this backdrop, the current organization of economic life does not appear sustainable, except perhaps in Kuwait, Qatar and some of the United Arab Emirates, which can supplement oil revenues by investment income. These countries have small indigenous populations, large oil revenues and huge financial resources.

After nearly 30 years of war economy, Iraq has an urgent need for civilian investment, but the country also has a considerable potential for developing a more diversified economy. The condition is political stabilization without foreign occupation. Iran already has a more diversified economy, but also has a large population and a need to create employment outside oil. Saudi Arabia's economy is not much diversified, and the country remains dependent on oil revenues. High population growth, rising unemployment and stagnant or declining living standards create an ever more urgent need for economic reforms. A priority is closer integration with the world economy and the lifting of US economic sanctions.

For these reasons, low oil prices in 1998 gave rise to not only a critical economic situation for Iran and Saudi Arabia, but also to some political change. In Iran, the outcome was further liberalization and a weakening of the conservative forces within the clergy. In Saudi Arabia, low oil prices strengthened reformist forces inside and outside the royal family. In both cases, high oil revenues since 2000 have made reforms less urgent and have muted their advocates.

In the Middle Eastern oil-exporting countries, political stability requires high oil revenues and a gradual development of representative institutions. On this latter point, Iran is the most advanced, Iraq the least. The risk of instability is embedded in a sudden decline in oil revenues before representative institutions are more developed, or in an external political event. Recent experience indicates that for Iran, a possible decline in oil revenues would help provoke a more liberal and democratic trend in politics and strengthen the private sector over the rentier state. This process has already been put in motion by generation change and globalization, but risks being reversed by the confrontation with the USA over the nuclear programme.

Also for Saudi Arabia, lower oil revenues would probably accelerate economic and political reforms and eventually open the country to increased foreign investment to create employment and income, but there are alternative outcomes. This would require, however, consensus within the royal family on the need for change and its direction, and that the élite surrounding the royal family voluntarily relinquish important privileges. Another way out could be to boost oil output, regardless of the consequences for oil prices and relations with Iran and Iraq. There is also a possibility of a more Islamist political development.

The 1997–98 low oil prices caused a severe economic predicament among the world's oil exporters, not least in the Middle East. The 1999–2000 oil price rebound has again improved the situation, but serious basic problems remain.

Postponing reforms through high oil revenues is hardly a durable solution. Maintaining high oil prices will require a persistently robust demand or agreement between the major oil exporters, preferably both, but neither is assured. Insofar as oil demand remains high and no significant investment is made in capacity expansion outside OPEC, and the leading Middle Eastern oil exporters agree on price levels and market shares, conditions could be favourable for oil prices to stay higher than during most of the 1990s. If oil demand falls, significant investment is made in capacity expansion outside OPEC, and the leading Middle Eastern oil exporters disagree on price levels and market shares, then the conditions could be ripe for another oil price decline.

The bad omen for Middle Eastern politics is that high oil revenues since 2000 have caused military spending to increase again. Indeed, after the end of the Cold War, the Middle East has become the world's leading market for arms, and is now its most militarized region, underlined by the US occupation of Iraq. For internal politics, high military expenditure means a lasting conflict between civilian and military priorities, resulting from a persistently powerful political position of the armed forces and a consequent unproductive use of scarce resources. Iran is currently an exception. For external politics, the rearmament indicates the persistence of regional threats, tensions and conflict potential.

The Rentier State

In the Middle East, oil has caused a special, capital-intensive mode of development. Briefly put, the political process is that the rulers do not tax citizens or businesses, but hand out selective privileges, financed by oil revenues, against loyalty and support from a largely parasitic private sector. Access to large oil revenues channelled through the treasuries is a distinctive feature of the state in the oil-exporting countries of the Middle East. These oil revenues make the state a distributor of economic rent from oil and therefore of privileges and transfers, instead of being a tax collector and redistributor. Most economic activities outside the petroleum sector depend on government permits, contracts, support and protection. This is usually coupled with an absence of taxes on property and income, except for the religious tax, *zakat*. Consequently, the Middle Eastern oil exporters have had no market economy, but rather a protected concessionary and distributive economy that is directed by the government. Private production, exports and investment have received reduced importance in the context of the state-run oil economy. The private sector has lost political weight.

The contrast with the independent capitalist development of the Western world is striking. In the developed capitalist economies, organized economic interests use the state for their political purposes. In the Middle Eastern oil-exporting countries, the state uses private business for its political purposes. This is a basic feature of the *rentier state*.

The absence of direct taxation has reduced the need for the state to prove its legitimacy to the population through democratic institutions. Instead, the state buys legitimacy by spending oil revenues. When the state does not impose taxes on wealth and income, the need for liberal and democratic reforms diminishes. Instead, the state can buy legitimacy and support by granting selective economic privileges. These selective favours have their counterpart in equally selective measures of discrimination. Those groups that do not benefit from the selective favours experience themselves as second-class citizens. In the Gulf countries, unlike the situation in Iran and Iraq, there are a large number of foreign workers with inferior economic, political and social status.

With huge oil revenues, capital accumulation could take place at a much higher rate in the public sector than in private business. Control of the accumulation process moved from private capitalists to public-sector bureaucrats and autocratic rulers. Oil money strengthened the state and the bureaucracy in relation to private business, creating a distinctive political system based on the centralization of petroleum revenues with the state (Cause III, 1994). Historically, in the key Middle Eastern oil-exporting countries there has been at least some connection between rising oil revenues and lagging political reforms. Today's regimes depend on oil revenues to prevent or delay reforms in the short term, and to survive in the long term. Rentier states need access to economic rent to survive. The politically conditioned need for revenues, to buy support and legitimacy, reduces oil policy discretion. The alternative is economic reform, with a more independent private sector and direct taxation, followed up by political reforms aiming at a more representative form of government.

Rising prosperity based solely on oil is a phenomenon of the past in the Middle East. With few exceptions, today's Gulf oil exporters face a race against time, as they have to develop away from oil dependence and their populations are rising quickly. Political implications are important, as rulers financed by erstwhile plentiful oil revenues are coming under increasing pressure to share power with representatives of the private sector—not only its bosses, but also its workers.

The oil importers have largely tried to balance their oil imports by arms exports. Since oil revenues started to rise in the early 1970s, the oil exporters of the Middle East and North Africa have become the dumping ground for the world's arms-makers. Even worse, the arms imports have stayed high even after the oil revenues started to decline in the early 1980s. The military priority is an essential aspect of the mismanagement of the region's petroleum wealth and an important reason for the present misery. It gives the arms-exporting countries in the West, including Russia, formerly the Soviet Union, a stake in the survival of the regimes in the Middle East and North Africa, as well as a responsibility for deteriorating economic and social conditions. Hence, it should be no surprise that opposition to the rulers in place often takes on an anti-Western accent, emphasizing Islam as the embodiment of local traditions. In the Middle East and North Africa, autocratic rule and mismanagement do not, however, require foreign intervention. Military rule has deep roots in the region's political traditions. There is no tradition of rulers being accountable to their population. Oil has strengthened autocratic rulers by providing huge revenues. There is little understanding in the West of how these strains could have their origins in oil-related issues and how they could eventually backfire on oil policies.

The ruling class, with a base in the public sector, including the armed forces and the nationalized oil industries, has the control of economic and political life. Its position is being challenged because of rising inequalities. This conflict is particularly bitter in countries that experienced a strong surge in oil revenues in the late 1970s and early 1980s. Their subsequent decline in the late 1980s and early 1990s produced strong discontinuities in development. At first, there were extensive disruptions of traditional society. Subsequently the attempt at technocratic modernization failed. The adaptation of a Western economic and social model, financed by oil revenues, was not successful. Algeria and Iran are the typical examples (Shirley, 1995). Oil revenues made an apparent modernization easy, but the easy solutions proved elusive. Since 2000, high oil prices have again contributed to political stabilization, and the social and political stability of the Middle Eastern and North African oil-exporting countries increasingly seems to hinge on high oil prices because of the failure to develop alternative sources of income and employment.

The result is the two-tiered economy. The public sector represents the developed part. It consists of the state apparatus, the national oil company, other key state enterprises and the leading financial institutions, all owned or controlled by the state. It accounts for most of the value added. The private sector, however, is less developed. It is dependent upon selective favours and transfers. Private businesses usually operate in imports, trade or services, but seldom in large-scale manufacturing. Agriculture is generally marked by low productivity and is dependent upon public support. The merchant class, the traders and craftsmen in the bazaar, needs differentiation. Some merchants have succeeded, through public favours and concessions, in gaining considerable wealth. Others have been marginalized by imports and large-scale trading. Nevertheless, the respect for private property and the link between the bazaar and the mosque are political essentials in present-day Muslim societies.

The growth and power of the military are salient features common to most countries of the Middle East, whether oil-exporting or not (Humphreys, 2001). Military officers have repeatedly intervened to keep countries and political systems together, so that military government has often been the rule rather than the exception (Richards and Waterbury, 1990). Iraq under Baathist rule is a good case in point. The social origins of the military, especially the junior officers, are largely in the urban middle and lower middle classes. This has been the case not only in Iraq. Historically, the military has been an exponent of social and political change, but over time, the military establishment has become a conservative force in the Middle East, defending its own privileges and its budgetary priorities. At the outset, military rule was socially radical, motivated by the aim of redistributing wealth and income, of carrying out profound reforms and asserting national interests against the colonial legacy. It has over decades acquired its own vested interests—meaning budgetary appropriations, training and the most modern equipment, apart from personal fringe benefits and political influence. In the oil-exporting countries the sudden influx of large oil revenues proved an irresistible temptation for the military establishment to demand more money. The military establishment represents a salient part of the new class of technocrats—wielding power, but not the ability to earn revenues. Like the technocrats of the public sector, the military establishment is largely professional, recruited by merit.

Indeed, the rise in military expenditure seems easier to explain by the level of oil revenues than by any sudden internal or external threats. Middle Eastern oil exporters have a preference for military spending not shared by oil exporters elsewhere. In 1998, Mexico spent less than 1% of its gross domestic product (GDP) on the military, Indonesia about 1% Malaysia, Norway and Venezuela about 2%, and Iran about 3%. By contrast, in Oman and in Saudi Arabia some 13% of GDP went to the military (SIPRI Database). In Islamic Iran the military evidently enjoys far less influence, privileges and money than was the case under the Shah.

External threats, internal enemies, the pressure from foreign arms manufacturers as well as the military complex can explain the military priority. The political instability of the Middle East means that practically all countries of the region face actual or potential threats from neighbours. Political instability also means that almost all Middle Eastern governments face internal threats as well. Foreign arms dealers, assisted by their governments, do their best to convince oil-exporting Middle Eastern rulers that they need to buy the most sophisticated and expensive military hardware. Finally, local officers, friends and family members of the rulers also promote arms purchases, against a commission. High military expenditure helps the armed services compete for personnel, drawing competence away from more productive civilian tasks. In theory, the military burden means that the oil-exporting countries have some flexibility in budgetary policies, provided that it is politically possible to cut expenditures on the armed forces and that no serious threats appear on the horizon.

The Islamist Critique

Islamism today to a large extent represents a social critique and a national revival, as well as a political revolt against a Westernized and technocratic ruling class. The ruling class, with a basis in the public sector, has the control of economic and political life. Its position is being challenged because of rising inequalities. This conflict is particularly bitter in countries that experienced a strong surge in oil revenues in the late 1970s and early 1980s. Their subsequent decline in the late 1980s and early 1990s produced strong discontinuities in development. At first there were extensive disruptions of traditional society. Subsequently the attempt at technocratic modernization failed. The adaptation of a Western economic and social model, financed by oil revenues, was not successful. Algeria and Iran are the typical examples.

With some exceptions, the oil-exporting countries were the most exposed to Western influence. This is where the subsequent frustration has been the most profound, due to the discontinuities of revenues. The hypothesis is that rising social inequalities can be criticized as transgressing basic political and religious principles of Islam. These principles are not always evident, because even classical Islam is a historically complex phenomenon. Nevertheless, the Bedouin society, in which Islam arose, was essentially conservative and egalitarian (Ruthven, 1991). The conservative tradition can today be invoked against Western influence. The egalitarian tradition, even if distant, can be invoked against wasteful and autocratic rulers. When present rulers appear as simultaneously wasteful, despotic and dominated by the West, they expose themselves to criticism based on ancient traditions from Islam's early age.

Islamic economic thinking, inspired by the sacred texts, the Koran, the *hadith*, the *sunna* and the *shari'a*, has developed in the 20th century as an opposition to the neo-classical economics of the Western colonialists and imperialists. It has been as prevalent in non-Arab Muslim countries, such as Iran and Pakistan, as in Arab countries.

Ideologically, Islam appears as a capitalist religion, with its emphasis on individual responsibility, private property and the private accumulation of wealth through trade and productive work, provided it is honest, *halal* (Rodinson, 1966). The ownership and accumulation of capital are ordered, as a requirement of efficiency, but Islam also positively prescribes social justice, the sharing of wealth and welfare for the poorer parts of society, institutionalizing compassion for the poor as a central element in the faith. Islam explicitly prohibits certain economic practices considered dishonest or harmful to the common good, *haram*. Consequently, Islamic economic thinking is normative, aiming at a balance between private initiative and social welfare. Honest work and inventiveness are honoured; compassion is mandatory; corruption, cheating and waste are prohibited. The key tenets are sharing wealth, prohibition, participation and sharing risk, and prohibition of interest charges and waste. In addition, the Shi'a tradition observes a religious income tax.

Sharing wealth is the primary economic principle of Islam (Mills and Presley, 1999). Alms, *zakat*, as a tax on capital, is one the five pillars of the religion (Anderson et al., 1994). Giving alms is part of the religious exercise and a duty even when there is no state to collect and redistribute it (Benmansour, 1995). The obligation of giving alms complements the prohibition of usury, *riba*. Both are redistributive mechanisms and parts of Islam's original social and political project.

The wealth tax, *zakat*, takes the form of ceding annually a part of the working capital. It appears as the community's share of wealth produced (Mannan, 1987). It is also a levy on property and savings. The purpose of *zakat* is both to redistribute wealth, for the benefit of the poor, and to counteract the hoarding of capital and prevent a passive participation in economic life by a rentier or leisure class (Hammad, 1989). Consequently, the objective is to redress the social balance, to finance charity and to provide incentives for the productive use of capital. *Zakat* is only applicable upon productive assets, here meaning equity held for at least one year. It is not levied upon personal consumption capital. The major exception is agriculture, where *zakat* is applicable to produce, not the land.

As a rule, the payment of *zakat* is in kind. On cash assets and goods intended for sale, it is usually 2.5% of the value. On produce from naturally irrigated land, *zakat* is usually 10%, from artificially irrigated land it is 5%. On mining of metals and exploitation of other buried treasures, *zakat* is usually 20% of the value. This is relevant for present petroleum exploitation. More recently, Islamic economic thinking has dealt with taxing industrial production. In this case, it has justified the principle of a *zakat* of 10%. It should, however, be exempt from craftsmen's tools (Mannan, 1989). Traditionally, zakat has not been levied on buildings. Modern Islamic economic thinking prescribes it to be levied on buildings for rent. For individuals, there is an exemption of 'zakatable' income. This is the money needed to sustain necessary consumption and to repay loans currently due (Choudhury and Malik, 1992). *Zakat* is to be imposed on productive assets left idle for a year, profits and windfalls from economic activity and inheritance (Choudhury, 1986). For corporations, working capital is exempt from *zakat*. The question of *zakat* in labour-intensive service businesses, where the human capital is of key importance, so far seems to have been largely overlooked.

Traditionally, as in many modern Muslim states, *zakat* has a supplement in other taxes. The most important are *jiziya*, the poll tax on non-Muslims, and the *kharaj*, land tax. The *jiziya* is often progressive, hitting the rich more than the poor. The *kharaj*, land tax, is usually applicable on lands conquered by military means. It is divided into a proportional tax on the produce and a fixed tax on the land. Another important tax is the *ushr*, tithe, collected on farmed land.

The prohibition of usury, *riba*, has caused different interpretations and is presently subject to dispute (Naqvi, 1994). A lenient interpretation is that the prohibition concerns unfairly high interest rates, usury in the Western sense. This would permit a fair rate of interest to make up for inflation and a modest return on capital invested. A stricter interpretation is that any kind of interest payment is prohibited. The majority of commentators seem to agree on the latter definition. The purpose is to prevent the rise of any rentier class in the economic system. A yet stricter interpretation is that Islam prohibits any unfair gain from a transaction between unequal partners (Hammad, 1989). A subtle differentiation is that manifest interest, by a delay in delivery, is prohibited. By contrast, hidden interest, such as profit-sharing or trading and selling, eventually the sale and repurchase of the same good, is tolerated. In practice, a hidden interest is charged through lending disguised as commercial operations. An example is the borrower selling a good to the lender, but with the obligation of repurchasing the same good at a given moment at a price agreed upon. Trade is tolerated in Islam, also as a substitute for interest.

The intention of forbidding usury is to provide for a minimum of social equity and justice and to prevent capital accumulation through lending money at a high cost to borrowers. The ethical objective is simultaneously to prevent the exploitation of the needy and enrichment through passive participation in the economic system. Implicitly this is also recognition of the fact that capital is idle unless actively used by labour. Against this backdrop, interest rates can be tolerated as a tool of measurement, but not as an objective of economic activity. A subtle modern understanding is that a return on capital equivalent to *zakat*, that is 2.5% on most assets, can be tolerated. The intention of *zakat* is also to encourage the usefulness of capital. Indeed, the rate of *zakat* of 2.5% annually can implicitly be seen as a natural value increase on capital assets. According to Islamic economic thinking, this natural growth should be distributed to the community. Any additional value growth of capital assets should be kept by the owner and be subject to normal taxation.

With the absence of interest, discount rates are redundant as a tool in monetary and economic policy (Choudhury, 1992). Monetary creation is the prerogative of the central bank. Commercial banks become investment managers for savings. The cost of capital becomes the real rate of return in business and vice versa. Hence, the rate of return in the financial sector is directly linked to the rate of profit in the non-financial sector, where the rate of profit measures the rate of growth of productivity and output. To sum up, in principle lenders and borrowers are to have the same rate of profit, giving incentives for investment in real assets rather than in financial assets.

In its practical orientation, the prohibition of usury, or interest in a strict interpretation, in Islamic economic thinking is a tool, not an objective for policy (Naqvi, 1994). The purpose is to replace interest payment by a more equitable financial mechanism. The absence of interest payment does not indicate a surplus situation where capital has a zero shadow price, nor does it necessarily indicate an indifferent or negative time preference for income (Mills and Presley, 1999). For private individuals, Islamic economic thinking recognizes the positive time preference. Present income can be invested profitably to enhance the future income base. Future income can at best be mortgaged to enlarge present purchasing power, but with the undesirable social result of subjecting the borrower to the lender. Consequently, Islamic economic thinking recognizes a positive private time preference for income. This can, however, be offset by a negative government time preference for income. An important purpose of a negative government time preference for income is to take the depreciation of the capital stock and the need for new investment into account. Practically, this means that the government will need higher revenues in the future than today in order to finance new investment and enhanced social services for a larger population. With a high demographic growth rate, the case for a negative government time preference for income strengthens. This point is essential for the review of oil depletion policies and the use of oil revenues in a situation of high population growth. The core of the critique is that capital itself is not productive, but that it requires human effort to generate output and income (Mills and Presley, 1999).

The counterpart to prohibiting usury or interest is to encourage the sharing of risk and profit, *mudarabah*. Participation with risk and profit-sharing is the Islamic substitute for the use of interest in financing new ventures. It associates unequal partners, but the lender, the stronger partner, generally takes the early risks and losses until the new venture is established and makes a profit (Mills and Presley, 1999). The arrangement provides the weaker ones with access to capital, when the joint ventures are successful. The objective is to bridge social differences through co-operation and to avoid conflict. The sharing of risk and profit is especially encouraged between labour and capital. The problems are the agreement on the ratio by which to share eventual profits and that some partners can bear losses more easily than others. In any case, co-operation is an important principle in Islamic economic thinking. An Islamic economic joint venture recognizes equal rights of workers and investors, applied to voting power as to the distribution of profits. The equity participation may be as subscribed capital or imputed wages forgone. It can also represent the value of labour time in production (Choudhury and Malik, 1992).

Islamic economic thinking prescribes external financing by an extension of the original joint venture and borrowing money, but with the lenders sharing the risk. The attractiveness to external lenders is not in an interest rate agreed upon *ex ante*, but profit is a function of the rate of return, established *ex post* over a number of years. This may deter investors from high-risk innovative ventures.

The prohibition of waste and idleness is another principle of Islamic economic thinking, *israf*. It concerns wasteful consumption, wasteful production and the idleness of productive resources, including capital. Wasteful consumption above reasonable needs is associated with luxury and injustice. It again engenders the use of productive resources for wasteful needs to the detriment of the daily needs of the population. The social cost of luxury consumption and production is fewer resources allocated to the production of goods and services with a higher marginal utility. The ethical imperative is that the productive resources should be used for the common good, not for the production of luxury articles for a minority. Correspondingly, hoarding is prohibited because it entails the use of productive resources for idle purposes. Finally, the hoarding of capital is prohibited as it entails the idleness of resources which otherwise could be used for the common good. In Islam the payment of interest on loans appears as waste, because it is compensation to the lender without any active effort. The subjective capitalization of risk by the lender is an unnecessary burden on investment.

In political terms, Islamic economic principles can also serve as a tool to fight or prevent the rise of a rentier or leisure class, living off capital, hoarding wealth and consuming conspicuously. The Islamic interpretation of private ownership finds its justification against this backdrop. In Islamic economic thinking, private property to the means of production and exchange is essentially a functional right; its justification is individual effort. Islam respects individual property when acquired through the individual's own labour, but much less so when inherited (Naqvi, 1994). In principle, all property belongs to God, but it is in the custody of private individuals as caretakers or trustees insofar as they respect Islam's ethical norms, which includes productivity. Islamic economic principles also tolerate managed markets, the co-operation of different sellers to set prices.

Insofar as these norms are not respected, the Islamic state has a sovereign right to confiscate private productive property. It can either keep it as state property or hand it over to other individuals. This principle also applies when the owner of productive capital does not get a certain return on the assets. The purpose is to enhance productivity for the common good. In addition to *zakat* as a capital tax, the threat of confiscation is a strong incentive to productivity. Furthermore, Islamic economic thinking insists on redistributive justice, providing all members of society with a minimum standard of living, regardless of their ability to earn it. Islamic economic thinking also tolerates various kinds of taxation to finance the social services and income transfers.

The Islamic concept of ownership of land and other natural resources is pertinent in this respect. The principle of private ownership of land is respected insofar as the proprietor is also working the land. Otherwise land should be in public ownership. Private property rights are limited. Otherwise they would deprive others of their rights (al-Mansour, 1995). Absentee landowners, living off land rent, are contrary to the letter and spirit of Islam. Likewise, natural resources can be in private ownership, but the economic rent must be shared by all members of the community (Mannan, 1987). Individuals are entitled to proper compensation for their efforts to improve the use and value of natural resources.

This principle can justify the state ownership of important natural resources, as for land. The Islamic view is that natural resources are a gift from God and belong to both present and future generations. Natural resources therefore belong to the state. It can delegate their commercial exploitation according to Islamic principles. Productivity is important in this respect. Exhaustible resources should not be misused by the present generation, and the revenues from their exploitation should be invested in other, lasting sources of income. The purpose is to enhance economic development to make revenues from exhaustible resources redundant once the resources are exhausted (al-Chalabi and al-Janabi, 1979).

In its normative approach, Islamic economic thinking at times seems to deal with ideals rather than actual situations. In an economy organized according to Islamic principles, the state is the preferable owner of natural resources, including land and minerals. Private initiative is encouraged in trade and manufacturing. Within the trading and manufacturing enterprises workers and owners share risk and profit, through co-operative joint venture based on a high degree of industrial democracy. Lenders also are to share directly risk and profit. Suppliers are permitted to co-operate, so that prices will be higher than under perfect competition, but lower than under monopoly. The absence of interest charges means that there is no rentier class and financial profits are never higher than productive ones. There are strong incentives to individual effort and capitalists owning means of production and trade. This essentially concerns capital accumulated through their active participation and sharing of risk. The economic surplus is created in both private and public sectors. Social equity and welfare are essentially ensured through the wealth tax.

This ideal economic model has its historical basis in Islam's social project. The crucial question concerns the effect of the sudden influx of oil revenues in Muslim countries, whether it has contributed to the realization of this model or not. The question is also how this objective eventually has fared during the subsequent economic adversity. The pivotal issues are the rate of extraction of oil, the organization of the oil industry and the use of petroleum revenues.

An extractive activity, such as the oil and gas industry, is in principle a finite process, because the resources are ultimately depleted. The present extraction is dependent upon the historical record and volumes already extracted. The present depletion again sets the limits for future extraction volumes. Even if exploration and technical and managerial progress augment volumes that can be commercially lifted, petroleum extraction is a historical process, and so is the flow of income, which raises the issue of equity over generations. This constraint is pertinent to the time preference for income, and not only for Muslim oil producers.

Oil revenues as rentier income differ qualitatively from productive income, because they have their origin in the extraction of a finite resource, not in human labour and productivity. The value of oil provides payment above factor costs, which includes a normal profit. The difference between the market value of the oil lifted and the costs of exploration, development and extraction, with a normal rate of return for capital, labour and materials, can be seen as a free gift of nature, an economic resource rent caused by the properties of crude oil (Dam, 1976). The condition is that the price of a commodity is substantially above production cost due to scarcity or imperfect competition or both. Oil in the ground represents resource capital for the landowner (Dasgupta and Heal, 1979). Lifting the oil means depleting the owner's resource capital. In most countries, oil in the ground is government property, so that depletion rates, the organization of the activity and the use of the revenues are public concerns.

Any government-landowner, Muslim or non-Muslim, first of all needs to decide on the rate of depletion, meaning how much petroleum to lift and how much to leave in the ground. The choice of depletion rates for oil and gas is the key policy parameter in any petroleum-producing country. The choice has to consider the current and future need for revenues. Simplistically, the depletion rate appears as a problem of portfolio management, where the options are to leave oil in the ground or to pump it out, eventually to reinvest the revenues. The critical intertemporal condition is that marginal utility, measured as the net present value of sales, must be equal over time (Gordon, 1981). Consequently, the timing of the extraction is crucial, depending upon the discount rate used. This argument is simpler for a private investor than for a government-landowner. From the perspective of Islamic economic principles it makes little sense.

In theory, a producer aiming at maximizing profit over time should be indifferent to pumping out oil today or in the future, provided the future revenues equal present ones adjusted for the discount rate. Therefore, in practice, an anticipated constant oil price represents an incentive to pump out oil quickly, provided the discount rate is positive. In this case, only the anticipation of oil prices rising at a pace above the discount rate or a negative discount rate could represent incentives to keep oil in the ground. For a private investor the alternatives are essentially to invest in the firm's assets, in external assets or to invest in oil in the ground (Jabarti, 1977). A fourth alternative is to pump out oil to finance current spending to maintain other activities.

From the perspective of a private landowner operating with a positive discount rate, the oil left in the ground can only yield a return when appreciating in value. On the other hand, the gradual depletion of a finite resource such as oil is likely to lead to rising costs and prices, because more marginal reserves have to be exploited. It presupposes that the market price and marginal cost are equal because of perfect competition (Hotelling, 1931). In this perspective, the choice of depletion rate is dependent upon the relationship between the expected development in real oil prices and the expected return from investing oil revenues (Dasgupta and Heal, 1979). As operations move to more marginal areas, the marginal cost of extraction and the oil price can be expected to increase. This can in theory represent an incentive to leave oil in the ground, if, as argued above, the expected price increase is above the discount rate.

If over the period considered, the rise in oil prices is expected to be higher than the rate of return on investing oil revenues, the choice is to leave relatively more oil in the ground. If investing oil revenues is expected to yield a higher return than oil prices are expected to rise, the choice is to pump out relatively more oil. In brief, expected oil price development should be weighed against the perceived cost of capital. This is essentially a problem of the time value of money, but also of risk propensity and value preferences, as well as market structures.

In practice, however, this easily makes an argument for pumping out oil quickly. Most of the time, the outlook is at best for constant oil prices in real terms. Experience is that oil prices seldom rise substantially, but increase dramatically in infrequent leaps. Therefore, the oil market has a persistent risk of a price decline, at least a temporary one. The market price of an exhaustible resource is essentially unsteady over time, due to exploration and discovery rates, depletion of old fields, technological progress, demand fluctuations and, not least, changing perceptions. Therefore, the usually reasonable risk consideration for a private oil investor is to pump out quickly and invest the revenues. Investor risk generally is lower in the wider capital market than in the more narrow oil market. For an oil-exporting government, risk considerations are more complex. Simplistically, for a government-landowner the alternatives are essentially to invest in domestic economic development, to invest in foreign assets or to invest in oil in the ground. A fourth alternative is to pump out oil to finance current consumption.

All governments, whether oil-exporting or not, have both current and future obligations to spend money. A private investor may sell oil assets in the market, to realize most of the net present value, the discounted cash flow from oil production, liquidate debts and divest loss-bearing activities. By contrast, a government cannot divest present or future budgetary obligations. Contrary to a private firm, a government is facing a continuity of expenditure obligations for administration, health, education, pensions, etc. Therefore, for an oil-exporting government realizing the discounted cash flow in order to reinvest the money in other assets involves serious risks. Future expenditure obligations must be matched by future revenues. For oil-producing governments, the notion of net present value for the oil assets may therefore be of limited meaning. The discount rate is arbitrary and some future budgetary obligations are difficult or impossible to shed. A government may sell an undeveloped oilfield, realizing the net present value at an early stage, but its budgetary obligations are not equally transferable to private investors, at least not without a high risk for the citizens concerned. Oil property is transferable in the marketplace, future budgetary obligations hardly.

A major risk is that spending gets the priority over saving and investment. By experience, the mere availability of oil revenues in any political system tends to stimulate pressures for spending. Access to oil appears as access to easy money. This can generate claims that otherwise would not have been voiced, and temptations to spend that without oil revenues would not have been considered. Another risk is that the oil revenues are invested badly. Even if the general investor risk in the capital market is less than in the oil market, any major investor, such as an oil-exporting government, runs a high unsystematic or subjective risk of not diversifying sufficiently. Different political systems might be more open to pressures to choose a higher-risk portfolio. Whatever the case, most portfolios of indirect, financial foreign investment seem to yield a fairly moderate return, which should be considered when deciding the depletion rate.

Against this backdrop, investment in domestic economic development may seem a better proposition for most oil-exporting governments. By experience, investment in health, education and infrastructure give a long-term return at a fairly modest annual rate. In a longer perspective, investment in education is probably the single factor that most clearly fosters economic growth (Denison, 1967). Investment in agriculture enhances domestic food supplies. Investment in manufacturing and services creates jobs and alternative sources of revenues. There are, however, limits to the amount of investment that the domestic economy can absorb without returns falling and the economy becoming over-heated. The issue of absorptive capacity of oil revenues, meaning the capacity to get a reasonable return on money invested in the domestic economy, is crucial to all oil producers (El Mallakh, 1968). The capital-surplus economy has no financial constraints, but other constraints appear, underlining the point that capital alone is not productive, but requires human efforts. From an Islamic perspective, depleting a finite capital asset, oil reserves, therefore should be synchronized with the creation of other capital assets, ensuring a continuity of income (al-Chalabi and al-Janabi, 1979).

If pumping out oil and reinvesting the revenues are not viable or appear as too risky, keeping oil in the ground to meet future budgetary needs is a sensible option. Furthermore, oil projects compete for capital with other sectors and have to meet certain basic criteria of return. This discussion shows the complexity of the issue, but for a government-owner pumping out oil at a maximum rate is not always compatible with long-term economic needs. Consequently, for an oil-exporting government, portfolio considerations should also consider intergenerational equity.

For a government exploiting finite natural resources, the time preference of money is a complex issue. It is not fully reflected in the discount rate. The government concerns are quite different from the perspective of a private investor concerned about short-term profit maximization. Even for private oil companies, oil in the ground represents an asset whose overall importance to the bargaining position and the stock value may exceed the discounted revenues. Oil in the ground does not deteriorate in quality. It is subject to a price risk. It may also increase in value because of technological progress, even with constant real prices. Oil represents a present and future source of foreign exchange. Consequently, a government-landowner has stronger reasons to leave oil in the ground than has a private investor. The fourth option, to pump out oil regardless of price expectations and return on investment, is an easy way for short-term income maximization. It is useful for governments shorter of revenues than of ambitions, but it leads to economic and political discontinuities.

For Islamic governments, the prohibition of interest, in a strict interpretation, makes calculations of net present value indifferent to the timing of the extraction. This is an argument for giving more consideration to intergenerational equity, to give a higher priority to the revenue needs of future generations. To the extent that the Islamic government prefers to use a negative discount rate, to offset the private sector's focus on immediate profits and to take population growth into account, it would have even stronger reasons for leaving oil in the ground. Even assuming constant oil prices, for an Islamic government there may be an economic sense in leaving part of the oil reserves for the future. Assuming rising real oil prices, any government not in dire financial distress would have strong arguments for keeping more oil in the ground. For Islamic governments, rising oil prices would weigh even more strongly against a quick depletion of oil reserves, as has indeed been the case when rising prices in the oil market have provided incentives for cutting output, causing a backward-bending supply function as countries have extracted oil to reach budget targets, not to maximize income.

The record of the Muslim oil-exporting countries considering Islamic economic principles is mixed on most accounts. The depletion policy of most Muslim oil exporters apparently has vacillated, but the petroleum policies and uses of oil revenues of Middle Eastern and North African oil-exporting countries are easy targets of Islamic criticism. However, the alternatives are not always evident.

The key point of criticism is an excessive extraction of oil and abuse of the revenues, referring to huge military budgets and conspicuous consumption by the ruling class. This amounts to an accusation of double *israf*, waste; squandering finite oil reserves for the illegitimate purpose of wasteful, luxury consumption and unnecessary military expenditure for the benefit of foreign arms manufacturers and their corrupt domestic importers. This coincides with a critique of too rapid depletion of the oil reserves, based on considerations of *riba*, as the prohibition of interest calculation would prescribe deferring extraction and revenues as much as possible for the benefit of future generations. Yet more dimensions of criticism are added; the priorities of military spending and the rulers' conspicuous consumption infringe on the imperative of *zakat*, of distributing wealth to the poor, and finally, reserving the oil industry for the public-sector technocrats, excluding the participation of the private-sector merchant class, infringes on the imperative of *mudaraba,* sharing risk and profit.

From this perspective, Islamic economic imperatives are not esoteric or radical, but often reflect common sense and experience of economic agents. The major issue is the relevance of the Islamic rejection of interest or usury for the time preference for income and petroleum revenues in particular. This concerns the depletion rates for oil and gas. Another important issue is the relevance of the Islamic respect for private property to the choice of company structure in the petroleum industry. A third important issue is the relevance for the Islamic prerogative of sharing wealth and avoiding waste in the use of petroleum revenues.

Concerns about resource depletion or the domestic economic balance give a case for producing oil according to income or budgetary targets. A country with limited oil reserves could prefer to stretch out their lifetime to secure a minimum future income base by reducing output as prices rise. Similarly, a country with a limited ability to absorb oil revenues could apply such considerations. The reason could be a rapidly declining marginal utility of oil revenues by a diminishing return on new investment, eventually accompanied by bottlenecks and inflationary pressures. Foreign investment could appear as an irrelevant or undesirable option. This could present a case for reducing oil production as prices increase. The argument is that tomorrow's income requirements are likely to be higher than today's, and the marginal utility of oil revenues could be higher in the future than at present. Consequently, oil in the ground in the future would be of greater value than it is today.

Depletion according to revenue targets takes marginal utility explicitly into account. It implies keeping oil in the ground once the ability to reasonably absorb oil revenues has been reached. Implicitly, depletion according to revenue targets means reinvesting oil revenues in other, durable sources of income, preferably foreign exchange. A minimum rate of return on investment puts a limit on the need for revenues and consequently on oil production. Furthermore, the rate of depletion becomes inversely tied to the price of oil, because the volume required to meet the revenue targets declines with a rising oil price and rises with a falling one. This amounts to a backward-bending supply curve, which is a negative price elasticity of oil supplies. This depletion principle is certainly compatible with Islamic economic principles as it takes intergenerational equity into account and seeks to avoid wasteful consumption and production. A minimum return on investment does not necessarily conflict with Islam and its rejection of interest, but can be seen as a measurement of social utility. Keeping oil in the ground is not idle use of reserves when the prohibition of interest makes the net present value indifferent to timing of the income, and especially when the marginal ability to absorb oil revenues is declining.

Adjusting oil depletion to demographic growth is likewise compatible with Islamic economic principles, as it takes intergenerational equity into account and seeks to avoid waste. Most Muslim oil-exporting countries have a high rate of population growth and the lack of alternative sources of income means that future oil revenue needs are likely to be larger than present ones. This makes inter-generational equity a pressing problem. Another urgent problem is to avoid wasteful depletion and consumption today, as rapid demographic growth may be an argument for depleting according to target revenues. It may also be a case for using a negative rate of interest in depletion calculations. The outcome would be that oil revenues in the future are more valuable than at present. The reasons are the rising population and the difficulty of developing other sources of income. Such a depletion principle would be compatible with Islamic economic principles as it would take intergenerational equity into account and at the same time seeks to avoid wasteful production and consumption.

Accelerating the depletion of finite oil reserves increases the risk that future generations are left with a poorer income base. Privatizing the oil industry raises the risk of individual preferences ruling a public asset. Using petroleum revenues primarily for consumption purposes, including the military, increases the risk of squandering wealth and neglecting long-term structural issues. Using petroleum revenues largely for individual benefits increases the risk of a worsening income distribution, undermining social and political stability. Critics advocating a lower depletion rate, organizing the oil industry with better accountability and using the revenues for investment and public welfare programmes, do not have to be Islamic, but they can refer to Islamic principles. The general criticism, based on secular considerations of intergenerational equity, efficiency and social justice, is relevant to most oil-exporting countries. It tends to coincide with an Islamic critique of oil policies and oil-financed economic policies in key Muslim coun-tries. The policies often appear as short-sighted, inefficient and socially unjust.

Historically, the advent of nationalist regimes, with or without an Islamist reference, has generally caused a slower rate of depletion of the oil reserves and stronger co-operation in OPEC raising the oil price. Salient cases are Libya after the 1969 revolution and Iran 10 years later. The Islamist opposition to the Shah of Iran for years criticized the oil policy for squandering resources, by pumping oil out too quickly, not taking the revenue needs of future generations into account. A further critique was that oil policy has benefited the new technocratic class based in the public sector, and that it had benefited the West, the consuming countries, first of all the USA, by pumping out quickly and keeping prices low. A similar criticism was voiced in Libya at the end of the monarchy.

Concerns for revenue continuity and future income requirements argue in favour of keeping more oil in the ground than otherwise would have been the case. This should be weighed against the risk that oil prices will decline, so that oil in the ground in the future will be of less value than today. Correspondingly, an accelerated depletion of the oil reserves should be weighed against the risk that oil prices will rise. Managing the oil market with the purpose of gradually moving the price of an exhaustible resource to the cost level of alternatives takes intergenerational equity into account for both producers and consumers and is certainly compatible with Islamic economic principles. The problem is that the cost level of alternatives is unknown and so is the time horizon required for the price of oil to move to that level (al-Chalabi and al-Janabi, 1977). The price path for oil chosen by the price leader and volume adjuster may not be compatible with the interests of other oil exporters, and the price and volume path chosen by the price leader may generate revenues exceeding the reasonable marginal utility of return on domestic investment projects. The alternative, to strictly extract oil by revenue targets, would require control of the market and price formation, unless supply volumes should be erratic, which again would engender instability. From this perspective, OPEC appears justified by Islamic economic principles, as by the consumers' need for oil-market stability.

Finally, from an Islamic economic perspective, unemployment is *israf*, waste of labour and human creativity. The drama in the Middle East is that the oil industry has caused a flow of money, but few jobs. At the same time, most Middle Eastern oil exporters just sell the raw material and import input factors for the oil industry as well as finished petroleum and petrochemical products. Investing in oil supply and service industries as well as in secondary and tertiary petrochemicals would help both job creation and the trade balance. Iran has embarked on such a path. Saudi Arabia has stated intentions in this direction in the eighth Five-Year Plan (for 2005–09—Khatib, 2004). This is evidently a domain where the private sector has a potential.

Islamic economic thinking when applied to oil corresponds to what on salient points appears as common sense in large parts of the rest of the world, not least in countries as different as Mexico, Norway, Russia and Venezuela. There is, however, a profound conflict with the oil policy that the US occupation authority has attempted to impose in occupied Iraq, aiming at large-scale privatization, raising volumes of extraction and using oil revenues to pay for the occupying force (Looney, 2003). Iraq's experience under US occupation raises the issue of whether the alleged clash of civilizations masks a clash of interests (Klein, 2005).

New Dilemmas

High oil prices around 2005–06 alleviate the predicament of the Gulf oil exporters, but they do not make the structural problems less serious. By the late

1990s it was evident that the Middle East had fallen behind economically. It is continuing to do so, in spite of the oil price recovery. By 2006, average income was high by Western standards only in Kuwait, Qatar and the United Arab Emirates. Countries such as Oman and Saudi Arabia have an average income level below that of poorer European countries, such as Greece or Portugal. Income distribution is less unequal among citizens than among the working population, which includes a large number of foreign workers. In Iran and Iraq, average income levels are much lower. Living conditions for the majority of the population are difficult by European or North American standards.

The oil price decline of 1986 led to a serious drop in oil revenues for most oil-exporting countries and a subsequent deterioration in social conditions, which has persisted for about 20 years. The oil-exporting countries, as a rule, are poor and becoming both relatively and absolutely poorer as their populations grow. Indeed, it is difficult to overemphasize the threat of the population time bomb, which has meant a rush against time in the effort to develop the Middle Eastern oil-exporting economies. Algeria finds itself in the same predicament.

All Middle Eastern oil exporters are now facing basic economic problems and difficult decisions in their oil policies, conditioned both by their own needs and interests and by relations to their neighbours. All these countries need high oil revenues, but they also need to reduce their dependence on oil. Low oil prices in 1998 revealed their economic vulnerability and political problems. Iran and Saudi Arabia experienced a dramatic deterioration of the balance of payments, making clear that the alternative to drastic budget cuts and profound economic and political reform was to stabilize oil prices at a significantly higher level. On the other hand, in both countries, low oil revenues triggered a process of economic reform, which seems to have been halted by higher oil prices since 2000.

The leaps in oil revenues in the 1970s and early 1980s enabled the rulers of most Middle Eastern countries to disengage their domestic economies from the world economy. Although this was especially the case with the oil exporters, similar tendencies were present also in the other countries. For the oil exporters, oil revenues were evidently seen as the ultimate solution to any budgetary or balance-of-payments problem. This is the case again.

Huge rentier revenues from the windfall profits from oil enable the rulers to square the circles of economic policy, although, so far, expenditure seems more prudent than in the late 1970s and early 1980s. Oil revenues again permit investment and consumption to increase simultaneously at high rates. Public expenditure can again be without raising taxes. Oil revenues permit selective and generous subsidies to consumers and producers alike. Domestic prices can once more be decoupled from those of the world market. Structural rigidities and market distortions can be maintained.

Historically, the return on public-sector investment in the Middle East has been generally poor (Pakravan, 1997). Reasons for low economic growth rates are stagnant or declining productivity and the absence of structural reforms. The outcome is declining average living standards and increasing social inequalities. Poverty is advancing, and unemployment rates are among the world's highest.

Equally seriously, the Middle East oil exporters do not seem to be able to manage any substantial diversification of their income base. With a few honourable exceptions, the region sells almost only crude oil, oil products and natural gas to the outside world. For this reason the Middle East is missing out on commercial and industrial opportunities in a more open and economically interdependent world.

In the Middle East the illusion of unlimited access to capital made the rulers overlook other problems on the road to economic development. The high oil revenues in the 1970s and early 1980s prevented measures and reforms that could have prepared the development of a more diversified economy. Consequently, oil also prevented more stable economic growth in the longer term.

The first cardinal error was the neglect of agriculture and domestic food supply. This was based on the illusion that oil-financed food imports were the long-term solution. Today, food imports weigh heavily in the trade balance of all Middle Eastern oil exporters—including in Iran and Iraq, which have potential for higher self-sufficiency in food.

The second major error was the neglect of mass education in many countries of the region. This was the case in Iran under the Shah, but not under the Islamic Republic, nor in Algeria, Iraq, Kuwait or Saudi Arabia. It was based on the illusion that the oil economy needed only a small number of experts, not mass literacy. Imperial Iran provided higher education to a small élite, neglecting mass literacy, but the Islamic Republic has emphasized education of the people. In other countries, such as Saudi Arabia, education is universal, but there are important quality differences.

The third error was to give priority to capital-intensive heavy industry instead of labour-intensive manufacturing. This choice was based on the illusion that the state should and could provide employment.

The fourth error was an overvalued exchange rate that stimulated imports at the expense of local businesses. This choice was also based on an illusion—that the oil economy did not need a productive and prosperous local merchant class. The illusion proved fatal to the Shah's regime in Iran, providing grounds for the alliance of clergy and merchants that overthrew the regime.

The key economic problems of the Middle East relate to population growth, inequity and economic stagnation. The unequal distribution of wealth means that the fruits of progress are unequally shared. Over time, this impedes the creation of a home market for industrial products and industrialization itself. The increasing concentration of wealth and income in the hands of a small number of people is unproductive. The very rich tend to expatriate part of their wealth, and concentrate demand on imported luxury items, impeding the growth of a wider home market for less sophisticated products. They also tend to keep part of their wealth idle, as in numerous luxury dwellings and cars, thereby diverting capital from more productive uses.

The experience of very low oil prices in 1998 and early 1999 revealed the vulnerability of the Middle Eastern rentier states and provided strong incentives to reach agreement to raise oil prices substantially. Saudi Arabia was a case in point. The lesson is simply that high oil prices stabilize the regimes and that low oil prices undermine them. Consequently, the rulers in place have an interest in maintaining high oil prices for the sake of regime survival.

Prospects are that Islamist governments, or governments under stronger Islamist influence, will accede to political power in the major oil-exporting countries of the Middle East. This is likely to coincide with rising demand for oil from the Middle East, as demand increases and extraction elsewhere stagnates or even declines (World Energy Outlook, 2004). The counterpart to a stronger call for Middle Eastern crude is stronger competition among the major oil importers to position themselves. This is the background for Chinese and Indian initiatives for comprehensive economic deals with Middle Eastern oil exporters, essentially Iran and Saudi Arabia, to have a first call for oil and natural gas in return for investment capital, industrial exports and arms. China and India's use of economic levers contrasts with the military efforts of the USA, which seems to have no other means (Stelzer, 2001).

Rising demand for Middle Eastern oil is likely to drive up prices, as the Middle Eastern oil exporters will have little incentive to raise output if revenue targets can be met by lower volumes when prices go up. Moreover, they are likely to give preferential treatment to trading partners with comprehensive economic deals, which appears detrimental to the USA. The risk is, therefore, that the political success of Islamist movements in the Middle East will lead to rising tensions with the USA over oil supplies and prices, giving the USA stronger reasons to stay in Iraq and even to threaten neighbouring oil-exporting countries, but at the same time, providing the Islamist movements with a useful enemy, as is to some extent the case with the Iranian government today (Ali, 2002). In return, the strengthening of Islamist movements or even governments in other Middle Eastern oil-exporting countries might provide right-wing US forces with a useful adversary, setting the stage for a prolonged conflict (Tertrais, 2004). The USA's plans to reform the Middle East appear to build on fantasy rather than insight (Salomon, 2004). The challenge is for Europe, together with China, India and others, to come to terms with the emerging Islamic political order in the Middle East, on the basis of international law, mutual respect and the right of self-determination (Leonard, 2005).

Bibliography

Ali, Tariq. *The Clash of Fundamentalists*. London, Verso, 2002.

Amuzegar, Jahangir. *Managing the Oil Wealth*. London, I. B. Tauris, 1999.

Andersen, Roy, Siebert, Robert F., and Wagner, Jon G. *Politics and Change in the Middle East: Sources of Conflict and Accommodation*. Englewood Cliffs, Prentice Hall, 1992.

Askari, Hossein. 'Oil, Not Islam, Is At Fault in the Middle East', in *The National Interest*, Jan. 2004.

Bamford, James. *A Pretext for War*. New York, Doubleday, 2004.

Barrington, Moore, Jr. *Social Origins of Dictatorship and Democracy.* Harmondsworth, Penguin Books. 1969, p. 413 ff.

Benmansour, Hacène. *Politique Economique en Islam.* Paris, Editions al-Qalam, 1995.

Burgat, François. *L'islamisme au Maghreb.* Paris, Payot, 1995a.

Burgat, François. *L'islamisme en face.* Paris, Editions La Découverte, 1995b.

Cappelen, Ådne and Choudhury, Robert. *The Future of the Saudi Arabian Economy.* Oslo, Statistics Norway, 2000.

Cause, F. Gregory III. *Oil Monarchies.* New York, Council on Foreign Relations Press, 1994.

Chaudhry, Kiren Aziz. *The Price of Wealth.* London, Cornell University Press, 1997a.

Al-Chalabi, Fadhil, and al-Janabi, Adnan. 'Optimum Production and Pricing Policies', in Journal of Energy and Development, Spring 1979, pp. 229–258.

Chaudhry, Kiren Aziz. Economic Liberalisation and the Lineages of the Rentier State, in Hopkins, Nicholas S., and Ibrahim, Saad Eddin (Eds), Arab Society, Cairo, The American University in Cairo Press, 1997b.

Chebel, Malek. *Le sujet en islam.* Paris, Seuil, 2002.

Chevalier, Jean-Marie. *Les grandes batailles de l'énergie.* Paris, Gallimard, 2004.

Choudoury, Musul Alam, and Malik, Uzir Abdul. *The Foundations of Islamic Political Economy.* London, Macmillan, 1992.

Choudoury, Musul Alam. *Contributions to Islamic Economic Theory.* London, Macmillan, 1986.

Choudoury, Musul Alam. *The Principles of Islamic Economic Theory.* London, Macmillan, 1992.

Choueiri, Youssef M. *Arab Nationalism.* London, Blackwell, 2000.

Dekmejian, R. Hrair. *Islam in Revolution.* Syracuse, Syracuse University Press, 1995.

Denison, Edward F. *Why Growth Rates Differ.* Washington, DC, Brookings, 1967.

Dam, Kenneth W. *Oil Resources.* London, University of Chicago Press, 1976.

Dasgupta, Partha S., and Heal, Geoffrey M. *Economic Theory and Exhaustible Resources.* Cambridge, Cambridge University Press, 1979.

Droz-Vincent, Philippe, and Salamé, Ghassan. *Moyen Orient : pouvoirs autoritaires, sociétés bloquées* (preface). Paris, Presses Universitaires de France, 2004.

El Mallakh, Ragaei. *Kuwait.* Chicago, The University of Chicago Press, 1968.

Ende, Werner. Auf der Suche nach der Idealen Gesellschaft, in Pawelka, Peter, Pfaff, Isabella, and Wehling, Hans-Georg, Die Golfregion in der Weltpolitik, Stuttgart, Kohlhammer, 1991.

Fargues, Philippe. 'Demographic explosion or social upheaval', in Salamé, Ghassan (Ed.), Democracy without Democrats, London, I. B. Tauris, 1994, pp. 156–79.

Fargues, Philippe, and Cambage, Y. *Chrétiens et Juifs dans l'Islam arabe et turc.* Paris, Fayard, 1992.

Fatamy, Samar. 'Les femmes en Arabie saoudite', in *Etudes Géopolitiques* 3, 2004 III, pp. 98–104.

Frachon, Alan, and Vernet, Daniel. *L'Amérique messianique.* Paris, Seuil, 2004.

Ghalioun, Burban. Le Moyen-Orient au bord de l'implosion?, in Boniface, Pascal, and Billion, Didier, Les défis du monde arabe, Paris, Presses Universitaires de France, 2004.

Gran, Peter. *Islamic Roots of Capitalism.* New York, Syracuse University Press, 1998.

Halliday, Fred. *Nation and Religion in the Middle East.* London, Saqi Books, 2000.

Hammad, Alam E. *Islamic Banking - Theory and Practice.* Cincinnati, Ohio, Zakat and Research Foundation, 1989.

Hartmann, Richard. *Die Religion des Islam.* Darmstadt, Wissenschaftliche Buchgesellschaft, 1992.

Hefner, Robert W. *Civil Islam Muslims and Democratization in Indonesia.* Berkeley, CA, University Presses of California, 2000.

Hidouci, Ghazi. 'Plaidoyer pour une transition politique dans le monde arabe, in Boniface, Pascal, and Billion, Didier, *Les défis du monde arabe*, Paris, Presses Universitaires de France, 2004.

Hobsbawm, Eric (1994). *The Age of Extremes.* New York. Pantheon Books, 1994.

Hotelling, Harold. 'The Economics of Exhaustible Resources', in Journal of Political Economy, Vol. 39, 1931, pp. 137–175.

Heisbourg, François. *La fin de l'Occident.* Paris, Odile Jacob, 2005.

Huband, Mark. *Brutal Truths, Fragile Myths.* Boulder, Col., Westview, 2004.

Humphreys, R. Stephen. *Between Memory and Desire.* London, University of California Press, 1999.

Ismael, Jacqueline S. *Kuwait: Dependency and Class in a Rentier State.* Gainesville, FL, University Press of Florida, 1993.

Jabarti, Anwar. 'The Oil Crisis: A Producer's Dilemma', in El Mallakh, Ragaei, and McGuire, Carl (Eds), U.S. and World Energy Resources: Prospects and Priorities, Boulder, Col., ICEED, 1977, pp. 130–131.

Kepel, Gilles. *Jihad*. Paris, Folioactuel, 2003.

Fitna – Guerre au coeur de l'Islam. Paris, Gallimard, 2004.

Khalaf, Roula. 'US democracy drive heartens the Islamists', in *Financial Times*, 20 May 2005.

Khalib, Farouk S. 'L'évolution économique du royaume d'Arabie saoudite, in *Études Géopolitiques* 3, 2004 III, pp. 111–118.

Khalidi, Rashi. *Resurrecting Empire*. Boston, Beacon Press, 2004.

Klare, Michael. *Blood and Oil*. New York, Henry Holt, 2004.

Klein, Naomi. *No War*. London, Gibson Square, 2005.

Lamchichi, Abderrahim. *L'islamisme politique*. Paris, L'Harmattan, 2002.

Lapidus, Ira M. 'The Separation of State and Religion in the Development of Early Islamic Society', in *International Journal of Middle East Studies*, No. 6, 1975, pp. 363–385.

Leonard, Mark. *Why Europe will run the 21st century*. London, Fourth Estate, 2005.

Lindholm, Charles. *The Islamic Middle East Tradition and Change*. London, Blackwell Publishers, 2002.

The Islamic Middle East. London, Blackwell, 2002.

Looney, Robert. 'Iraq's Economic Transition: The Neoliberal Model and its Role', in *The Middle East Journal*, Autumn 2003, Vol. 57, No. 3, pp. 568–587.

Luders, Michael. 'Mit deco Koran in die Moderne', in *Die Zeit*, 22 December, 1995.

Mahfoud, Ahmed. 'La religion islamique justifie-t-elle la confusion entre spirituel et temporel?', in *L'Islamisme*, Paris, Éditions La Découverte, 1994.

Mannan, Muhammad Abdul. *Islamic economic principles: Theory and Practice*. Boulder, Col., Westview Press, 1987.

Mansfield, Peter. *A History of the Middle East*. New York, Penguin Books, 1991.

Mills, Paul S., and Presley, John R. *Islamic Finance: Theory and Practice*. London, Macmillan, 1999.

Naim, Mouna. 'L'islamisme, alibi des régimes répressifs', in *Le Monde*, 22 February 1996.

Naqvi, Syed Nawab Haider. *Islam, Economics and Society*. London, Kegan Paul International, 1994.

Owen, Roger. *State, Power and Politics in the Making of the Modern Middle East*. London, Routledge, 1992.

Owen, Roger, and Pamuk, Sevket. *A History of the Middle East Economies in the Twentieth Century*. Cambridge, MA, Harvard University Press, 1999.

Pakravan, Karim. 'The Emerging Private Sector: New Demands on an Old System', in Sick, Gary G., and Potter, Lawrence G. (Eds), *The Persian Gulf at the Millennium*, New York, St Martin's Press, 1997, pp. 115–126.

Pawelka, Peter. 'Der Irak als "Rentierstaat"', in Pawelka, Peter, Pfaff, Isabella, and Wehling, Hans-Georg, *Die Golfregion in der Weltpolitik*, Stuttgart, Kohlhammer, 1991.

Penrose, Edith, and Penrose, E. F. *Iraq, International Relations and National Development*. London, Ernest Benn, 1978.

Planbol, Xavier de. *Les nations du prophète*. Paris, Fayard, 1994.

Pott, Marcel. *Allas falsche Propheten*. Köln, Bastei Lübbe, 2001.

Richards, Alan, and Waterbury, John. *A Political Economy of the Middle East: State, Class and Economic Development*. Boulder, CO, Westview Press, 1990.

Roberts, John. *Visions and Mirages*. Edinburgh, Mainstream Publishing, 1995.

Oil and the Iraq War of 2003. Boulder, CO, ICEED, 2003.

Rodinson, Maxime. *L'Islam et capitalisme*. Paris, Editions du Seuil, 1966.

Ruthven, Malise. *Islam in the World*. Oxford, Oxford University Press, 2000.

Rutledge, Ian. *Addicted to oil*. London, I. B. Tauris, 2005.

Salomon, Jean-Jacques. 'Un fantasme américain: la démocratie au Grand Moyen-Orient', in *Futuribles*, No. 302, Nov. 2004, pp. 5–28.

Shirley, Edward G. 'Is Iran's Present Algeria's Future?', in Foreign Affairs, May–June 1995, pp. 28–58.

Sivan, Emmanuel. *Radical Islam*. London, Yale University Press, 1985.

Stelzer, Irwin M. 'Can We Do Without Saudi Oil?', in *The Weekly Standard*, 19 November 2001.

Tertrais, Bruno. *La guerre sans fin*. Paris, Seuil, 2004.

Tertrais, Bruno. *Quatre ans pour changer le monde*. Paris, CERI/Autrement, 2005.

Toscane, Luiza. *L'Islam, Un autre Nationalisme?* Paris, L'Harmattan, 1995.

Vogt, Kari. *Islams hus*. Oslo, Cappelen, 1992.

Waterbury, John. 'Democracy without Democrats? The potential for political liberalisation in the Middle East', in Salamé, Ghassan (Ed.), *Democracy without Democrats*, London, I. B. Tauris, 1994, pp. 23–47.

World Energy Outlook. Paris, IEA/OECD, 2004.

Yetiv, Steve A.. *Crude Awakenings*. London, Cornell University Press, 2004.

Oil Politics and Environmental Conflict: The Case of Niger Delta, Nigeria

CHUKWUMERIJE OKEREKE

Introduction

This essay examines the link between oil politics and environmental conflict in Nigeria. The specific focus is on the environmental conflict in the Niger Delta region from where the bulk of the country's oil is extracted. The essay provides a concise account of the ways in which the scramble for the control of oil money has led to one of the most violent environmental conflicts in known history.

There are several accounts of this issue which have generally tended to suggest that environmental conflict in the Niger Delta arises mainly from the efforts of the oil-bearing communities to resist the big oil companies whose central aim is construed as wanting to take as much oil as possible with the least regard for the environmental consequences of their activities. But most of these accounts misrepresent the complex issues in the Niger Delta by providing a simplistic picture. For while it is true that the big multinational oil companies are major players both in political economy and social conflicts connected to oil politics in the region, the true character of the Niger Delta conflict is none the less best understood in terms of the historical development of the country and the larger political economy under which the oil companies and the other main actors interact. Indeed, virtually the whole of Nigerian politics since the country gained independence from Britain in 1960 is intricately connected with the quest for oil control by both internal and external forces, such that an understanding of this politics of oil is critical in explaining not only the environmental conflict, but also almost all other aspects of politics in this country, including its constitution, institutions, economy and foreign policies.

For the purpose of analysis, the rest of the essay is divided into four short sections. In the first section, I provide general information on the area, the people and the strategic nature of oil exploratory activities in the Niger Delta. In the second section, I provide an account of the various dimensions of environmental conflict in the Niger Delta and in the process indicate the main justifications under which these acts of violence are committed. In the third section, I show how the politics of oil in Nigeria leads to wide-scale environmental destruction as well as the inability of relevant authorities to successfully stem the damage. I also explain how the perspectives and the responses of main actors to the issue are shaped by the peculiar historical development of the country. I then end with some concluding remarks.

The Strategic Importance of the Niger Delta Oil

Oil was first drilled in Nigeria by Shell in 1956, just four years before the country's independence.[1] Since then, many other oil companies, such as Elf, Texaco, Mobil and Agip, have joined Shell in prospecting and drilling for oil in the country. The company is the biggest oil operator in Nigeria, accounting for around one-half of the nation's output of 2.6m. barrels per day (b/d).

Nigeria is about the 10th largest producer of oil in the world, with a production rate of well over 2m. b/d.[2] The country has the largest oil reserves in the whole of Africa (an estimated 22,000m. barrels), with more than 90% of this resource located in the Niger Delta region. The Niger Delta, with an area of about 36,000 sq km, is one of the largest wetlands in the world (Ibeanu, 2000: 20). It is composed of four main ecological zones, including coastal barrier islands, low-land rain forests, freshwater swamp forests and mangrove forests. Thus, the Niger Delta has a very high biodiversity, with many unique species of plants and animals. The region provides home to most of the oil companies operating in Nigeria and is thus said to be the proverbial hen that lays the golden egg. Proceeds from the sale of oil drilled in the Niger Delta account for more than 80% of all federal revenues and more than 95% of all foreign exchange earnings (Forrest, 1995: 133). Hence, oil is actually the lifeblood of the Nigerian economy. As Cyril Obi puts it, it 'is the fiscal basis of the Nigerian state' (Obi, 1998: 261).

At the same time, oil production in the Niger Delta has important international significance. Nigeria is already the fifth largest producer of oil among OPEC nations. The country is equally the fifth largest supplier of oil to the USA and large quantities are also sold to China, Japan and Europe. Furthermore, with the current plan of the US government to diversify its energy supply from the Middle East, it is estimated that production in the Niger Delta, as well as in the entire Gulf of Guinea (comprising Gabon, Chad, Equatorial Guinea and Angola), will account for up to 25% of all US foreign oil by 2015 (Hoyle, 2005). Surely, then, it is not a surprise that the global oil market has been responding with increasing sensitivity to situations in the Niger Delta, more especially since the Iraq war in 2003 and the subsequent political tension in the Middle East (De Capua, 2006). Multinational oil companies, eager for a supply from outside the Middle East, want to increase production from Africa. Nigeria is generally considered to be part of the solution to the insatiable demands for more oil from the USA and fast-growing China and India. On a visit to Nigeria in May 2006,

---

[1] Shell has been prospecting for oil in Nigeria since 1938, but it was in 1956 that the company, then known as Shell D'Arcy, drilled the first well at Oboibiri Bayelsa State. ('Shell under fire from Nigerian ethnic groups', 24 May 2006, *Mail&Guardian*: http://www.mg.co.za/articlepage.aspx?area=/breaking_news/breaking_news__africa/&articleid=272685)

[2] Nigeria sold 198m. barrels between January and 1 March 2006. This amounts to an average of 3.3m. b/d.

Chinese President Hu Jintao signed deals to increase Chinese exploration and production.[3]

Part of the drive by the West to increase and maintain production in Nigeria stems from the fact that the crude oil from the Niger Delta, popularly known as *Bonny Light*, is one of the best in the world. Apart from having a very low sulphur content, it is also one of the easiest crudes to extract and to refine (Bearman, 1998).[4] Expectedly, Shell and the rest of the oil companies operating in the Niger Delta have sought to make the most of this situation. Nigeria is Shell's third biggest country of production after the USA and the United Kingdom. Drilling in Nigeria accounts for more than 11% of Shell's annual global production and this is set to rise in the coming years. For quite some time now, Shell has been drilling more than 1m. b/d of oil from the Niger Delta. In general, it is estimated that Shell earns about US $600,000 a day and between $200m.–$600m. from its concessions in the Niger Delta (Greenpeace, 1995: 19).

But while the pockets of Shell and most of the Nigerian politicians are bulging with oil money, the vast majority of the people of the Delta still live in severe and visible poverty. Most of the indigenes, whose traditional means of livelihood are farming and fishing, are unable to fend for themselves as their lands and rivers have become heavily polluted by regular oil spillages as well as by outright dumping of waste waters from oil-drilling activities. A vast majority lives in mud and thatched houses and many of these are regularly swept away by the high-intensity floods that arise from the indiscriminate deforestation of the area by the oil companies. In many of the villages in this area, there is virtually no government presence, except, in some cases, scattered oil flow stations and abandoned oil-drilling equipment. Most of the people in this area, thus, lack basic amenities such as water, medical care and electricity.

Hence, while hunger, disease and poverty remain the defining features of the Niger Delta, the military and politicians in power, as well as the employees of the oil companies, regularly display incredible levels of opulence. It is this huge and sharp contrast in the quality of life of the people in the oil-bearing communities and those of the oil workers and politicians in the centres of power across Nigeria that constitutes the major substratum upon which the violent conflict in the region thrives. One of the first activists to speak out against this disparity was businessman, TV writer and activist Ken Saro-Wiwa, from the Ogoni region, east of Nigeria's oil capital, Port Harcourt. Saro-Wiwa advocated non-violence, but Nigeria's then military government charged him with having 'counselled and procured' the murder of four Ogoni elders, and in 1995 hanged him, to international condemnation.

---

[3] S. Robinson, 'Nigeria's Deadly Days', *Time*, 5 June 2006: http://www.time.com/time/europe/magazine/printout/0,13155,1193987,00.html

[4] Average production cost is about US $2.50 per barrel. This is a bit higher than the Persian Gulf but lower than the Gulf of Mexico and the North Sea.

Dimensions of Environmental Conflict in the Niger Delta

There are at least three main dimensions to the environmental conflict and the violence that occur in the Niger Delta. The first is the aggression of the multi-national oil companies against the ecosystem. The assault against nature is characterized by largely unregulated and indiscriminate construction of canals in the region. The random construction of canals and other causeways to facilitate oil-exploration activities leads to the destruction of the hydrology and the delicate balance of the ecosystem. Canalization, further, has led to saltwater intrusion, which is the main reason for the death of many species in the fresh water and which renders such waters largely unfit for drinking and household use.

Most of the landscape in the Niger Delta is covered by deeply laid, partially visible, and surface-laid high-tension pipelines carrying oil and gas from one section of the community to the other. Spills and leaks from these pipes, most of which are ill maintained, occur with regular frequency. In some cases, the spills and leaks are followed by huge explosions, which raze buildings and kill thousands of villagers. All of the oil companies operating in the region flare huge volumes of gas daily. The result is heavy air pollution as well as drastic changes in weather conditions in the region. Indeed, the collective activities of the oil companies in the Niger Delta, described by the late Ken Saro-Wiwa as 'ecological war' (Saro-Wiwa, 1995),[5] have made the Niger Delta one of the world's most threatened human ecosystems (Greenpeace, 1995). But violence against nature often translates into violence against the people, given that those who have traditionally depended on this ecosystem, are, by the destruction of their immediate environment, subjected to diverse forms of hardship, including malnutrition, forced eviction, impoverishment, social disarticulation and untimely death.

The second dimension of environmental conflict in the Niger Delta is the violence directed against the oil companies and the federal government by the oil-bearing communities. This aspect is characterized by the harassment of oil workers, hostage-taking, the seizing of barges, aggressive disruption of production activities and vandalization of oil installations. For example, between November 2005 and April 2006, more than 200 oil workers were taken hostage by various youth groups and militias operating in the Niger Delta. These groups, which claim to be fighting for the liberation of the people of Niger Delta, demand large sums from the government and oil companies as compensation for environmental damage arising from oil-exploration activities. In January 2006, a group that goes by the name of the Movement for the Emancipation of Niger Delta (MEND) seized one flow station in the region and demanded the payment of US $1,500m. as compensation. The group also demanded the release of the leader of the Niger Delta People's Volunteer Force, Mujahdin Asari Dokubo, who the government had earlier arrested for leading similar acts of violence in the area (Oduniyi and Ezeigbo, 2006). In February 2006, Shell reported that it was losing up to 37,800 barrels of crude oil and up to $2.27m. a day to bunkering and the

---

[5] Ken Saro-Wiwa in his final statement before the military tribunal that condemned him to death in November 1995.

outright destruction of its oil pipelines in the Niger Delta. However, federal government sources claim that the government is losing about 200,000 barrels of oil and billions of naira daily to violence and environmental conflict in the region (US $1 = naira $200).

Violence in the region is nothing new. Tribal conflict has plagued it for years. Well-armed and organized gangs have been present almost as long as the oil companies, making tens of millions of dollars in 'bunkering' actions in which oil is illegally siphoned. The gangs have also extracted money by kidnapping oil workers and providing 'security' services in exchange for not attacking oil installations. Oil-producing communities often claim that these acts of violence result from the frustration and desperation prevalent in the region. They argue that decades of neglect by the oil companies, the extremely high rate of unemployment in the area and the general political marginalization of the region by successive regimes at the federal level have left the people of the Niger Delta with no option other than to literally fight for their survival. Hence community leaders consistently refrain from blaming those responsible for these acts of violence, claiming that a realistic assessment must begin by analysing and removing the causes of these acts of aggression.[6] Yet another popular line of argument is that the government actually instigated these acts of insurgence by the ruthless way in which it seeks to crush every form of organized peaceful protest or voice of complaint in the region. A notable illustration is the way the Nigerian military government under Gen. Sani Abacha handled the protest from the Saro-Wiwa-led Movement for the Survival of the Ogoni People (MOSOP) in the early and mid-1990s. The government sought to quell every form of opposition by incessantly intimidating and harassing the leaders of this Movement. When this tactic did not achieve the desired results, the government brought fabricated charges against the most vocal of the leaders and saw to it that they were convicted and promptly executed. The junta also commissioned a joint military task force which occupied Ogoniland for several months. Within this period, the task force brutally plundered about 102 Ogoni villages, killing as many as 2,000 Ogonis and forcing many thousands more to flee the state (Okonta and Oronto, 2001).

Therefore, the third dimension of oil-motivated environmental conflict in the Niger Delta is the violence directed against the people by the government. This dimension of violence is mostly perpetrated under the pretext of the need to protect oil installations or to maintain law and order. Government agents, sometimes in collaboration with the oil companies, frequently raid communities in the Niger Delta to arrest, maim and kill people simply for showing the slightest resistance to the smooth operation of the multinational oil companies. Occasionally, as in the case of the Ogoni mentioned above, they plunder a whole village, burning down hundreds of houses and rendering thousands destitute. In 2000, the current civilian administration led by Olusegun Obasanjo promptly called in the

---

[6] See, for example, the interview with the president of the Ijaw National Council, Dr Kimse Okoko with Sam Onwuemedo of *The Vanguard* on 16 September 2000.

army with a shoot-at-sight directive when aggrieved youths clashed with some policemen in the small oil-bearing town of Odi in Bayelsa state. At the end of the one-week operation, the entire town of Odi lay in ruins as houses, trees, and all cultural artefacts were completely levelled by the military. More than 100 inhabitants were killed in the same operation and properties worth US $200m. were destroyed.

It is these acts of violence by the government against its own citizens that tend to endorse the perception that the Nigerian government is a mere lackey of the oil companies and a puppet in the hands of the forces that are bent on ensuring the perpetual subjugation of the Niger Delta people by the dominant tribes and ethnic groups within (Saro-Wiwa, 2000). The federal government, however, insists that most of the people organizing protests in the Niger Delta are self-serving individuals whose primary aim is to destabilize the entire country. They point to scattered developmental projects in the Niger Delta and conclude that pro-testers are greedy elements bent on fomenting trouble and claiming for them-selves alone the oil wealth that nature has bestowed upon the Nigerian state as a whole.[7]

Oil politics and the environment of Niger Delta

It is not possible to understand the environmental conflict in the Niger Delta outside the historical and political development of Nigeria. When the British mercantilists first arrived at the present-day Nigeria, what they met was more than 250 ethnic groups, most of which had distinct languages, cultures and religious belief systems. Of these groups, the Yoruba-speaking people dominated on the western side, the Ibos dominated in the eastern part, while the Hausa Fulanis were the dominant tribe in the north. The people of Niger Delta, comprising the Ijaws, the Urhobos and the Ogonis, together with the other ethnic groups, were interspersed among these dominant three. But in 1914, the British colonial office decided, contrary to the wish of the people, to thrust all of the different ethnic and culturally heterogeneous groups into one political unit. This decision was motivated solely by the economic interests of the British mercantilists and the colonial government.

The contact of the early British traders and colonial agents with the various regions had shown clearly that the north, with its desert-like environment, generally constituted a financial drain on the foreign government. The southern part, on the other hand, with its high biodiversity, had plenty of resources, including assorted types of economic trees and a nearby sea, which made for

---

[7] On 25 September 2003, the United States Agency for International Development (USAID) Mission to Nigeria and the Shell Petroleum Development Company (SPDC) signed a five-year, US $20m. Memorandum of Understanding (MOU) to share their common goals of promoting democracy, stability and economic prosperity in Nigeria. USAID/Nigeria will contribute US $5m. and SPDC will contribute US $15m.: (http://www.usaid.gov/ng/pressrelease.htm). Critics, however, claim that it is all very well for Shell to argue that it will be improving the local environment, but it was Shell that despoiled much of it in the first place.

the easy transportation of these resources back to England. It therefore made economic sense, to the colonial office, to amalgamate these two regions, not only to save administrative costs but also to ensure that the resources from the south could be used to sustain the newly annexed protectorate in the north (Osadolor 1998: 35–36).

But there is perhaps a more important reason why the British colonialists thought it expedient to thrust all the groups together into one political unit. This has to do with their desire to ensure uninterrupted access to the rich resources in the south even after granting political independence to the new state. In their association with the southerners, which lasted for more than 200 years before they made contact with the north, the British mercantilists and the colonial agents had discovered to their greatest discomfort that the southerners were very enterprising and highly independently-minded. Historical accounts record series of cases showing how the people of the south managed to frustrate the British traders in their attempt to appropriate palm oil, timber, rubber and other valuable resources from the region at little or no cost (Khan, 1994). Most of the kingdoms, for example, made the British traders sign treaties that clearly vested the rights of ownership of resources in the natives. Some coastal communities, in addition, enacted rules against monopoly of trade while others sought to establish themselves as middlemen by making it illegal for the merchants to trade directly with the communities in the hinterlands. Furthermore, these people also set up various courts of equity where erring traders were tried and punished (Okonta and Oronto, 2001). It took the official annexation of these areas as a British protectorate; the forceful deposition of the more resistant kings; and, in some cases, the complete destruction of whole villages to eventually cow these people into submitting to whatever terms of trade were dictated by the British mercantilists.

Given this experience, and owing also to the fact that the majority of the politicians pushing for Nigeria's independence were from the southern region, the colonial government was extremely concerned for the unity of the country but also anxious that it might lose unlimited access to the rich resources in the south after granting independence to the forcibly amalgamated state. This anxiety was heightened all the more by the discovery of crude oil in the south and Shell's desire to acquire exclusive concessions over all the oil reserves in the area.

The way this problem was 'solved' was to create artificial political imbalances in the country by allocating to the more compliant north federal legislative seats equal in number to those of all the other regions and ethnic groups put together (Tamuno, 1998). To consolidate this plan, the colonialists equally engineered a highly convoluted and anfractuous constitution meant to keep all the various ethnic groupings at each other's throats (Nnoli, 1978). In this way, the British government knew it would guarantee that the northern politicians would always be in the position to govern the country and to grant them access to the resources in the south on favourable terms. Idahosa (1999: 211) was therefore very correct when he asserted that the 'latent function of the exercise (amalgamation) was to ensure administrative convenience necessary for the facilitation of the exploitative mission of the colonizers'.

However, the result of this lopsided political arrangement has been a deep-seated mistrust and resentment among the various ethnic groups in the country. This inequitable political arrangement equally accounts for the series of political tensions in the country since independence. The climax was the attempt by the southerners to secede from the country in 1967 and a 30-month brutal civil war in which millions of lives were lost. In the build up to the war, the British government unsurprisingly downplayed the equity arguments by the south and even supplied the federal side with arms and logistics with which the secession attempt was effectively quashed.

The points to pin down from the foregoing are, first, that the oil industry in Nigeria developed during a turbulent period in the nation's political history, such that no attention could have been given to adequate environmental protection and equity concerns. Further, quite unlike the countries in the Caspian region, the Nigerian government did not have the benefit of hindsight necessary to establish the robust environmental regulatory framework needed to manage the consequences of oil production. Second, even if the environmental consequences of oil-exploratory activities were well known, it would still have been difficult to rein in Shell, which at that time operated very much as an arm of the colonial administration. Of course, it can be argued that official corruption, incessant political crisis and administrative incompetence remain the greatest causes of the inability of successive Nigerian governments to solve the environmental crisis in the Niger Delta, but it should not be forgotten that the enabling environment (especially that of ethnocentrism) was created, and sustained up to the present by Western colonialists and other agents of imperialism, such as the MNCs.

Indeed, the greedy, all-or-nothing mentality of the first British mercantilists and the divide-and-rule tactics of the colonial government have consistently provided the dominant frame from which the issue of environmental degradation in the Niger Delta is handled by the various governments. Although millions of dollars accrue to the government daily from the sale of crude oil, little or no attention is given to the environmental consequences of the very activities that yield this income. Rather, government officials, most of whom hail from the north (as well as a number of their southern counterparts), maintain fabulous foreign bank accounts and enjoy indescribable affluence.

The main sentiment this provokes amongst the people of Niger Delta is that they are still being treated as a conquered territory plundered by both foreign companies and their internal agents in the north. This feeling is fuelled by the fact that most of the developed cities in the country are far removed from the place of actual production and the communities which bear the brunt of the environmental degradation which results from oil-production activities. It is this logic that animates the violent dimensions of environmental activism in the Niger Delta. Shell is mostly targeted because the company (despite its claims to neutrality) is still seen by many as an ally of the oppressive northern-dominated military regimes, and, as the most prominent symbol of several decades of ruthless exploitation of the Niger Delta by Western imperialists. As a Nigerian proverb goes, if a man cannot get at the chief, he can still maim the chief's goat.

Conclusion

This essay demonstrates that the environmental crisis in the Niger Delta is directly related to the quest for control of oil money in Nigeria both by internal and external forces. It has been argued that although poor governance and a weak political system are at the root of the crisis, the British government laid the foundation for this state of affairs by forcibly amalgamating all the ethnic groups into one political unit solely for British economic gains. Successive federal governments have fed on this substratum of injustice and added to it a matchless lifestyle of profligacy in which all efforts are geared towards the spending of oil money on foreign goods without taking care of the environment of the communities in the areas where oil is drilled. Many years of poverty in the midst of affluence and the continual deterioration of the environment have finally provoked so much frustration that many in the Niger Delta are now willing to take up arms against the oil companies and their own government. This is part of an attempt to bring to the attention of the world what is considered to be the most outrageous dimension of environmental injustice in history and the effort by the federal government in conjunction with the oil companies to protect what is obviously the fiscal basis of the Nigerian state.

A–Z Glossary

By Bülent Gökay

A

Aceh

The mainly Muslim province of Aceh enjoyed a long history as an independent sultanate, before becoming first part of the Dutch East Indies and later the Republic of Indonesia. The British formally recognized Aceh as an independent state in 1819. While identifying all of Sumatra as a Dutch sphere of influence, the 1824 Anglo-Dutch Treaty of London continued to recognize Aceh's sovereignty. In 1871, Britain effectively reneged on its agreement with the Acehnese when it signed the Treaty of Sumatra, which offered the Dutch an entirely free hand in Aceh. The great majority of Acehnese never accepted Dutch rule. Such was the antipathy towards the Dutch that the Japanese invasion was initially greeted with even greater support than it received elsewhere in the archipelago. The Acehnese played a crucial role in the independence struggle in 1945–49. Because of the difficult conditions of that moment and Sukarno's promise of far-reaching autonomy and freedom, Aceh's leaders made a strategic decision to work under the umbrella of Indonesian independence. During the Suharto years (1965–98), resentment against rule from Jakarta was fuelled by the use of the army to keep order. The separatist Gerakan Aceh Merdeka (GAM—Free Aceh Movement) was formed in 1976 and has led calls for Aceh to break away from Indonesia. Hopes for peace were raised on 9 December 2002, when the two sides signed an agreement which offered autonomy and free elections in 2004 in exchange for the rebels disarming. But the deal collapsed in May 2003 when both sides failed to fulfil their side of the bargain. The rebels refused to give up their weapons, and the Indonesian military failed to withdraw to defensive positions. Indonesia has declared martial law and launched an all-out military offensive. GAM has vowed to continue its fight for full independence. At least 10,000 people, mainly civilians, have been killed in the decades-long conflict. Persistent abuses of civilians by troops and police have alienated much of the local population. The discovery of large reserves of oil and gas in Aceh has increased dissent because the Indonesian government has taken most of the proceeds. Under the failed autonomy agreement, the future provincial government would have been allowed to keep 70% of oil and gas profits. *Shari'a* law was introduced in Aceh in 2002, a move which the government hoped would appease the faithfully Muslim population. Aceh supplies an estimated 30% of Indonesia's total oil and gas exports, or

11% of the country's total exports. Mobil Oil Indonesia is a joint venture between Mobil Oil Inc. (USA) and Pertamina (Indonesia's state oil company). Mobil Oil carries out exploration for and exploitation of gas and oil, which is later channelled to PT Arun for production. Mobil Oil also owns shares in PT Arun, though only a small percentage. Aceh was one of the few places to be struck in December 2004 by both the massive earthquake that occurred in southern Asia and the tsunamis it caused—a double blow that killed thousands and wreaked so much devastation that separatists fighting a decades-long insurgency called a temporary cease-fire. But there has been no movement towards new peace negotiations, and several dozen people are still killed every week in clashes.

AGIP

AGIP, which stands for Azienda Generale Italiana Petroli (Italian Oil Company), is an Italian automotive gasoline and diesel retailer. It is a subsidiary of multi-national **petroleum** company Eni. Eni operates in the refining and marketing of petroleum products through its Refining & Marketing Division. The Division's activities are mainly concentrated in Italy, Europe and Latin America. The marketing activities of the Refining & Marketing Division also include the sale of fuels, combustibles and lubricating oils to the industrial, agricultural and transport sectors, as well as to public administrations and for civilian heating purposes. Eni owns a number of production plants for finished lubricants and greases in Italy, Europe, North and South America and the Far East. AGIP has also undertaken crude oil exploitation operations in **Nigeria** since the 1960s and has some 17 oil wells in the locality. In 2000, AGIP signed a co-operation contract with the China National Petroleum Corporation (CNPC) for exploring oil and gas in the Sebei Block in west China's Qaidam Basin. Through its AGIP Gas brand, Eni also markets liquefied petroleum gas (LPG) for domestic, heavy and light industrial and agricultural uses. The entire chain of refining and marketing activities is made possible by crude trading activities, for the procurement of supplies for the company's refining operations but also involving sales on international markets.

Alaska

The name 'Alaska' derives from an Aleut word meaning 'great land', although some believe the Aleut word meant 'mainland' for those residing on the Alaska Peninsula. Alaska today refers to the entire state as well as to the Peninsula. 'Alyeska' survives as the name of a ski resort in Girdwood, and also as the name of the Anchorage consortium overseeing the **Trans-Alaska pipeline** company. When Alaska's oil boom began in the early 1970s, native leaders negotiated with the US Congress to settle land claims and ensure that some of the oil wealth trickled down. They formed 13 native corporations, including Arctic Slope Regional Corporation, which encompassed eight Inupiat villages, including Kaktovik. The oilfields in Alaska are important because the USA's dependency on **petroleum** imports has risen considerably in the past 20 years. The so-called **'oil shocks'** of 1973 and 1980, and the Islamic revolution in **Iran** in 1979 had serious repercussions for the USA, where Americans had to queue for hours to buy gasoline. The war in the Persian (Arabian) Gulf in 1991 put the USA's access to two-thirds of the world's oil reserves in great danger. Opening oilfields in Alaska is considered significant as it would decrease US dependency on petroleum imports from the Middle East and Latin America, boost the revenue of American oil companies, create many American jobs, lower the price of oil for American oil consumers, and increase federal, state, and local tax revenues.

Alberta Oil Sands

Oil sands are deposits of bitumen, molasses-like viscous oil that will not flow unless heated or diluted with lighter hydrocarbons. They are contained in three major areas beneath 140,800 sq km of north-eastern Alberta—an area larger than the state of Florida, twice the size of New Brunswick, more than four-and-a-half times the size of Vancouver Island, and 26 times larger than Prince Edward Island. However, only about 2% of the initial established resource has been produced to date. Alberta's oil sands industry is the result of the investment of thousands of millions of dollars in the infrastructure and technology required to develop the non-conventional resource. In 2003 Alberta's oil sands were the source of about 52.7% of the province's total crude oil and equivalent production, and of about 34.8% of all crude oil and equivalent produced in Canada. Output of marketable oil sands production increased to 858,000 barrels per day (b/d) in 2003, compared with 741,000 b/d in the previous year. It is anticipated that soon Alberta's oil sands production may account for one-half of Canada's total crude output, and for 10% of North American production. It is expected that Alberta's oil sands will have become one of the most important sources of new oil in the world by 2010 as conventional crude dries up. Alberta will possess one of the most valuable energy sources in the world by that time, and one of the few still open to private investment.

Alternative Fuels

Substitutes for traditional liquid, oil-derived motor vehicle fuels like gasoline and diesel. Alternative fuels include mixtures of alcohol-based fuels with gasoline, methanol, ethanol, compressed natural gas, and others. Fuels that are used in place of **petroleum**-based fuels such as gasoline and diesel are commonly considered 'alternative fuels'. The US Department of Energy classifies the following fuels as alternative fuels: biodiesel, electricity, ethanol, hydrogen, methanol, natural gas, propane, p-series, and solar energy. Some of these fall into the category of renewable energy. Renewable energy includes electricity generation for the home, while the term alternative fuels tends to refer to mobile energy. Sometimes 'non-conventional oil' is considered in this category. Non-conventional oil is another source of oil separate from conventional or traditional oil. Non-conventional sources include tar sands, oil shale and bitumen. Potentially significant deposits of non-conventional oil include the Athabasca oil sands site in north-western Canada and the Venezuelan Orinoco tar sands. Oil companies estimate that the Athabasca and Orinoco sites contain as much as two-thirds of total global oil deposits, but they are not yet considered proven reserves of oil because of the high cost involved in the production process. Therefore, extracting a significant percentage of world oil production from tar sands may not yet be feasible. The extraction process requires a great deal of energy for heat and electrical power, which is at present obtained from natural gas (itself in short supply). There are proposals to build a series of nuclear reactors to supply this energy. Non-conventional oil production is currently less efficient, and has a larger environmental impact than conventional oil production. A possible solution to a potential future energy shortage would be to use some of the world's remaining fossil fuel reserves as an investment in renewable energy infrastructure such as wind power, solar power, tidal power, geothermal power, hydropower, thermal depolymerization, ethanol and biodiesel, which do not suffer from finite energy reserves, but do have a finite energy flow. The construction of sufficiently large renewable energy infrastructure might avoid the economic consequences of an extended period of decline in fossil fuel energy supply per capita. Most alternative fuels assume a source of renewable energy or at least sustainable energy (such as nuclear power) as a source of the fuel. A few alternative fuels (for example, hydrogen) may be made by sustainable or non-sustainable means. If they are made by non-sustainable means, such fuels are offered as alternatives usually because they would potentially cause less pollution at the point of use, and perhaps less pollution overall.

American Petroleum Institute

The American Petroleum Institute, often referred to as the API, is the USA's principal trade association for the oil and natural gas industries. Based in Washington, DC, the API is a 'major research institute ... committed to using the best available scientific, economic and legal analysis to guide and support' its policy positions. The API represents the US oil and gas industries to the government. It has adopted positions on such issues as exploration, taxes, trade regulation, environmental regulation, sanctions, industry security and climate change. Each year the API also distributes more than 200,000 publications prepared by a committee of leading industry professionals.

Angola

Angola is sub-Saharan Africa's second largest oil producer after **Nigeria**. The country's oil and oil derivatives industry is the source of 91.92% of its total exports. In 2004 **petroleum** and petroleum products were the source of almost US \$9,700m. in state revenues. Angola fulfils a leading role in Africa's oil industry, as both a major producer and exporter. Angolan crudes have an API gravity that ranges from 32 degrees to 39.5 degrees and a sulphur content ranging from 1.12% to 0.14%. Angola's economy is characterized by its high degree of dependence on the oil sector, from which 40% of the gross domestic product and 80% of government revenues derive. The majority of the country's crude oil is produced off shore in the northern Cabinda province. Other crude reserves include those located onshore near the city of Soyo, off shore in the Kwanza Basin north of Luanda, and off shore of the northern coast. There have been significant discoveries since the mid-1990s. Oil companies currently seek ways to reduce their costs and to develop the cost-efficiency of producing from the high-risk deep-water areas. Leading foreign oil companies with operations in Angola are US-based ChevronTexaco and ExxonMobil, France's Total, the United Kingdom's BP, Royal Dutch/Shell, and Italy's **AGIP**/Eni oil company.

Anti-Trust Laws (USA)

In the late 19th century, rapid consolidation occurred within the booming US economy. 'Trusts' (or holding companies) were established to join together all of the firms in a particular industry—e.g. the Sugar Trust, the Tobacco Trust, the Steel Trust. These holding companies operated on a huge scale, dominating their industries at home and, in some instances, global output. Standard Oil, owned by John D. **Rockefeller**, was the largest of these trusts. In 1910 Rockefeller's individual net worth equalled almost 2.5% of the entire US economy, representing some US $250,000m. in current terms, or at least twice as much as Bill Gates. Opposition to the trusts, especially from farmers who objected to the high cost of transporting their products to the cities by rail, led to the adoption of the Sherman Act in 1890—the first piece of anti-trust legislation. However, it was not until 20 years later, after a campaign had been directed by so-called 'muckraking' journalists, that Standard Oil was arraigned before the courts. In 1911 an historic judgment divided Rockefeller's company into six main entities, including Standard Oil of New Jersey (Esso, now Exxon), Standard Oil of New York (Socony, now Mobil), Standard Oil of Ohio, Standard Oil of Indiana (now Amoco, part of BP) and Standard Oil of California (now Chevron), and facilitated the entry into the oil industry of new participants such as Gulf and Texaco, which struck oil in Texas. The so-called 'Seven Sisters' were subsequently involved in mergers. In 1984 Chevron acquired Gulf in what was, at the time, the largest corporate merger ever in the USA. Ironically, however, in the 1990s the oil industry recombined. Exxon, for example, merged with Mobil, formerly part of the Standard Oil empire, to establish a company twice the size of its closest rival, BP Amoco, which is similarly made up of two former Standard Oil companies (Amoco and Standard Oil of Ohio) and has attempted to merge with a third (Arco, formerly Atlantic Petroleum of Pennsylvania). The market share of the three big oil companies now rivals that achieved by Rockefeller.

Arab–Israeli Wars

The Arab–Israeli wars were those waged in 1948–49, 1956, 1967, 1973–74 and 1982 between Israel and surrounding Arab states. Arab–Israeli tensions have been further complicated and sometimes aggravated by the political, strategic, and economic interests of the great powers in the region.

The 1948–49 Arab–Israeli War: The 1948–49 Arab–Israeli War is known by Israelis as the 'War of Independence' or the 'War of Liberation'. For Palestinians, however, the war marked the beginning of the so-called 'Catastrophe' that was to befall them. Having refused to accept the division, by the United Nations, of the territory of the British Mandate of Palestine into two states, one Jewish and one Arab, the Arab states of Egypt, Syria, Transjordan, Lebanon and **Iraq** attacked the newly established State of Israel. As a result of this war, the first in the Arab–Israeli conflict, the region was divided among Israel, Egypt and Transjordan.

The 1956 Arab–Israeli War: From 1949 to 1956 a truce between Israel and the Arab states, partly enforced by UN forces, was periodically interrupted by raids and reprisals. The USA, Great Britain and France took the side of Israel, while the Soviet Union expressed support for Arab demands. During 1956 tension increased as Israel became convinced that the Arabs were preparing to go to war. Egypt's nationalization of the Suez Canal in July further estranged Great Britain and France, which concluded new agreements with Israel. On 29 October, Israeli forces commenced a combined air and ground assault on Egypt's Sinai Peninsula. The success of the Israeli forces early in the assault was strengthened by an Anglo-French invasion along the Canal. Although many countries denounced in strong terms the action taken against Egypt, the cease-fire of 6 November, which had the backing of the United Nations, the USA and the Soviet Union, came only after Israel's capture of a number of key objectives, such as the Gaza Strip. In 1957 Israel abandoned these positions to a UN emergency force, after access to the Gulf of Aqaba and, consequently, the Indian Ocean, had been guaranteed.

The 1967 Arab–Israeli War (the Six-Day War): Following an interlude of relative calm, border incidents between Israel, Syria, Egypt and Jordan increased during the early 1960s. In May 1967, President Nasser of Egypt requested the withdrawal of UN forces from Egyptian territory, mobilized units in the Sinai, and denied Israel access to the Gulf of Aqaba. Israel's response was to mobilize its armed forces. In June, after a period in which threats and provocations had escalated, Israel launched an attack that virtually wiped out the combined Arab air capability. Having thus obtained air superiority, Israel gained control of the Sinai Peninsula within three days and turned its attention to the Jordanian frontier, capturing Jerusalem's Old City; and to the Syrian border, taking the strategically located Golan Heights. The war, which ended on 10 June, is frequently referred to as the Six-Day War. The Suez Canal was closed by the war, and Israel declared that it would not relinquish Jerusalem and that it would retain the other territories it had captured until significant progress in Arab-Israeli relations had been achieved. Conventional fighting subsequently gave way to frequent artillery duels along the frontiers and to clashes between Israelis and Palestinian guerrillas.

The 1973–74 Arab–Israeli War (the Yom Kippur War): During 1973, the Arab states, believing that their grievances against Israel were being ignored, discreetly prepared for war, under the leadership of Egypt's President Sadat. On 6 October, the Jewish holy day of Yom Kippur, in a two-pronged assault on Israel, Egyptian forces struck eastward across the Suez Canal and pushed the Israelis back, while Syrian forces advanced from the north. Iraqi forces also participated in the war and, in addition, Syria received assistance from Jordan, **Libya**, and the smaller Arab states. The attacks took Israel by surprise and the country did not mobilize fully for several days. Then, however, Israel was able to repel the Syrian and Egyptian forces and establish a salient on the west bank of the Suez Canal. US, Soviet and UN diplomacy had achieved a tenuous cease-fire by 25 October. In November, Israel and Egypt concluded a cease-fire agreement, but fighting between Israel and Syria continued until the negotiation of a further cease-fire in 1974. Thanks, largely, to diplomacy undertaken by US Secretary of State Henry **Kissinger**, Israel retreated across the Suez Canal and several miles inland from the east bank to behind a UN-supervised cease-fire zone. On the Syrian front also, Israel relinquished territorial gains that it had made during the war. Following the war Egypt and Syria resumed diplomatic relations with the USA, and the clearance of the Suez Canal began. The 1973–74 War led to a major revision of the balance of power in the Middle East and culminated, some years hence, in the negotiation of the Camp David Accords. US support for Israel provoked an Arab oil embargo and American car owners found themselves having to queue to buy gasoline. Oil prices rose sharply as a result of the embargo, enabling Arab producers to reduce exports without any corresponding loss of revenue. Market shortages gave rise to fear and anxiety among consumers; oil companies embarked on panic-buying of oil, bolstering their inventories and causing demand to rise. Price increases of 40% and 'gas lines' were interpreted as signs of the USA's loss of independence over its oil supplies.

The 1982 Arab–Israeli War: In 1978 Palestinian guerrillas based in Lebanon launched an air raid on Israel. In retaliation, Israeli troops occupied a strip of southern Lebanese territory about 6–10 km deep. Eventually a UN peace-keeping force was set up there, but sporadic fighting continued to occur. In 1982, Israel launched a major offensive with the aim of destroying all Palestinian military bases in southern Lebanon. Following a 10-week siege of the Muslim sector of west Beirut, a stronghold of the Palestine Liberation Organization (PLO), Israel succeeded in forcing the Palestinians to accept a US-sponsored plan whereby the PLO guerrillas would evacuate Beirut and relocate to several Arab countries that had agreed to accept them. In 1985 Israel withdrew from Lebanon, but still maintains a Lebanese/Christian-policed 'buffer zone' north of its border.

Arab League

The Arab League or League of Arab States is an organization of Arab states. The League's charter declares that the League shall co-ordinate economic affairs, including commercial relations; communications; cultural affairs; nationality, passports, and visas; social affairs; and health affairs. The charter also forbids Arab League members from resorting to force against each other. The permanent headquarters of the League are located in Cairo, Egypt. At the time of its formation by seven states on 22 March 1945, the Arab League defined its main goals as to: *Serve the common good of all Arab countries, ensure better conditions for all Arab countries, guarantee the future of all Arab countries and fulfil the hopes and expectations of all Arab countries.* Like the Organization of American States, the Council of Europe and the African Union, the aims of the Arab League are primarily political; each of these organizations may be viewed as a regional version of the United Nations. However, Arab League membership is based on common cultural background rather than geographical location, and in this respect it bears comparison with such organizations as the Latin Union or the Nordic Council. Unlike some other regional organizations, however, such as the European Union, the Arab League has not achieved any significant degree of regional integration and the organization itself has no direct relations with member states' citizens. All members of the Arab League are also members of the Organization of the Islamic Conference. Among the League's most important activities have been its attempts to co-ordinate Arab economic life, through, for example, the Arab Telecommunications Union, the Arab Postal Union, and the Arab Development Bank. In 1965 an Arab Common Market open to all member states was established. The common market agreement provides for the eventual abolition of customs duties on natural resources and agricultural products, free movement of capital and labour among member states and co-ordinated economic development. In 2003, Egypt signed an energy co-operation agreement with three Arab League states—Jordan, Lebanon and Syria.

Arctic National Wildlife Refuge (ANWR)

The 8m.-ha Arctic National Wildlife Refuge (ANWR) is located in the north-eastern corner of **Alaska**, lying wholly north of the Arctic Circle and 2,000 km south of the North Pole. The Coastal Plain area, which covers some 600,000 ha on the ANWR's northern edge, is bordered on the north by the Beaufort Sea, on the east by the US-Canadian border, and on the west by the Canning River. The Kaktovik Inupiat Corporation and Arctic Slope Regional Corporation own about 38,000 ha in the Coastal Plain around the village of Kaktovik. At its widest points, the Coastal Plain extends for some 160 km in width and about 48 km in depth, covering an area slightly larger than the state of Delaware. The Native population comprises about 220 residents at Kaktovik, a village on Native-owned lands at Barter Island, adjacent to the Coastal Plain and within the boundaries of ANWR. Less than 160 km west of the ANWR, located along similar geologic trends, lies Prudhoe Bay, the largest oilfield in North America. The output of Prudhoe, together with that of Kuparuk, Lisburne and Endicott, accounts for about 25% of US domestic oil production. Geologists believe that the Coastal Plain of the ANWR is the onshore area with the highest **petroleum** potential that remains to be explored in North America. This potential is believed to run to thousands of millions of barrels of recoverable oil and may rival that of the Prudhoe Bay field. US output of crude, which declined from almost 9m. barrels per day (b/d) in 1985 to some 6.6m. b/d in early 1995, is projected to fall to less than 5m. b/d in 2010. Even if US crude oil demand increases only modestly, the deficit in US supplies will run to about 10m. b/d, and will need to be met by new discoveries or imports. The ANWR will therefore make a crucial contribution to meeting the USA's energy requirements.

Australian Oil

Australia accounts for about 0.2% of global production of conventional oil and for some 2% of gas output world-wide. More than 80% is located off shore, there are few 'giant' fields and those that do exist lie at the lower end of the 'giant' spectrum. Some gas discoveries have been made well off shore, in deep water, and will be costly to develop. Their Energy Profit Ratios (EPRs) are likely to be low. Australia is a net importer of crude oil and both imports and exports refined **petroleum** products. Natural gas is exported in the form of liquefied natural gas (LNG). At present, Australia is able to meet about 80%–85% of its crude oil needs from domestic output. Bass Strait is the source of about 44% of Australia's crude oil and condensate, followed by the Carnarvon Basin, off the north-west coast of Western Australia, which contributes around 41% of total production. The Gippsland Basin in Victoria is Australia's main source of natural gas (with a 33% share) and liquefied petroleum gas (69%), while most of the country's LNG is sourced from the North West Shelf Development Project.

Azerbaijan

Azerbaijan regained its independence following the collapse of the Soviet Union in 1991. The country has a Turkic and majority-Muslim population. Although a cease-fire took effect in 1994, Azerbaijan's conflict with Armenia over the Azerbaijani Nagorno-Karabakh enclave (largely Armenian-populated) has yet to be resolved. As a result of the conflict, Azerbaijan has lost 16% of its territory and must accommodate some 571,000 internally displaced persons. Corruption is omnipresent and the potential for wealth-creation from the country's undeveloped **petroleum** resources remains largely unrealized. Oil is Azerbaijan's principal export. Output fell in the years up to 1997, but there has been an increase in every year since then. The negotiation of **production-sharing agreements (PSAs)** with foreign companies, which have so far committed US $60,000m. to long-term oilfield development, should generate the funds required for industrial develop-ment in the future. Oil production under the first of these PSAs, with the **Azerbaijan International Operating Company**, commenced in November 1997. A consortium of Western oil companies is scheduled to begin pumping 1m. barrels per day from a large offshore field in 2006, transporting the oil via a $4,000m.-pipeline it has constructed between Baku and Turkey's Mediterranean port of Ceyhan. It has been estimated that by 2010 revenues from this project will have doubled the country's current gross domestic product. Although Azerbaijan is confronted by the same challenges as the other former Soviet republics in switching from a command to a market economy, the country's substantial energy resources improve its long-term prospects. The government has only recently begun to make headway in economic reform, and old economic ties and structures are gradually being replaced. Other obstacles that impede Azerbaijan's economic progress include the need for accelerated foreign investment in the non-energy sector, the continuing conflict with Armenia over the Nagorno-Karabakh region, and persistent corruption. Trade with **Russia** and the other former Soviet republics is declining in significance, while that undertaken with Turkey and the nations of Europe is growing. In the long term Azerbaijan's economic future will be determined by international oil prices, the construction of new pipelines in the region, and Azerbaijan's ability to manage the wealth that accrues to it from oil.

Azerbaijan International Operating Company (AIOC)

Azerbaijan International Operating Company (AIOC) is a consortium comprising 10 major international oil companies and the **State Oil Company of the Azerbaijan Republic (SOCAR)**. AIOC is developing the Azeri, Chirag and deep-water portion of Gunashli fields in the **Azerbaijan** sector of the Caspian Sea. Their 30-year **production sharing agreement (PSA)** was concluded in September 1994, ratified by parliament on 2 December, and took effect on 12 December. The oil reserves of the contract area have been estimated at more than 4,000m. barrels. In what has been described as 'the deal of the century', an international consortium, AIOC, signed an 8,000m.-euro, 30-year contract in September 1994 to develop three fields—Azeri, Chirag, and the deep-water portions of Gunashli—with total reserves estimated at 3,000m.–5,000m. barrels. Oil revenues are projected to be roughly 80,000m. euros over the 30-year life of the AIOC and Azerbaijan will realize 80% of these revenues. Almost all of Azerbaijan's oil production increases since 1997 have come from AIOC, which is operated by BP. From November 1997 until the end of 2001, AIOC produced a total of 133.5m. barrels of oil, mostly from the Chirag-1 stationary platform.

B

Baku-Ceyhan Pipeline

The Baku-Ceyhan (Bakhu-Tblisi-Ceyhan) pipeline is 996 mm in diameter, 1,760 km in length, and was opened, finally, in 2005. The decision to build the pipeline was first made by **Azerbaijan**, Turkey, **Kazakhstan** and **Georgia** on 18 November 1999. At that time, they signed a document called the 'Istanbul Declaration'. US President Bill Clinton was present in Turkey at that time on a formal visit and signed the Istanbul Declaration as a witness. They agreed that Baku-Tbilisi-Ceyhan would be the main export pipeline for oil produced in the Caspian Basin. The biggest interests in the construction of this pipeline belong to Britain's BP oil company, which has a 34.7% share, followed by the **State Oil Company of the Azerbaijan Republic (SOCAR)**, which has a 25% share. The construction of the pipeline is generally considered to be one of the major developments in the Caspian region since the collapse of the Soviet Union. The pipeline project offered wide-ranging benefits. As far as Turkey was concerned it meant a major role in the export of oil from the Caspian region; the transportation of Caspian oil to the Turkish port of Ceyhan, thus avoiding the pollution-sensitive area on the other side of the Bosphorus and the Dardanelles; expansion of Turkey's political and economic ties with the concerned countries in the Caucasus and **Central Asia**, especially with Azerbaijan; transit rights and a good source of financial gain. As far as the Republic of Azerbaijan was concerned, it meant a great achievement in the pipeline diplomacy of the Caspian Sea; financial gains from the export of Azeri oil to Western markets; the establishment of Azerbaijan as a reliable source of energy for the industrialized countries, thus helping Azerbaijan in its struggle to become more involved in international affairs as a European country, and a possible step towards the acceptance of Azerbaijan as a full member of NATO. As far as land-locked Kazakhstan was concerned, it meant a possible route for oil exports; better relations with Western countries; a step towards its long-declared policy of 'multiple pipelines' with its special interpretation. Georgia was seeking transit rights for the export of oil from other countries, and was becoming more important for regional peace, especially taking into consideration the role of Chechen rebels and Russian plans for them. As far as the USA was concerned, it meant a step towards the export of oil from the Caspian resources to Western markets in order to reduce the degree of dependence on

Persian (Arabian) Gulf oil; a step in line with the policy of the US government seeking to prevent **Iran** and the Russian Federation from benefiting from the oil and gas pipelines of the Caspian region in order to block the expansion of their influence; the reduced dependence of Caspian countries on the existing network of Russian pipelines; and help for the countries politically close to the USA (Azerbaijan, Turkey and Georgia). However, the Baku-Ceyhan pipeline has been confronted by some serious problems, including: a) its high cost—it was originally estimated that it would cost US $3,000m.–4,000m.; b) some sources claimed that the Baku-Ceyhan pipeline was a 'political pipeline' and that the project would eventually collapse under the pressure of economics. Some thought that the political barriers in relations between Iran and the USA might be removed by developments in Iran. In that case, the USA might cease its opposition to the Iranian route, which was the most economical way to export Caspian oil and gas products. For the same reason, the Iranian officials in charge of Caspian affairs stated decisively after the conclusion of the Istanbul Declaration that the Baku-Ceyhan pipeline would never be built; c) some experts argued that there was not enough oil in the concerned areas to justify the Baku-Ceyhan pipeline; d) the 1,760-km pipeline was too long and crossed politically volatile areas, such as Georgian territory, where there was instability; e) the route taken by the Baku-Ceyhan pipeline crossed too many countries.

'Big Oil'

'Big Oil' refers to the economic power of the major multinational oil and gasoline companies, and their perceived political influence, especially in the USA. Examples of the companies that collectively constitute Big Oil include Exxon-Mobil, Chevron Corporation, BP, Royal Dutch/Shell and ConocoPhillips. Usually used pejoratively, the term Big Oil is now used with reference to the huge impact crude oil has on first-world industrial societies. The term may also be utilized in discussions of consumers' relationship with oil production and **petroleum** use, as both US and European consumers generally respond to increases in the international price of petroleum by purchasing relatively fuel-efficient vehicles. By the same token, consumers tend to lose interest in fuel efficiency and the oil debate as pump prices stabilize. In 2005, the term Big Oil was used frequently in the media as the US pump price for regular, unleaded gasoline rose above US $2.00 per gallon (*c.* 3.8 litres), and then, in the early autumn, above US $3.00. These increased fuel costs have been attributed to the effects of 'Hurricane Katrina' and 'Hurricane Rita', as well as to the uncertain status of crude oil supply and continued instability in **Iraq**. A current issue is whether the petroleum industry has taken advantage of meteorological and political unrest to indulge in profiteering by recording alleged windfall profits. The response of the oil industry has been to emphasize its extensive costs and market uncertainties, and to undertake a campaign of public education regarding the industry's background and how transactions made on commodity futures markets affect pricing. In defence of the industry, its supporters and many fiscal conservatives have pointed to its status as an example of free-market economics. On the other hand, the oil industry's detractors have drawn attention to allegations that it has taken advantage of unrest to enrich itself unfairly.

Blue Stream Pipeline

Blue Stream, a major trans-Black Sea gas pipeline operated by the Russian gas monopoly Gazprom, transports natural gas from **Russia** to Turkey. Constructed with the aim of diversifying gas sources, by 2010 Blue Stream is expected to be operating at maximum capacity, with annual deliveries of 16,000m. cu m of gas. The pipeline extends over a total of 1,213 km. The cost of its construction amounted to US $3,200m., including expenditure of $1,700m. on its underwater section. For various reasons, the financial returns from the pipeline have been disappointing. As Turkey is a monopsony, it exercises a large degree of control over the terms of purchases from Gazprom. Concessions made by Gazprom to the Turkish government have substantially reduced envisaged revenues from the pipeline. In late August 2005, Russian President Vladimir Putin and Turkish Prime Minister Tayyip Erdoğan discussed the construction of a second pipeline, or an expansion of Blue Stream. A 'strategic partnership' between Russia and Turkey was meant to be founded on Blue Stream, including such elements as joint participation in the development of oil, energy, and transport projects. The agreement to sell Russian gas to Turkey was concluded in December 1997, when the two parties endorsed a corresponding inter-governmental agreement whereby Russia undertook to supply Turkey with 364,500m. cu m of gas in 2000–25. The existing gas transit route traversed Bulgaria, Moldova, **Romania** and Ukraine. However, transportation via this land route added substantially to the cost of the gas, and it was frequently reported that gas was being illicitly siphoned off *en route* through Moldova and Ukraine. Russia believed that the solution to these problems lay in the construction of a pipeline across the Black Sea floor. Blue Stream's construction also provoked protests by environmentalists, but, lacking the support of official environmental assessments, these made little impact. Some Russian economists have argued that the construction of a pipeline to Ankara linked Russia with a monopolist consumer, and questioned Turkey's reliability. A political goal of the Blue Stream project was to prevent competing countries from using Turkey as part of a route to transport Middle Eastern and Caspian gas to Europe. In November 1999, **Turkmenistan**, Turkey, **Azerbaijan** and Georgia signed an inter-governmental agreement to construct a competing Trans-Caspian gas pipeline, and within a few months General Electric, Bechtel and Royal Dutch/ Shell had set up a joint venture with this objective. However, Turkey had no interest in a second pipeline project. By the spring of 2000, however, a dispute had surfaced among the Trans-Caspian participant nations concerning the alloca-tion of quotas for Azerbaijan's use of the pipeline. Consequently, all construction work ceased. Blue Stream, therefore, emerged victorious in the struggle for the Caspian. As Blue Stream's opening ceremony approached, the USA was openly critical of the pipeline, urging Europe to avoid greater reliance on Russia for its energy supplies.

Buraimi

Buraimi is a group of small oases in south-east Arabia, on the border between Abu Dhabi (United Arab Emirates—UAE) and Oman. In the 1950s **Saudi Arabia** claimed this oil-rich area. The origins of the tension over Buraimi may be traced back to 200 years ago, when the an-Nahyans of Abu Dhabi (who now rule Abu Dhabi, the UAE's leading emirate) and the as-Sauds, who now rule Saudi Arabia, were no more than competing tribes. The an-Nahyans, who subsisted as pearl-divers and herdsmen, accepted domination by the as-Saud tribe although they did not adopt Wahhibism, the as-Sauds' strict interpretation of Islam. Much of their competition was focused on the Buraimi oasis. A little more than 50 years ago, Saudi forces took control of the Buraimi oasis, supported, reportedly, by US oil companies which had promoted Saudi Arabia's claim to the territory. Following the failure of international arbitration, Abu Dhabi and Omani forces, with British support, expelled the Saudi invaders. In 1974, the recently formed UAE concluded a treaty with King Faisal of Saudi Arabia, under whose terms Saudi Arabia received a coastal strip lying between the UAE and Qatar, and control over the then as yet unexploited Shaybah oilfield, together with all of the revenue accruing from it. The Buraimi oasis seems to have been ceded to the UAE, where it is referred to as al-Ain. However, a map available on the website of the Saudi Arabian Ministry of Foreign Affairs shows Buraimi still to lie in Saudi Arabian territory, together with parts of neighbouring Oman and Yemen. Indeed, this is the shape of Saudi Arabia as depicted in sketches on the pages of Saudi Arabian passports. After years of diplomatic frustration, the oil-rich federated state of the UAE has reignited a quarrel with Saudi Arabia concerning two sections of their common border. A map included in the 2006 edition of the official UAE Yearbook depicts the UAE as extending to the west as far as Qatar, crossing territory that is under Saudi control. The map published in the previous year's edition of the Yearbook does not show this. Less obvious, but also portrayed, is a southern border that extends to include most of the Shaybah oilfield. Any diplomatic quarrel could jeopardize US commercial interests as US companies have substantial commitments in both the UAE and Saudi Arabia. In addition, the UAE's ad-Dhafra air base is used by US transport and investigation aircraft, having partly replaced former US facilities in Saudi Arabia. The UAE's port of Mina Jebel Ali is also generally used by US naval ships.

C

Camp Bondsteel

The largest 'from scratch' foreign US military base since the time of the **Viet Nam** War, located in the hills east of the southern Kosovo town of Uroševac. The USA arranged to supply approximately 7,000 US personnel as part of the NATO Kosovo Force (KFOR) to help sustain a capable military force in Kosovo and to ensure the safe return of Kosovar refugees. The USA supported KFOR by providing the headquarters and troops for one of the four NATO sectors. US forces entered Kosovo in June 1999 following NATO Operation Allied Force. Headquarters for US forces are positioned at Camp Bondsteel, built on some 300 ha of former farmland near Urosevic. Bondsteel has a perimeter of about 10 km. The 400-ha camp was constructed from the ground up on a former field. Basecamps Bondsteel and Monteith were set up in June 1999 in Kosovo to be used as staging points for the bulk of US forces stationed in the Multi National Brigade-East. About 4,000 US service personnel were stationed at Camp Bondsteel, and another 2,000 were at Camp Monteith, near Gnjilane. Both camps are named after Medal of Honour recipients, Army Staff Sgt James L. Bondsteel, honoured for heroism in Viet Nam, and Army First Lt Jimmie W. Montieth, Jr, honoured for heroism in France during the **Second World War**. Camp Able Sentry, located near the Skopje Airport, Macedonia, serves as a point of entry for supplies and personnel into Kosovo. Another 500 Americans support the operation from Camp Able Sentry in the Former Yugoslav Republic of Macedonia. Camp Bondsteel is located close to vital **oil pipelines** and energy corridors presently under construction, such as the US-sponsored **Trans-Balkan pipeline project**. Defence contractors were involved in the construction of the camp—in particular Halliburton Oil subsidiary Brown & Root Services. In 1992 Dick Cheney, as US Secretary of Defense in the administration of George Bush, awarded the company a contract providing support for the US army's global operations. Cheney left politics and joined Halliburton as CEO between 1995 and 2000. He later became US Vice-President in the administration of George W. Bush. Camp Bondsteel is known as the 'grande dame' in a network of US bases running along both sides of the border between Kosovo and Macedonia. In less than three years it has been transformed from an encampment of tents into a self-sufficient, high-tech base camp housing nearly 7,000 troops—three-quarters of all the US troops stationed in Kosovo. It is so big that it has downtown, mid-town and uptown districts, retail outlets, 24-hour sports halls, a chapel, library and the best-equipped hospital in Europe. At present there are 55 *Black Hawk* and *Apache* helicopters based at Bondsteel and although it has no aircraft landing strip, the location was chosen for its capacity to expand. It has been suggested that it could replace the US air force base at Aviano, Italy. The Bondsteel template is now being applied in Afghanistan and at the new bases in the former Soviet Republics. In April 1999, Gen. Michael Jackson, the British commander in Macedonia during the NATO bombing of Serbia, explained to the Italian newspaper *Sole 24 Ore* that, 'Today, the circumstances which we have created here have changed. Today, it is absolutely necessary to guarantee the stability of Macedonia and its entry into NATO. But we will certainly remain here a long time so that we can also guarantee the security of the energy corridors which traverse this country.' The newspaper added, 'It is clear that Jackson is referring to the eighth corridor, the East-West axis which ought to be combined to the pipeline bringing energy resources from **Central Asia** to terminals in the Black Sea and in the Adriatic, connecting Europe with Central Asia.'

Carter Doctrine

For more than 40 years, US foreign policy has been guided by America's growing dependence on Middle Eastern oil supplies. Adopted by both Republicans and Democrats, this policy is known as the Carter Doctrine because it was articulated most clearly by President Jimmy Carter in 1980. Control of Middle Eastern oil resources has always been a matter of strategic focus to the USA. In his famous speech of 1947, when he initiated the Cold War and articulated the doctrine that now goes under his name, US President Truman referred to the Middle East with its 'great natural resources' as among the considerations that greatly motivated the campaign against 'communism'. In 1974–75, in the midst of the **OPEC** oil price increases and the threat of extended oil embargoes, the US administration considered the possibility of undertaking military action against Middle Eastern oil-producing states. With the sudden fall in 1979 of the Shah of **Iran**, who had been installed in a US Central Intelligence Agency-backed coup against the nationalist Mossadegh government in 1953, the USA became increasingly concerned about threats to its interests in the region. Accordingly, in his January 1980 State of the Union address, President Carter warned: 'An attempt by an outside force to gain control of the Persian Gulf region will be regarded as an assault on the vital interests of the United States of America, and such an assault will be repelled by any means necessary, including military force.' Although this quote refers to an 'outside force' (such as the Soviet Union), the Carter and Reagan administrations were obviously, if perhaps simplistically, concerned that the ideas behind the Iranian Revolution might lead to hostile forces from inside the region gaining control over Persian (Arabian) Gulf oil. When Ba'ath-controlled **Iraq** emerged noncompliant from the **Iran–Iraq War**, this anxiety shifted to the point where the 1996 National Security Strategy included the reference that forces internal to the Persian Gulf region demonstrating a threat to US vital national interests would be countered by force. This new policy was explained to be necessary owing to the 'overwhelming dependence of Western nations on vital oil supplies from the Middle East'.

Central Asia

Central Asia is a vast, land-locked region of Asia. Though a variety of definitions of its exact composition exist, no one definition is universally accepted. Despite this uncertainty in defining borders, it does have some vital overall character-istics. For one, Central Asia has historically been intimately tied to its nomadic peoples and the Silk Road. As a result, it has acted as a junction for the movement of people, goods, and ideas between Europe, the Middle East, South Asia, and East Asia. It is also sometimes recognized as Middle Asia or Inner Asia, and is within the scope of the wider Eurasian continent. The history of Central Asia is identified by the area's climate and geography. The aridness of the region made agriculture challenging and its distance from the sea cut it off from a great deal of trade. Thus, few major cities developed in the region; instead the area was for millennia subjugated by the nomadic horse peoples of the steppes. Relations between the steppe nomads and the settled people in and around Central Asia were long defined by conflict. The dominance of the nomads came to an end in the 16th century, as firearms allowed settled peoples to expand their control of the region. **Russia**, China, and other powers expanded into the region and had gained control of the bulk of Central Asia by the end of the 19th century. After the Russian Revolution of 1917 the Central Asian regions were incorporated into the Soviet Union. Mongolia remained independent but became a Soviet satellite state. In the Soviet areas of Central Asia there was much industrialization and con-struction of infrastructure, but there also took place the suppression of local cultures and hundreds of thousands of deaths from forced collectivization programmes, bequeathing a lasting legacy of inter-ethnic tensions and severe environmental problems. With the collapse of the Soviet Union five Central Asian countries achieved independence. Central Asia has long been significant for its rich oil and gas resources. The region itself never held a principal stationary population, nor was it able to make use of its rich natural resources. Thus, it has hardly ever throughout history become the seat of power for an empire or influential state. Central Asia has functioned more as the battleground for external powers than as a power in its own right. In the post-Cold War era, Central Asia is an ethnic cauldron, prone to volatility and conflicts, without a sense of national identity, but rather a complicated mixture of historical cultural influences, tribal and clan loyalties, and religious fervour. Projecting authority into the area is no longer just Russia, but also Turkey, **Iran**, China, Pakistan, **India** and the USA. Russia continues to dominate political and military affairs throughout the Caucasus, and former Soviet republics, although as these countries shed their post-Soviet authoritarian systems, Russia's influence is slowly waning. Turkey has some influence because of ethnic and linguistic ties with the Turkic peoples of

Central Asia, as well as serving as an oil pipeline route to the Mediterranean. Iran, the seat of historical empires which dominated parts of Central Asia, has historical and cultural links to the region, and is vying to build an oil pipeline from the Caspian Sea to the Persian Gulf. China, already controlling Xinjiang and **Tibet**, projects significant influence in the region, especially in energy/oil politics. And the USA, with its increasing military involvement in the region, and oil diplomacy, is also significantly drawn into the region's politics.

Chad

The great majority of Chad's 10m. people depend on subsistence agriculture for their livelihoods. Living standards in the country are among the lowest in the world. Chad is currently ranked in the bottom five out of nearly 180 nations rated by the United Nations in its yearly human development index review. Yet the country has one major source of wealth, oil, which has begun to be tapped in the last few years. The fighting in Chad is not only and directly about oil, but oil has made control of the government there a political prize much more worth fighting for. As so often in Africa, political tensions are part of a scramble for the profits from rich mineral wealth. Chad has been exporting oil on a large scale since 2003. It is estimated to have reserves of up to 1,000m. barrels. That is not large in comparison to major oil producers in **OPEC**, but by local standards the potential rewards are huge. The key to unlocking Chad's oil wealth has been the building of a 1,600-km pipeline from Chad through Cameroon to the coast. That project received crucial support from the World Bank, which offered money and other assistance on the basis that much of the resultant income would be spent on poverty alleviation. This was written into Chad's laws. A few months later, however, the Chadian government changed the law, giving itself greater discretion to use oil revenues as it saw fit. Inevitably, it seems possible that some of the money has been spent on arms. The World Bank consequently froze large sums of development aid to Chad as a mark of its disapproval. It has been one of the most contentious episodes in the organization's history. Campaigners claim that Chad has become yet another African country where mineral wealth is contributing to insecurity and making life worse for most people, rather than bringing them higher living standards.

Chávez Frías, Hugo Rafael

Leader of **Venezuela**, who has been President of that country since 1999. Educated at the Military Academy. After graduating in 1975, Chávez pursued a career as an army officer, rising to the rank of lieutenant-colonel. From a young age, Chávez was profoundly affected by the deep-rooted conflicts in Venezuelan society, particularly the dire conditions of the poor, and was attracted to revolutionary ideas. He was influenced by a wide spectrum of world leaders and philosophers, ranging from Mao Zedong to John F. Kennedy, and from Nietzsche to Che Guevara. But, most importantly, the pursuit of Simón Bólivar's objective to expel imperialism and unify the peoples of Latin America made the biggest impact on him. Chávez first formed his own revolutionary group within the army in 1977, at the age of 23, and began to establish contacts with other revolutionary and radical groups in the country, developing his critical stance towards the government, which he considered to be corrupt. Later, in 1982, Chávez was central in forming a powerful civilian-military movement, the Revolutionary Bolivarian Movement (MBR-200). The unsuccessful coup attempts in 1992 against the government of President Carlos Andrés Pérez and its neo-liberal policies were essentially the result of the activities of this political network. Even though the 1992 coups had widespread popular support among the Venezuelan poor and lower ranks of the army, largely due to a lack of planning they failed. The leader of the coups was Chávez (then a lieutenant-colonel), who was imprisoned until 1994. Following his release from prison, Chávez continued his political activities, and subsequently, in 1998, established the Movement for the Fifth Republic (MVR). MVR quickly became the platform for creating a revolutionary popular movement, which successfully campaigned in the 1998 congressional elections. Voter turn-out was more than 80% and Chávez's movement won the elections with 56% of the vote. Chávez assumed the presidency in February 1999. After taking office, Chávez began to implement a radical reform agenda. With the new 1999 Constitution, drafted by Chávez and his close associates, the official name of the country was changed from Venezuela to the Bolivarian Republic of Venezuela. The new Constitution also established the principles of participatory democracy for all citizens of Venezuela, banned all kinds of discrimination, guaranteed free speech and the rights of the indigenous population, and established that 50% of electoral candidates must be women. In the subsequent elections, held in July 2000, the Chávez's coalition won a landslide victory, obtaining a two-thirds' majority, which gave Chávez a strong mandate to move ahead with his new revolutionary course. The oil wealth of Venezuela, currently the world's fifth largest producer, has been central to Chávez's revolutionary agenda. Half of the state's revenues and about one-third of Venezuela's gross domestic product come from oil. Even though Venezuela had nationalized its oil industry in 1976, a new policy, known as *Apertura Petrolera* (opening up the oil sector to private investors), pursued in the 1990s relaxed nationalization significantly, permitting foreign companies to enter the Venezuelan oil sector. Under Chávez, Venezuela's oil sector underwent a very significant change of policy. First, Chavez made a number of top appointments to the management of the national energy company, *Petróleos de Venezuela* (PDVSA), thereby increasing his control of the company. Chávez also introduced a number of contractual changes regarding the operations of foreign-owned corporations, greatly increasing state revenues and limiting foreign companies' power and profits. In this way, Chávez's reforms initiated, effectively, the nationalization of Venezuela's oil sector. On 12 April 2002, key business leaders, angered at Chávez's handling of the Venezuelan oil industry, organized widespread strike action, which soon turned into large-scale clashes between anti-Chávez protesters and Chávez's supporters. The resultant chaos prompted the army to intervene (allegedly with the support of the US intelligence services) and to arrest Chávez, who it blamed for the violence. But within two days Chávez was restored to power owing to mass protests in his favour and support from key army units. The US administration was quick to hail the anti-Chávez coup, presenting it as a necessary step to establish tranquillity and democracy. In his foreign policy, Chávez is openly promoting a shift in the political orientation of the Latin American continent away from US-centred neo-liberal policies towards a popular socialist model. In line with this goal, Venezuela helped Argentina to pay a significant part of its debt to the Internatinal Monetary Fund, and thus, effectively, restricted US influence over Argentina. Even though Venezuela is currently selling a large proportion of its oil to the USA (the USA depends on Venezuela for nearly one-sixth of its oil), the country is taking a number of significant steps to reduce its reliance on the USA. In 2005, Chávez's government signed a series of extensive agreements with China, whereby the PDVSA agreed to supply China National Petroleum Corporation (CNPC) with 160,000 barrels of oil per day. Venezuela's PDVSA and China's CNPC are also developing a number of joint projects for the marketing, transportation and sale of oil products in South-East Asia.

China National Offshore Oil Corporation (CNOOC)

China National Offshore Oil Corporation (CNOOC) is the third-largest National Oil Company (NOC) in the People's Republic of China after China National Petroleum Corporation (CNPC) and Sinopec. It has a virtual monopoly over the potentially vast and largely unexplored oil reserves in China's coastal waters. It has also been buying up reserves and expertise overseas. It essentially focuses on the exploitation, exploration and development of crude oil and natural gas off shore of China. Shares of its listed arm, CNOOC Ltd, are traded in Hong Kong and New York. China Oilfield Services (COSL) is a fellow subsidiary of CNOOC Ltd listed in Hong Kong. CNOOC is a state-owned oil company, 70% of whose shares are owned by the government of the People's Republic of China, and the State-Owned Assets Supervision and Administration Commission of the State Council performs the rights and obligations of shareholder on behalf of the government. CNOOC is not the typical communist, command-economy-era dinosaur that still troubles corporate China. In early 2001, it sold a 30% stake in the company to the public, and these shares trade freely on the Hong Kong and New York stock exchanges. CNOOC officials take pride in their success at running an outward-looking firm that generally operates without Beijing's direction. A strong, eight-person board that includes four foreigners as non-executive, or outside, directors, manages the company. As of 2005 CNOOC was engaged in oil and gas exploration and development, the exploitation of overseas resources, the development of midstream and downstream business and in the establishment of a modern business system in order to achieve the strategic goal of building a world-class integrated energy company.

China's Pursuit of Oil

In little more than a decade, the People's Republic of China has changed from being a net exporter of oil into the world's second largest importer after the USA. Concern is mounting about the future prospects for China's domestic oil production, which supplies about two-thirds of the country's crude oil needs. China's government estimates that it will need 600m. metric tons of crude oil a year by 2020, more than triple its expected output. World-wide, the best oilfields have already been claimed. For the USA, Europe and Japan, the **'oil shocks'** of the 1970s supplied the lessons that have shaped their thinking about energy. China is a latecomer to the already unstable global energy business. It is grappling with how to manage dramatic growth and soaring demand for energy at the same time as it confronts the implications of interventionist US foreign policy. Throughout China's modern history, and particularly under Communist Party rule, the country's leaders have sought self-sufficiency. This was a drive fuelled by nationalist pride and the experience of colonialism, which fed notions that the outside world seeks to prevent China's rise as a great power. Under the rule of Mao Zedong, China focused on oil production in its north east, near the city of Daqing. The government's current push to secure foreign oilfields is driven by worries that there may one day be too little oil to meet demand world-wide and that foreign powers will choke China. **China National Offshore Oil Corporation's (CNOOC)** aggressive efforts to secure reliable supplies of oil and natural gas around the world reflect just how strong China's thirst for fossil fuels has become. Its booming economy and burgeoning appetite for cars and other modern conveniences have caused energy demand to soar. China's oil imports doubled over the past five years and surged by nearly 40% in the first half of 2004 alone. These increases vaulted the Chinese mainland ahead of Japan and into second place among the world's biggest oil consumers, behind only the USA. With oil in short supply, growing demand from China is clearly having an unwelcome impact on the oil market. The country accounts for about one-third of the increase in world oil consumption currently, more than any other single nation. While many of the factors that have caused the oil price spike appear to be fleeting, there may be no respite from Chinese demand for the foreseeable future. The country's industrial base is consuming vast amounts of petrochemicals for manufactures ranging from fertilizers to Barbie dolls. The number of cars on mainland roads was expected to increase by 2.5m. in 2004 alone. Even if China's growth in gross domestic product of 9.4% in 2004 moderates to 8% in 2005, as the Chinese Academy of Social Sciences predicts, the country is now a permanent major player in the global competition for oil. And just as oil is seen as driving US foreign policy, so too are China's geopolitical strategies increasingly influenced by the country's search to meet its energy needs. China was not always so heavily dependent upon imported oil. The discovery in 1959 of the Daqing oilfields under the Manchurian grasslands meant that the once largely agrarian country was for decades able to produce more crude than it required—a happy circumstance that the government celebrated as a political victory. Oil and gas discoveries in the

South China Sea and Bohai Gulf, where drilling began in 1979, made China seem all the more invulnerable to **'oil shocks'**, and the country remained an oil exporter until 1993. Today, however, output from China's top four oilfields is in decline. By some estimates, the country's current proven reserves will be depleted in as few as 14 years. Meanwhile, largely untapped **petroleum** pools believed to lie beneath western China's desolate Tarim Basin are currently uneconomic to drill, even with today's high oil prices. China's leaders are forced to seek ever-greater supplies of petroleum from overseas. More than half of China's oil imports currently come from the volatile Middle East, making oil security a pressing concern in Beijing. China has begun to build up a strategic oil reserve that it hopes to fill with at least 30 days' worth of supplies, and the country has several pipelines planned that would theoretically receive supplies from fields in **Russia**, **Central Asia** and Burma. But China's state-controlled oil industry, comprising three major companies (CNOOC, Sinopec and China National Petroleum Corporation), has yet to develop a clear, comprehensive energy policy. The process of Chinese overseas exploration began in 1997, when Premier Li Peng encouraged state-run oil concerns to look outside China's borders for investment opportunities, and in the past few years the search has ranged all over the world. Since then China's intensified oil diplomacy and its increasingly competitive stance in world oil markets have already created friction with countries such as **India**, which like China has a rapidly expanding economy and growing oil needs to satisfy. Currently, production from China's overseas investments supplies just 5% of imports—the rest is purchased on the open market. The fields that Chinese companies have so far bought into are already mature, and many experts feel that they have been overvalued. For China's leaders, however, buying foreign oil- and gasfields in the name of energy security has become a central mission. Throughout the 1990s, China made deals to lock in long-term supplies and buy installations from Africa to Latin America. In 2002, CNOOC became the largest offshore oil producer in Indonesia when it bought a field from the Spanish firm Repsol YPF SA.

Chechnya

A mountainous region, Chechnya has important oil deposits, as well as natural gas, limestone, gypsum, sulphur, and other minerals. Its mineral waters have made it a spa centre. Major production includes oil, petrochemicals, oilfield equipment, foods, wines, and fruits. For centuries, the Chechen people's history and relationship with the regional power, **Russia**, has been full of turmoil. Recognized as a distinct people since the 17th century, Chechens were active opponents of the Russian conquest of the Caucasus during 1818–1917. In 1858 tsarist Russia defeated leader Imam Shamil and his fighters who were aiming to establish an Islamic state. After the 1917 Russian Revolution, a declaration of independence by the Chechens was met with occupation by the Bolsheviks. During the fighting the oilfields of Grozny were set on fire. The fire was not extinguished for nearly 18 months. As many as 5,000 people reportedly fled

Grozny. The collapse of order in the region led the Bolsheviks to come out openly in favour of Soviet power. The Grozny Bolsheviks were active among the workers in the Grozny oilfields, setting up armed workers' detachments. The Bolsheviks assumed control in the Chechen territory at the end of 1917 and a Soviet republic was formed in the region in March 1918. It was designated the Terek Soviet Republic after the Terek River which cuts across the Northern Caucasus. The White Army occupied the area in early 1919 and it was not until 1920 that Soviet rule was re-established. In 1924, a Chechen-Ingush Autonomous Region was established. In the mid-1930s, it became an autonomous republic. Like their Ingush neighbours, Chechens are predominantly Sunni Muslims. During the **Second World War**, Stalin (on the basis of allegations that the Chechens had collaborated with the Germans) deported the entire Chechen population to **Central Asia**, **Kazakhstan** and Siberia. Their territory was jurisdictionally divided among the Russian and Georgian Soviet Republics. The real motivation was undoubtedly related to the fact that the majority of the Chechen people obstinately refused to bow to Soviet central authority. Following the deportation, Chechen place names were replaced by Russian ones and the land was allocated to new, mainly Russian, settlers. This is evidence of the degree of alarm with which the Soviet government viewed the 'conquered' North Caucasus. With the Soviet Union's collapse in 1991, a number of regions managed to break away and gain independence. Ingushetia voted for separation from Chechnya in a referendum and became an autonomous republic within the Russian Federation in the following year. Gen. Dzhokhar Dudayev, having seized power in the capital Grozny in 1991, led Chechnya's drive for independence. The President of the newly formed Russian Federation, Boris Yeltsin, refused to recognize Chechnya's declaration of independence, sending in troops instead, only to withdraw them when they were confronted by armed Chechens. The events subsequently developed into a very volatile and confrontational power struggle between Grozny and Moscow. During the past 15 years the Russian army has established a brutal dictatorship in Chechnya based on naked terror. Ten years ago Chechnya had a population of 2m. Today it numbers 800,000. At least 80,000 have died since 1994. All major towns, including the capital Grozny, have been razed to the ground. Chechnya was probably not granted independence for geopolitical and economic reasons. A major oil pipeline carries oil from fields in Baku on the Caspian Sea and Chechnya towards Ukraine. Grozny has a major oil refinery located along this pipeline. For Russia the **oil pipelines** and the routes they take are important, so that oil can be sold to Western markets and their needs met. The loss of this small republic would decisively weaken Russian influence in the North Caucasus—a region with vast international significance because of its rich oil deposits and its strategic proximity to the key oil pipeline routes.

Churchill, Winston

Winston Churchill was a British politician and author, best known as Prime Minister of the United Kingdom during the **Second World War**. At various times a soldier, author and politician, Churchill is generally regarded as one of the most important leaders in modern British and world history. He won the 1953 Nobel Prize for Literature. Prior to the **First World War**, Winston Churchill, then the most senior civilian representing the British Navy, oversaw a series of programmes to convert Britain's fleet from coal to oil. The switch made the British fleet a faster, more agile counter to the increasingly adversarial German navy. But without its own indigenous oil supply, Britain's conversion irrevocably tied it to the Persian (Arabian) Gulf, its cheapest source of oil. Shortly before the First World War, the Anglo-Persian Oil Company (which was founded in 1908), after lengthy negotiations, promised Winston Churchill, then First Lord of the Admiralty, secure supplies of oil. In exchange the British government injected £2m. of new capital into the company, acquired a controlling interest and became *de facto* the hidden power behind the oil company. In 1922, Churchill, as British Colonial Secretary, was charged with finding a way through the morass of what he often called Mesopotamia. He was referring to the British mandate of **Iraq**, whose borders he had drawn a year before, carving the country out of the defeated Ottoman Empire. Some critics claim that Churchill and Britain seized Iraq for its oil; oil there was, but Britain's oil supply had already been guaranteed (with Churchill's help) through **Iran**.

Colombia

Colombia, officially the Republic of Colombia, is a country in north-western South America. It is bordered to the east by **Venezuela** and Brazil, to the south by Ecuador and Peru, to the north by the Caribbean Sea, and to the west by Panama and the Pacific Ocean. Colombia is a free-market economy with major commercial and investment ties to the USA. Transition from a highly regulated economy has been under way for more than a decade. Colombia is well endowed with minerals and energy resources. It has the largest coal reserves in Latin America and is second to Brazil in hydroelectric potential. The country's **petroleum** reserves were estimated at 3,100m. barrels in 1995. It also possesses significant reserves of nickel, gold, silver, platinum, and emeralds. The discovery of 2,000m. barrels of high-quality oil at the Cusiana and Cupiagua fields, about 200 km east of Bogotá, has enabled Colombia to become a net oil exporter since 1986. Total crude oil production averages 620,000 barrels per day (b/d); about 184,000 b/d is exported. The Pastrana government has extensively liberalized its petroleum investment policies, leading to an increase in exploration activity. Refining capacity cannot satisfy domestic demand, so some refined products, especially gasoline, must be imported. Plans for the construction of a new refinery are under development.

COMECON—Council for Mutual Economic Assistance

COMECON, the Council for Mutual Economic Assistance, was an economic organization of communist states, created in 1949, and dissolved in 1991 after the collapse of the Soviet Union. After COMECON's creation, the relationship between the Soviet Union, on the one hand, and Albania, Bulgaria, Czechoslovakia, Hungary, Poland, and **Romania**, on the other, was largely unchanging. In return for fuel, non-food raw materials and semi-manufactures ('hard goods'), Eastern Europe furnished the Soviet Union with so-called 'soft goods', including finished machinery and industrial consumer goods. Economic relations of this kind were founded on an economic problem which confronted the East European communist states in the 1950s. Eastern Europe had scant energy and mineral resources, and this scarcity was aggravated by the poor energy-efficiency of Eastern Europe's industrial sectors. As late as mid-1985, Eastern European factories used 40% more fuel than their Western counterparts. Eastern European countries were heavily dependent on the Soviet Union for oil. From the early 1950s until the early 1970s, accordingly, the Soviet Union supplied its East European clients with hard goods at low cost, in exchange for finished machinery and equipment. Attached to Soviet economic policies were political and military support. While these economic relations prevailed, the Soviet Union could be confident that there would be relative political stability within the Eastern bloc, obedience to the Soviet Union's international strategy, and military support for Soviet objectives. By the 1980s, both parties had grown used to this arrangement, which remained especially advantageous to the Soviet Union, since it could expand its energy and raw materials complex quickly and at relatively low cost. In the 1970s, the Soviet Union's terms of trade had improved. **OPEC**'s oil price for oil had risen astronomically, favouring the oil-rich Soviet Union. The soaring price of oil raised the cost of providing Eastern Europe with oil at prices lower than those set by OPEC. Moreover, extraction and transportation costs for oil, much of which came from Siberia, were also rising. Responding to the market, the Soviet Union reduced its exports to its East European partners, and began to buy more soft goods from these countries. This change in policy obliged the East European countries to approach the West for hard goods, even though they had fewer goods to export in exchange for hard currency.

D

Druzhba ('Friendship') Pipeline

The Druzhba pipeline is the largest of **Russia**'s export pipelines to Europe. In the 1960s, **COMECON** undertook a number of bilateral and multilateral investment projects between the Soviet Union and other state-socialist countries in Eastern Europe. The most notable project was the co-ordinated construction of the Druzhba pipeline for the transport and distribution of crude oil from the oil-rich Soviet Union to its satellite states in Eastern and East-Central Europe. Spanning more than 4,000 km with a capacity of 1.2–1.4m. barrels per day (b/d), the pipeline is split into two sections: one running through Belarus, Poland and Germany; and the other through Belarus, Ukraine, Slovakia, the Czech Republic, and Hungary. The Druzhba pipeline system begins in Samara where it collects oil from fields in West Siberia, the Urals, and the Caspian Sea. From Belarus to where the pipeline divides in two at Mozyr, the system is currently only approximately 50% utilized. After Mozyr, though, both branches are fully operational, and the area between Belarus and Poland is where work has recently begun to increase the pipeline's capacity. One proposal to extend the pipeline into Germany would cut tanker traffic in the Baltic Sea. Also, it would potentially allow for exports of Russian crude to the USA via Germany.

E

Energy Crisis

Energy crisis refers to a situation in which a state (or a number of states) suffers from a disruption of energy supplies (in this case, oil) accompanied by rapidly increasing energy prices that threaten economic and national security. The threat to economic security is represented by the possibility of declining economic growth, increasing inflation, rising unemployment, and lost investment. Looking at the two energy crises of 1973 and 1979, one can identify some common elements. Both events started with political turmoil in some of the oil-producing countries; were associated with low oil stocks; were associated with high import concentration from a small number of suppliers; were associated with declining US **petroleum** production; were associated with high dependency on oil imports; were associated with a low level of oil-industry spending; led to speculation; caused an economic downturn; limited policy options in the oil-producing countries of the Middle East.

Equatorial Guinea

Equatorial Guinea, which has been characterized as the '**Kuwait** of Africa', is a tiny state located on the west coast of Africa. Equatorial Guinea has long been one of the poorest and most neglected countries in the world, but has the potential to achieve within a few years oil output of as much as 500,000 barrels per day (b/d) and, thereby, the rank of sub-Saharan Africa's third-largest producer, after **Nigeria** and **Angola**. Owing to its oil resource, the economy of Equatorial Guinea was projected to grow by 34% in 2005, more than twice the rate of any other country. It is also as a result of oil that Equatorial Guinea's relations (and those of the government of Teodoro Obiang Nguema Mbasogo, who came to power in a coup in 1979) with the USA have begun to flourish: the USA buys almost two-thirds of Equatorial Guinea's oil. Equatorial Guinea's enhanced significance is a consequence of political instability in the Persian (Arabian) Gulf and other regions which supply the USA with oil. In combination with a small population, wealth derived from oil offers Equatorial Guinea the opportunity to break the mould in a region plagued by tyrannical regimes and rampant corruption. That potential seems likely to remain unfulfilled, in the short term at least, however, as the Obiang regime is widely considered to be one of the worst in the world—an indictment endorsed by the US Central Intelligence Agency. The Agency's current *World Factbook* states that Equatorial Guinea is a country 'ruled by ruthless leaders who have badly mismanaged the economy'. In the Cold War period, one way in which the USA competed with the Soviet Union was by providing thousands of millions of dollars' worth of military and economic aid for Africa. Following the collapse of the Soviet Union, however, the USA showed less interest in the continent. In 1995, a report by the Pentagon stated that the USA had 'very little traditional strategic interests in Africa'. More recently, however, Africa has become a larger supplier of US oil imports—in particular West Africa, deemed to include Angola, Nigeria, the Republic of the Congo, Gabon, Cameroon and Equatorial Guinea. Together, these countries supply 15% of the USA's oil imports—almost as much as the USA imports from **Saudi Arabia**—a figure that has been forecast to rise to 20% within the next five years and, according to the US National Intelligence Council, to as high as 25% by 2015. The energy policy that the US administration is currently pursuing forecast that West Africa would become one of the US market's fastest growing sources of oil and gas. Until recently, Equatorial Guinea was entirely ignored by the USA. Roughly the size of Maryland, the country comprises several islands—including Bioko, home to Malabo—and territory on the continent, between Gabon and Cameroon. Equatorial Guinea, Spain's only former colony in sub-Saharan Africa, obtained independence in 1968. The country was first ruled by Francisco Macías Nguema (who has been compared to Uganda's former dictator, Idi Amin), who outlawed political opposition and in 1970 appointed himself as 'President for Life'. Some 50,000 people, about 10% of the population, were murdered during the Macías years and 80,000 fled into exile. In 1979, Macías was deposed. He was subsequently executed by Obiang, his nephew, who, as head of the National Guard and, later, commander of the armed forces, had been instrumental in implementing the repression of the Macías years. While his rule has been less brutal than that of his predecessor, Obiang's regime has been cruel enough for one Western diplomat to refer to him as 'a known murderer'. Obiang's regime's economic record is also dismal, and it is only the discovery of oil which has saved the country from destitution. After substantial reserves of oil were discovered off the coast of Equatorial Guinea, multinational oil companies such as ExxonMobil and Chevron, as well as smaller independents like Ocean Energy, Vanco and Triton, decided to invest a total of US $5,000m. in the country.

Exxon Valdez Oil Spill (1989)

Located at the head of a deep, stillwater fjord in the north-east section of Prince William Sound, Valdez is the northernmost ice-free port in North America. The town covers some 700 sq km and had a population of approximately 4,000 in 2000. The Valdez area was sparsely populated until the winter of 1897–98, when gold-seekers travelled to the town in order to follow the 'All-American Route' over the Valdez Glacier into the interior. Some intended to prospect in the Copper River Basin, while others planned to travel on to the Klondike. Valdez was formed out of an initial tent city at the head of the bay. Four thousand stampeders passed through Valdez in that year. Some remained onshore to establish businesses, while others carried themselves and their equipment over the glacier, some dying in the attempt. Valdez was a busy town in the first two decades of the 20th century. As well as its main industries of mining and shipping, fox farming, fishing, and tourism provided additional employment and revenues. By the 1920s, however, Valdez's first boom had ended. With the completion of the **Alaska** railroad from Seward to Fairbanks, via Anchorage, in 1924, the Valdez route was no longer the only way to access the interior; mining was no longer profitable and in 1925 even the army withdrew. The population of Valdez declined to 400–500. On 27 March 1964, at 5:36 p.m., an earthquake lasting more than four minutes and registering 9.2 on the Richter Scale struck 45 miles west of Valdez, triggering an underwater landslide, which in turn created several tremendous waves. The first waves washed away the Valdez waterfront and drowned the 30 people who had been standing on the dock. In the whole of Alaska, 114 people died as a result of the earthquake.

The town of Valdez was condemned when it was discovered that it had been built on unstable ground. In 1967, the town was relocated to its present site, four miles east of its original location. Fifty-two buildings were moved and the other structures were burned and the ground razed. In 1973, Congress approved plans for a **Trans-Alaska pipeline** with its southern terminus at Valdez. Thousands of people moved to Valdez to take part in the construction boom. The town's population soared to 8,000 people, but had settled at 3,500 by 1989. On 24 March 1989, 25 years after the 1964 earthquake, the *Exxon Valdez* oil tanker ran aground at Bligh Reef, discharging 10.8m. gallons (*c.* 41m. litres) of crude oil into Prince William Sound in the largest oil spill in North American history. No crude oil was in fact carried into the port of Valdez, as Bligh Reef lies some 40 km south of the port. However, the oil was carried by winds and tides further south into the Sound and onto beaches. Oil covered more than 1,900 km of rocky beaches. The population of Valdez trebled almost overnight. Hotel accommodation was created all over the city. Food and clothing stores were established and prices soared. Temporary buildings were erected for Exxon's office space, and rents rose dramatically. Money flowed through Valdez in unprecedented quantities. On average, it cost Exxon US $1,000 each day to support one worker in a beach clean-up crew. That figure multiplied by 10,000 rises to a huge sum of money. Exxon employed many people in the Prince William Sound area to move supplies to the villages in the Sound, and to support the clean-up crews throughout the areas contaminated by oil. Press crews covered every aspect of the spill. Environmental groups attempted to rescue wildlife affected by the oil. Alyeska Pipeline Service Company, the non-profit company that manages the Trans-Alaska pipeline, incorporated a new division into its ranks: SERVS (Service Escort Response Vessels), which was intended to help prevent another spill and to supply an immediate response should one occur. Today, the population of Valdez is about 4,200. Most of the residents are employed by the city, the oil industry, in tourism, fishing, or transportation and shipping.

F

The First World War (and Oil)

Oil's importance to modern industrial society increased swiftly due to the proliferation of motor vehicles in the early 20th century. However, the turning point for oil's significance was the First World War. By switching the fuel used by the British navy from coal to oil, the British First Lord of the Admiralty **Winston Churchill** created a crucial advantage for Britain and its allies over their enemies. After the Allied victory, British foreign secretary Lord Curzon stated, 'The Allies floated to victory on a wave of oil.' In the years that followed the war, the epicentre of oil production shifted from Texas, USA, and the Caribbean basin to the Middle East, where vast reserves had been discovered. From then on France, Britain, and the USA became competitors in the apportionment of what came to be perceived as the greatest prize of the century. Britain, which had already had control of all of **Iran**'s oil since 1901, emerged initially as the best-placed contender. Frustrated with the British government's attempt to obstruct every US company's efforts to obtain concessions in Iran and **Iraq**, the president of Standard Oil of New Jersey (now Exxon) complained, 'British domination would be a greater menace to [Standard Oil of] New Jersey's business than a German victory would have been.'

G

Georgia

Thanks to its location, between the Black Sea, **Russia**, and Turkey, Georgia's strategic significance is disproportionate to its size. The country is developing as the principal route from the Black Sea to the Caucasus and the wider Caspian region, but it also acts as a buffer between Russia and Turkey. Historically, Georgia has had a close relationship with Russia, but it is reaching out to its other neighbours and looking to the West for alternatives and opportunities. Traditionally, Georgia's economy has been based on Black Sea tourism, the cultivation of citrus fruits, tea and grapes, mining of manganese and copper, and small-scale industrial production of wine, metals, machinery, chemicals and textiles. Georgia meets most of its energy requirements through imports. The country's only sizeable domestic energy resource is hydropower. Although the economy has suffered from civil conflict and political instability, since 1995, with the help of the International Monetary Fund and the World Bank, a substantial recovery has been made, in which the gross domestic product (GDP) has been increased and inflation reduced. The Georgian economy continues to suffer from large budget deficits due to a failure to collect tax revenues. Although energy shortages still occur, in 1998 Georgia privatized the distribution network and deliveries have gradually improved since then. The development of an international transportation corridor for Caspian oil through the key Black Sea ports of Poti and Batumi figures prominently in Georgia's hopes for recovery in the long term.

Global Warming

Global warming refers to the increase in average world temperatures caused by the so-called 'greenhouse effect'. Certain gases in the atmosphere act like glass in a greenhouse, allowing sunlight through to heat the earth's surface but preventing the heat from escaping back into space. As the greenhouse gases accumulate in the atmosphere, the Earth becomes hotter. Carbon dioxide (CO_2) is one of the principal greenhouse gases. As trees grow they absorb CO_2 from the air. When they die the CO_2 is returned to the air. Deforestation and wood burning (such as occurs in tropical rainforests) is increasing the latter part of the process, causing CO_2 to accumulate in the atmosphere. Deforestation is now out of control: in

1987 an area of the Amazon rainforest as large as Britain was burned, discharging 500m. metric tons of CO_2 into the atmosphere. Deforestation also means that there are fewer trees to absorb CO_2. Burning 'dirty' fossil fuels (oil, coal and gas) to power cars, homes and industry releases heat-trapping, global-warming gases into the atmosphere, altering the Earth's climate and disrupting weather systems. Scientists have warned that global warming will cause an increase in the temperature of ocean waters that fuels hurricanes, leading to stronger winds, heavier rainrall and larger storm surges, and that doing nothing to reduce global warming pollution will magnify the severity of these extreme weather events. According to recent findings of the United Nations Intergovernmental Panel on Climate Change, in order to stabilize greenhouse gases in the atmosphere, global emissions must be reduced to at least 60% below 1990 levels. Such a reduction implies a radical change in the way energy is used world-wide. Such change may require nothing less than a new industrial revolution, in which societies diminish their reliance on oil, gas and coal which have provided the energy for the global economy for more than 100 years.

Greenpeace

Greenpeace is a non-profit organization established in 40 countries across Europe, the Americas, Asia and the Pacific. In order to maintain its independence, Greenpeace will not accept donations from governments or corporations, relying instead on contributions from individuals and foundation grants. As a global organization, Greenpeace focuses on the most serious world-wide threats to the world's biodiversity and environment. Greenpeace has been campaigning against environmental degradation since 1971 when a small boat crewed by volunteers and journalists sailed into Amchitka, an area north of **Alaska** where the US government was conducting subterranean nuclear tests. This established a tradition of 'bearing witness' in a non-violent manner that continues today, and Greenpeace ships play an important role in all of the organization's campaign work. Greenpeace's flagship, the *Rainbow Warrior*, is named after a North American Cree Indian legend. The legend portrays a time when human greed has made the Earth sick. At that time, a tribe of people known as the Warriors of the Rainbow rise up to defend it. As one of the longest banners Greenpeace has ever made summarized, 'When the last tree is cut, the last river poisoned, and the last fish dead, we will discover that we can't eat money . . . .'

H

Hirsch Report

The Hirsch Report was prepared for the US Department of Energy and published in February 2005. It discussed the likelihood of **peak oil** occurring and how soon mitigating action needs to be taken. The Lead Author, Robert Hirsch, published a brief summary of this report in October 2005 for the Atlantic Council. The report describes how the peaking of world oil production presents the USA and the industrialized world with an unprecedented risk management problem. As peaking is approached, liquid fuel prices and price volatility will increase dramatically, and, without timely mitigation, the economic, social, and political costs will be unprecedented. Viable mitigation options exist on both the supply and demand sides, but to have substantial impact, they must be initiated more than a decade in advance of peaking. The report concludes: world oil peaking is going to happen; oil peaking could cost the US economy dearly; oil peaking presents a unique challenge; the problem is liquid fuels; mitigation efforts will require substantial time; both supply and demand will require attention; it is a matter of risk management; and government intervention will be urgently required.

Hitler and Oil

Adolf Hitler made oil central to his plans for conquest in the **Second World War**. Germany's relatively insignificant supplies of crude **petroleum** were wholly insufficient for modern mechanized warfare; in 1934, for instance, about 85% of the country's finished petroleum products were imported. The Standard Oil group of companies, in which the **Rockefeller family** owned a controlling interest of 25%, gave crucial assistance by providing oil to Nazi Germany in preparation for the Second World War. Hitler's ill-conceived incursion into the Soviet Union was halted just before it reached the oil-rich Caucasus. In 1941, Hitler sought to use Caspian oil to fuel his army. He launched a campaign to take control of the region and its mineral reserves. He had earlier declared that if he failed to seize the Caucasus, he would be forced to end the war. Although it is not really known to what extent it contributed to the end of the war, Germany's defeat in its quest for Caucasus oil in late 1942 was the first important reversal it had suffered since the beginning of the war.

I

India

India has significant reserves of oil and natural gas, and four of India's top six revenue-generating companies produce oil and natural gas. Indian oil was first discovered in commercial quantities in Assam in the late 19th century. In 1954 the country established an Oil and Natural Gas Commission as a department of the Geological Survey of India, but a 1959 act of parliament transformed it into the country's national oil company. Oil India Ltd, in which the government at one time had a share of one-third, was also set up in 1959 and established an oilfield that had been discovered by the Burmah Oil Company. By 1981 the Indian government had acquired all of the Burmah Oil Company's Indian assets and completely owned Oil India Ltd. In 1959 the Oil and Natural Gas Commission discovered oil in Gujarat and brought other fields into operation in the 1960s and 1970s. The early oilfields discovered in India were of humble size. In 1974 the Oil and Natural Gas Commission discovered a large field—called the Bombay High—off shore of Bombay. Production of oil from that field fuelled rapid growth in the country's total output of crude in the late 1970s and during the 1980s. In the 1989 financial year, oil production peaked at 34m. metric tons, of which Bombay High accounted for 22m. tons. In the early 1990s, wells were closed in offshore fields that had been inefficiently exploited, and production declined to 27m. tons in the 1993 financial year. That amount was insufficient to meet India's needs, and 30.7m. tons of crude oil was imported in the 1993 financial year. India currently has 35 major fields onshore, mainly in Assam and Gujarat, and four major offshore oilfields, near Bombay, south of Pondicherry, and in the Palk Strait. In 1990, of the country's 4,828 wells, 2,514 were producing at a rate of 664,582 barrels per day (b/d). The oilfield with the greatest output is Bombay High, with production of 402,797 b/d in 1990, about 15 times the amount produced by the next largest fields. Total reserves today are estimated at 6,100m. barrels. The government has approved ambitious exploration plans to raise output in line with demand and to rapidly bring new discoveries into production. In the late 1980s and early 1990s, encouraging discoveries were made in Tamil Nadu, Gujarat, Andhra Pradesh and Assam, many of them off shore. It was estimated that these new fields might contribute as much as 15m.–20m. tons in new production and that total output of crude oil could increase to

51m. tons. Nevertheless, India's need for oil and **petroleum**-based products— about 40m. tons per year—far exceeded its annual domestic production capacity of 28m. tons in the 1990s.

International Energy Agency (IEA)

The International Energy Agency (IEA) is a Paris-based intergovernmental organization founded by the Organisation for Economic Co-operation and Development (OECD) in 1974 in the wake of the oil crisis in 1973. The IEA acts as energy policy adviser for its 26 member countries in their effort to secure affordable and reliable energy. Its initial role was to co-ordinate measures in times of oil emergencies. In recent decades, however, the energy markets have changed, and so has the IEA. Its remit now extends far beyond oil crisis management to include broader energy issues, including climate-change policies, market reform, energy technology collaboration and outreach to the rest of the world. With a staff of around 150, comprising mainly energy experts and statisticians from its member countries, the IEA conducts a broad programme of energy research, data compilation, publication and public dissemination of the latest energy policy analysis and recommendations on effective practices. The IEA is determined to provide realistic policies in times of disruption to the supply of oil, as well as to act as a source of information and statistics about the international oil market and other energy sectors. The agency has a secondary role in promoting and developing alternative energy sources, rational energy policies, and multinational energy technology co-operation. The one sector in which it does not involve itself and carry out detailed research, except as a contribution to the overall energy balance and economy, is nuclear fission, which is instead covered by the International Atomic Energy Agency. The IEA holds a combined stockpile of 4,000m. barrels of oil, 1,400m. of which governments control for emergency use. Much of the oil is held in the form of **petroleum** products which need no further processing. IEA publications are considered world-wide as reliable source of information. The European Commission also participates in the work of the IEA.

Iran

Known as Persia until 1935, Iran became an Islamic republic in 1979 after the ruling Shah was overthrown and forced into exile. Shi'ite Islamic forces established a theocratic system of government with ultimate political authority nominally vested in a learned religious scholar. Throughout its history, Iran has been of great geostrategic importance due to its central location in Eurasia. Iran is a member and co-founder of the United Nations, the Organization of the Islamic Conference, and of **OPEC**. Iran also plays a very important role in international politics on account of its large supply of **petroleum** and other resources. Iran's economy is a mixture of central planning, state ownership of oil and other large enterprises, agriculture and other sectors of the rural economy, and small-scale private trading and service ventures. The current administration continues to follow the limited market reform policies of its predecessor and has indicated that it will diversify Iran's oil-reliant economy. It is attempting to do this by investing revenues in areas such as motor vehicle manufacturing, aerospace industries, consumer electronics, petrochemicals and nuclear technology. Iran also hopes to attract large-scale foreign investment by creating a more favourable investment climate, through reduced restrictions and duties on imports, and the creation of free-trade zones such as those in Chabahar and the island of Kish. Contemporary Iran has a solid middle class and a growing economy but continues to be plagued with high inflation and unemployment. Iran is OPEC's second largest oil producer, exporting 4m.–5m. barrels per day, and it holds 10% of the world's confirmed oil reserves. Iran also possesses the world's second largest natural gas reserves (after those of **Russia**). The strong oil market in 1996 helped ease financial pressures on Iran and allowed the country to make timely debt-service payments. The history of Iranian oil began, in a sense, with the British government's control of resources through the UK-owned Anglo-Persian Oil Company that commenced operations in 1908. Britain's disregard for Iranian interests and its staunch refusal to negotiate changes in the oil concession led to a rising anti-British nationalist opposition. When Mohammed Mossadegh, a respected elder statesman, become Prime Minister in 1951, he finally succeeded in nationalizing the Iranian oil industry, but Britain demanded a reversal, cutting off Iran's foreign sales of oil. As British power waned and that of the USA grew, a coup (allegedly staged by the US Central Intelligence Agency) in 1953 ousted Mossadegh and installed in power the authoritarian, pro-American Shah, Reza Pahlavi. Soon thereafter, US companies took a large share of the oil concession and the USA replaced Britain as the most influential foreign hegemonic power in the region. For 25 years, Iran served as a close ally of the USA in the Middle East, buying expensive US military hardware. However, a popular revolution finally overthrew the Shah in 1979, leading to a new and hardline Islamic government. When student militants in Tehran seized hostages at the US Embassy in November of that year, the USA severed diplomatic and economic relations with Iran, imposing extensive sanctions. US oil companies have not been able to return to Iran since then, but a number of European and Asian companies have large and growing operations in Iran, especially in the oil and gas sector. In 1980–88, Iran fought a bloody, extremely costly, and indecisive war with **Iraq** that eventually expanded into the Persian (Arabian) Gulf and led to clashes between the US Navy and Iranian military forces between 1987 and 1988. Iran has been designated by the US administration as a state sponsor of terrorism for its activities in Lebanon and elsewhere and remains subject to US economic sanctions and export controls. Following the election of a reformist President and Majlis (legislative assembly) in the late 1990s, attempts to foster political reform in response to popular dissatisfaction floundered as conservative politicians prevented reform measures from being enacted. Parliamentary elections in 2004 and the inauguration in August 2005 of Mahmoud Ahmadinejad, a hardline populist, as President completed the reconsolidation of conservative power in Iran's government. Iran's economy is characterized by a bloated, inefficient state sector, over-reliance on the oil sector, and statist policies that create major distortions throughout. Relatively high oil prices in recent years have enabled Iran to amass some US $40,000m. in foreign exchange reserves, but have not totally eased economic problems such as high unemployment and inflation. The proportion of the economy devoted to the development of nuclear technology remains a contentious issue with leading Western states.

Iran Hostage Crisis

The **Iran** hostage crisis, during which Iranian students held captive 52 diplomats and citizens of the USA, took place between 4 November 1979–20 January 1981. At the beginning of November 1979 Iranian leader Ayatollah Khomeini incited Iranians to demonstrate against US and Israeli interests. On 4 November 500 Iranian students styling themselves the *Muslim Students Following the Line of the Imam* took control of the main US Embassy building, seizing as hostages 66 of its occupants, 52 of whom would not be released until January 1981. The demands on which their captors made their release conditional included the surrender by the USA of the deposed Shah to face trial in Iran; and the release of Iranian assets frozen by the USA in response to the hostage-taking. All of the demands issued by the student captors were rejected by the US government. Two unsuccessful attempts were made to rescue the hostages, one of which was partially executed and the other planned. Among the consequences of the US response to the hostage crisis were US economic sanctions imposed on Iran which included a ban on imports of Iranian oil from 12 November 1979.

Iran–Iraq War

The Iran–Iraq War was waged between September 1980–August 1988 at a cost of some 1m. casualties and more than US $1,000,000m. Regional and international politics were irrevocably altered by the war, an indirect consequence of which was **Iraq**'s invasion of **Kuwait** in 1990.

Iranian Oil Bourse

The French word '*bourse*' refers to a stock exchange for securities trading. The proposal to establish an Iranian **petroleum** bourse was included in **Iran**'s development plan for 2000–05. In 2005–06, the Iranian government expressed its intention to begin competing with the New York Mercantile Exchange (NYMEX) and the London-based International Petroleum Exchange (IPE) in the international trading of oil, utilizing a euro-denominated trading mechanism. (It should be noted that both the IPE and NYMEX are owned by US corporations.) The Iranian oil bourse officially opened in May 2006. One of the more difficult technical obstacles impeding a euro-based oil transaction trading system has been the lack of a euro-denominated oil pricing standard, or oil 'marker' as it is referred to in the industry. Existing oil 'markers'—West Texas Intermediate

(WTI) crude, North Sea Brent crude, and Dubai crude produced by the United Arab Emirates (UAE)—are all denominated in US dollars. However, since the spring of 2003 Iran has required payments for its European and Asian/ACU exports to be made in euros—although the pricing for trades is US dollar-denominated. The Iranian Oil Bourse, located in the free-trade zone of Iran's Kish Island on the Persian (Arabian) Gulf, remains a potential destabilizing factor for the US economy. Oil is priced in dollars because the dollar is the world's **reserve currency**. When a trusted alternative appears, the dollar is likely to lose its reserve currency role. Today, about 70% of the world's international foreign currency reserves are held in dollars. If the petroeuro begins to challenge the **petrodollar**, this percentage could diminish drastically. An oil bourse that utilized euros would cause a shift away from the dollar, initiate a fall in the value of the dollar, and eventually cause a 'dollar crisis' to develop. This, according to some strategic analysts, is a probable motive for the USA's apparent refusal to exclude the possibility of taking military action against Iran in order to resolve the international dispute over the country's nuclear programme, among other issues. Some observers point to the fact that the American-British invasion of **Iraq** in 2002 took place after Saddam Hussain had refused to accept dollars in payment for Iraq's oil exports under the Oil For Food programme, choosing euros instead. As no weapons of mass destruction have been discovered in Iraq, there has been speculation that the main reason for the invasion was the US administration's fear of the possible financial repercussions of Saddam Hussain's plan to substitute euros for dollars. In economic terms, the Iranian Oil Bourse represents a much greater threat to the hegemony of the US dollar than Saddam Hussain's plan did, because it will allow anyone willing to either buy or sell oil for euros to trade on the exchange, thus circumventing the US dollar altogether.

Iraq

Iraq possesses the world's second largest proven oil reserves, currently estimated at 112,500m. barrels, about 11% of the world total, and also disposes of immense natural gas resources. Many experts believe that Iraq has additional undiscovered oil reserves, which might raise total reserves well beyond 250,000m. barrels when serious prospecting resumes, positioning Iraq closer to **Saudi Arabia** in terms of reserves, and far above all other oil-producing countries. Iraq's oil is of high quality and is very inexpensive to produce, making the country one of the world's most profitable sources of oil. Iraq's economy is dominated by the oil sector, which has traditionally provided about 95% of foreign exchange earnings.

Formerly part of the Ottoman Empire, Iraq was occupied by Britain during the **First World War**. In 1920, it was declared a League of Nations mandate under UK administration. In stages, over the next dozen years, Iraq attained its independence as a kingdom in 1932. A 'republic' was proclaimed in 1958, but in reality a series of military strongmen ruled the country thereafter, of whom the last was Saddam Hussain. Territorial disputes with **Iran** led to an inconclusive and costly eight-year war (1980–88). In August 1990, Iraq invaded and annexed

Kuwait, but was expelled by a US-led multinational coalition force during the Gulf War of January–February 1991. Following Kuwait's liberation, the UN Security Council called for Iraq to destroy all of its weapons of mass destruction and long-range missiles, and to allow UN weapons inspections to be conducted. On 6 November 2000, the Iraqi government announced that it would no longer accept dollars for oil sold under the UN's Oil For Food Programme, opting instead to adopt the euro as the currency in which Iraq's oil exports would be priced. This was the first time that an **OPEC** country had dared to violate the dollar-price rule. Since then, the value of the euro has increased and the value of the dollar has steadily declined. The USA, in alliance with Britain, intervened in Iraq militarily in March 2003, and installed its own authority to run the country. Two months after the invasion, Iraqi euro accounts were switched back to dollars, and it was announced that payments for Iraqi oil would once again be required to be made exclusively in US dollars. After the invasion, US and UK oil companies gained privileged access to Iraq's oil resources. Excluded from control over Iraqi oil since the nationalization of 1972, Exxon, BP, Shell and Chevron now receive the lion's share of the world's most profitable oilfields.

Iraq Petroleum Company (IPC, formerly Turkish Petroleum Company)

Formed in 1914 as the Turkish Petroleum Company (TPC), the Iraq Petroleum Company (IPC) brought together interests which for more than a decade had been contesting each other for a firm foothold in the Middle East. From the outset, the purpose of the IPC was to consolidate existing rights under common ownership and to preclude competitive rivalry for future rights. Under an agreement adopted at the British Foreign Office on 19 March 1914, the British-Dutch groups accepted a 'self-denying clause', stipulating that they 'would not be interested, directly or indirectly, in the production or manufacture of crude oil in the Ottoman Empire ... otherwise than through the Turkish Petroleum Co ...' Following the defeat of the Ottoman Empire in the First World War and its subsequent dismantlement, shareholding in the Turkish Petroleum Company (TPC) became a major issue at the San Remo Conference in 1920, as the war had demonstrated to the big powers the importance of having their own sources of oil. One of the original partners had been a German oil company, and the French had seized its shares as enemy property and demanded entrance into the TPC by virtue of their seizure. Both the Italian and the US government demanded that their national oil companies should be partners as well. After prolonged and sharp diplomatic exchanges, US oil companies were permitted to buy into the TPC, but it would take several years for the negotiations to be completed. In 1925 the TPC was granted a concession to prospect for oil, on condition that a royalty, payable to the Iraqi government, was levied on all oil extracted after a period of 20 years. In October 1927 oil was discovered north of Kirkuk. As a result of the discovery negotiations on the distribution of shares in the TPC were accelerated, and in July 1928 the shareholders concluded a formal arrangement whereby the Anglo-Persian Oil Company (from 1935 the Anglo-Iranian Oil Company (AIOC) and from 1954 BP), Royal Dutch/Shell, the Compagnie française des pétroles (CFP, from 1991 Total), and the Near East Development Corporation (a consortium that included Standard Oil) each received a share of 23.7%, while the remaining 5% share was allocated to an Armenian entrepreneur, Calouste Gulbenkian. The company's refining operations and sales were restricted to **Iraq**'s internal market so that it would not compete with its parent companies. Although it had been agreed at the San Remo Conference that a 20% share in the company should be reserved for Iraqis wishing to invest in it, the oil companies were to able to exclude Iraqi participation. The TPC was renamed as the IPC in 1929. The interests of the IPC's shareholders were at variance. The Anglo-Persian Oil Company, Royal Dutch/Shell and Standard Oil all disposed of abundant supplies of crude oil outside of Iraq and sought, accordingly, to maintain the Iraqi concessions as reserves. The other companies, including CFP, which had no access to major crude resources elsewhere, favoured the swift development of crude oil production in Iraq. These varying interests were responsible for delaying the development of oil production in Iraq. In 1934, the construction of a pipeline from Kirkuk to Al-Hadithah was completed. At Al-Hadithah the pipeline bifurcated, with one branch running to Tripoli, Lebanon, and the other to Haifa, Palestine. Production from the Kirkuk field commenced in the same year. However, it was not until 1938 that IPC began to export significant quantities of crude oil. Prior to the **Second World War**, annual production from Kirkuk averaged 4m. metric tons, but fell sharply during the War. In the 1940s and 1950s, the IPC was granted concessions to prospect for oil in Dubai and elsewhere in the Persian (Arabian) Gulf region. In 1961 the Iraqi government headed by Gen. Qassem nationalized 99.5% of the IPC's concessions.

K

Kazakhstan

Historically, the Kazakhs, comprising Turkic and Mongol nomads who began to populate the region from the 13th century, seldom cohered as a unified nation. **Russia** gained control of the region in the 18th century and in 1936 Kazakhstan became a Soviet Republic. As part of the agricultural 'Virgin Lands' programme undertaken in the 1950s and 1960s, the active participation of Soviet citizens in the cultivation of Kazakhstan's northern pastures was fostered. Accordingly, non-Kazakhs (mainly Russians, but including some other nationalities) came to outnumber the native Kazakhs. After independence in 1991 many non-native Kazakhs departed. Contemporary Kazakhstan is confronted by the need to develop national unity; to develop its energy resources and find markets for its energy exports; to develop in a sustainable way its non-energy sectors; and to reinforce its international relations. Kazakhstan possesses huge reserves of fossil fuels, on which, together with the country's other mineral and metal resources, its industrial sector is based. Kazakhstan's booming energy sector made a substantial contribution to the achievement of a rate of economic growth of greater than 10% in 2000–01, and to annual growth of more than 9% in 2002–05. Oil export capacity has increased considerably since the inauguration of the Caspian Consortium pipeline—running from western Kazakhstan's Tengiz oilfield to the Black Sea—in 2001. Work is also under way, in collaboration with China, to construct an oil pipeline that will run from Kazakhstan's Caspian coast eastwards to the border with China. Current industrial policy aims to reduce Kazakhstan's dependence on the oil sector, and to reduce the leverage gained by foreign investors and foreign personnel. Disputes have arisen between the Kazakh government and foreign oil companies over the terms of production agreements. The local currency, the tenge, has been subjected to upward pressure in recent years owing to a huge influx of oil-derived foreign exchange.

Kissinger and the Politics of Oil

Henry Kissinger was born into a Jewish family in Bavaria, Germany, in 1923. His family relocated to New York, USA, in 1938. In 1977 Kissinger officially retired from political life, having, by that time, gained recognition for his shrewd political acumen. He was able, for example, to distance himself sufficiently from the Watergate and other scandals that occurred during the presidency of Richard Nixon, whom he served as Secretary of State, to retain office throughout the presidency of Gerald Ford. When the Western oil-importing countries were plunged into economic crisis as a result of the actions of **OPEC** in the 1970s, Kissinger's diplomacy and his assertion that 'oil is too important to leave it to the Arabs' appeared impractical, not least because US intervention would have been likely to provoke Soviet counter-measures.

Kuwait

Kuwait's reserves of crude oil, at some 96,000m. barrels, represent about 10% of total reserves world-wide. **Petroleum**, from which 95% of export revenue and 80% of government income is derived, accounts for almost one-half of the country's gross domestic product (GDP). According to the Central Bank of Kuwait, in 1997 the country's reserves of natural gas, at some 1,484,000m. cu m, accounted for 1.1% of total reserves world-wide. Britain supervised foreign relations and defence for the ruling Kuwaiti as-Sabah dynasty from 1899 until independence in 1961. The country's oil industry was dominated by foreign interests until 1973, when production of (low-priced) oil peaked at 3.3m. barrels per day (b/d). The industry had been nationalized by 1977 and measures were taken to conserve oil resources and reduce production. Output fell to a low of 1.25m. b/d in 1981, but recovered to 2m. b/d in 1990. In August 1990 Kuwait was invaded and subsequently annexed by **Iraq**, remaining under Iraqi occupation until February 1991, when the country was liberated by a US-led multinational coalition. Damage to the country's oil industry during the Iraqi occupation was extensive, affecting hundreds of oil wells and gathering stations and rendering useless Kuwait's three refineries. The cost of repairs to the damaged infrastructure was more than US $5,000m. By mid-1994, however, Kuwait's nominal daily oil production capacity (including the country's share of the Neutral Zone) had recovered to some 2.4m. b/d, and refining capacity had been restored to its pre-invasion level. The state-owned Kuwait Petroleum Corporation (KPC), estimated to be the world's seventh largest oil company, conducts extensive operations overseas, administering refineries and sizeable downstream distribution networks in Western Europe. Some 90% of Kuwait's crude oil is marketed via term contracts, and its price is linked to that of Saudi Arabian Medium (for Western customers) and a monthly average of Dubai and Oman crudes (for Asian buyers).

L

Libya

Libya's oil reserves, at some 40,000m. barrels, are equivalent to about one-eighth of those of **Saudi Arabia**, the world's largest producer. Oil was first discovered in Libya in 1959 by foreign companies conducting exploration and drilling activities under concessions that covered an area of some 600,000 sq km. Production commenced in September 1961, and by the end of 1969 Libya accounted for 15.4% of **OPEC**'s total and 7.5% of global output. Since he took power in a military *coup d'état* in 1969, Libyan leader Col Muammar Abu Minyar al-Qaddafi has developed a distinctive political system based on his own 'Third Universal Theory'. The system, which attempts to combine socialism and Islam, derives partly from tribal customs and is meant to involve the Libyan people in a unique form of 'direct democracy'. In the 1970s and 1980s Qaddafi used revenues accruing from oil to disseminate his ideology abroad, lending support to foreign subversives and terrorists with the aim of accelerating the demise of both Soviet-style communism and Western capitalism. From 1973 Qaddafi involved Libya in a military campaign in **Chad**'s Aozou Strip, but was forced to withdraw in 1987. In 1982, as a consequence of UN sanctions imposed after the destruction by a Libyan agent of Pan Am Flight 103 over Lockerbie, Scotland, Libya entered a period of international isolation. Following the imposition of sanctions, Libya apparently reduced its support for terrorism, and in the 1990s the country began to restore relations with Europe. The UN suspended sanctions in 1999 and finally lifted them in September 2003 after a resolution of the Lockerbie affair had been achieved. In late 2003, Libya announced that it would disclose details of and terminate its programmes for the development of weapons of mass destruction, and considerable progress has subsequently been achieved in the normalization of relations with the West. In 2004 Qaddafi travelled to Western Europe for the first time in 15 years. In that year a number of outstanding actions against the Libyan government in respect of terrorist activities carried out in the 1980s were resolved by Libya's payment of compensation to the families of victims of the UTA and La Belle disco bombings. Almost all of Libya's export revenue and about one-quarter of the country's gross domestic product (GDP) are derived from the oil sector. Per capita GDP is one of the highest in African, but the income that the country earns from oil is not widely distributed. In recent years progress has been made in the implementation of economic reforms as part of a programme to reintegrate Libya into the international community. Most US unilateral sanctions against Libya were removed in 2004, prompting increased foreign direct investment.

M

Mauritania

Mauritania, an increasingly significant African oil producer, constitutes a bridge between the Arab Maghreb and western sub-Saharan Africa. Under French domination from 1914, the country became independent in 1960. In 1976, Mauritania annexed part of the territory of the former Spanish Sahara (now Western Sahara), but was forced, some three years later, to relinquish it as a consequence of guerrilla action by the Frente Popular para la Liberación de Saguia y el-Hamra y Río de Oro (Frente Polisario—Polisario Front), which was fighting for independence for the territory. In 1984 Maaouya Ould Sid Ahmed Taya took power in a coup. A new constitution was introduced in 1991 and opposition political parties were permitted to operate. Two multi-party presidential elections that were subsequently held were widely regarded as compromised, but legislative and local elections held in October 2001 were deemed, generally, to have been free and fair. In August 2005, as the result of a bloodless coup, President Taya was replaced by a military council led by Col Ely Ould Mohamed Vall, which announced its intention to hold power for up to two years pending its creation of conditions for genuine democratic institutions and elections. Meanwhile, Mauritania remains an autocratic state that is vulnerable to tensions between the various ethnic components—including white Moors, black Moors, and non-Moor groups—of its population. Economic weakness has led to Mauritania's marginalization in regional affairs. It is hoped that the exploitation of Mauritania's offshore reserves of oil and natural gas may initiate economic development. Production and export of oil are scheduled to begin on a substantial scale in 2006.

Mexico

The discovery and commerical production of **petroleum** in Mexico dates back to the beginning of the 20th century. In 1911 exports commenced. According to Article 27 of the 1917 Constitution, the Mexican government had a long-term and incontestable right to all subsoil resources. Having none the less long challenged this right, foreign oil companies operating in Mexico were nationalized in the late 1930s. In spite of disruption caused by the Revolution, the country's output of oil, at 193m. barrels—representing about one-quarter of total production world-wide—peaked in 1921, largely in response to the increase in international demand caused by the **First World War**. Mexico was the world's leading exporter and its second largest producer of petroleum (after the USA) for much of the 1920s. In the early 1930s, however, partly as a consequence of economic depression world-wide, failure to find new sources of oil and the development of **Venezuela**'s oil industry, Mexico's production declined to about one-fifth of the level achieved in 1921. A recovery was initiated through the discovery, in 1932, of the Poza Rica oilfield near Veracruz, which remained Mexico's principal source of oil until the late 1950s. In 1938, the petroleum industry was nationa-lized, the Mexican government taking complete control of exploration, produc-tion, refining, and distribution in both the oil and natural gas industries, and of manufacturing and sales in the petrochemical products sector. In response, US oil companies sought to persuade the US government to impose an embargo on all imports from Mexico in order to discourage similar nationalizations elsewhere. The boycott was short-lived, however, as the US government favoured an accommodation between the oil companies and the Mexican government in accordance with the 'Good Neighbour Policy' pursued by US President Franklin D. Roosevelt, and in view of security requirements that had arisen as a result of the Second World War. This was achieved in 1943 when the oil companies received US $24m. as part of a final settlement. In 1938–71 Mexico's production of oil output grew at an average annual rate of 6%. Output rose from 44m. barrels in 1938 to 78m. barrels in 1951. In 1957, however, in order to meet domestic demand that had gradually outstripped production, Mexico became a net importer of petroleum products. In 1971, thanks to the development of new oilfields in the isthmus of Tehuantepec, output increased to 177m. barrels, but domestic demand continued none the less to surpass production. However, this situation was ameliorated by extensive oil discoveries in the 1970s: virtually every exploration attempt carried out after 1972 was successful. In 1973 output rose above the level of *c*. 190m. barrels that had been achieved in 1921. In 1974 the national oil company, Pemex, announced new discoveries of oil in Veracruz, Baja California Norte, Chiapas, and Tabasco. By 1975 domestic production of oil had outstripped demand, thus creating an exportable surplus. In 1976 Mexico's proven reserves of hydrocarbons were assessed at 11,000m. barrels. By 1983 they were estimated to total 72,500m. barrels. In 1983–91, Mexico exported, on average, at a rate of some 1.4m. barrels per day (b/d), while output rose from 2.7m. b/d to 3.1m. b/d. The contribution of the oil sector to Mexico's gross domestic product increased from 5% in 1985 to more than 6% by 1992. In the following year oil was the source of almost 30% of central government revenue. Production of oil rose steadily from 2.5m. b/d in 1989 to 2.7m. b/d in 1991, spurred in part by the crisis in the Persian (Arabian) Gulf. From early 1993, however, output began to decline. Mexico's consumption totalled 61m. metric tons of oil equivalent in 1992. Total petroleum consumption amounted to 1.8m. b/d in that year. During the first 10 months of 1995, total output of minerals (including oil) contracted marginally, by 1%. In the whole of 1995, output declined to average 2.6m. b/d, compared with

2.7m. b/d in 1994. In the first quarter of 1996, however, production of oil increased by 6% compared with the corresponding period of 1995, to an average of 2.8m. b/d. By the early 1990s Mexico refined some 40% of its own production. This rate was achieved thanks to government policy of heavily investing in the augmentation of existing refinery capacity and the construction of new facilities in order to retain as much value added accruing from petroleum processing as possible. At current levels of production Mexico's reserves will last for a further 50 years. Since nationalization of the oil industry in 1938, state-owned Pemex has exercised a monopoly in the production and marketing of hydrocarbons.

N

National Front of Iran (NFI)

The National Front of Iran (NFI—Jebhe Melli) was founded as a political opposition party by leading Iranian nationalists, including Mohammed Mossadegh, in the late 1940s. It remains active, both within **Iran** itself and in exile. Shortly after it had been founded the NFI assembled a coalition of political parties in support, among other reforms, of nationalizing Iran's oil industry, which was dominated at that time by the Anglo-Iranian Oil Company (AIOC). In 1951, in response to the NFI's demands, the Shah of Iran appointed Mossadegh as the country's Prime Minister. Mossadegh immediately enforced the Oil Nationalization Act, which had been approved by the Iranian Majlis (assembly) earlier in 1951. The response of Great Britain was to initiate a boycott of Iranian oil, which effectively paralysed the Iranian oil industry. Britain's challenge to the legality of the nationalization was rejected by the International Court of Justice, but the AIOC persisted none the less in seeking an accommodation with Iran. Mossadegh, however, confident of ultimate victory, dismissed all of the company's proposals. Meanwhile, Iran was plunged into economic crisis for lack of foreign exchange and oil revenues. The outcome was the Abadan Crisis and a *coup d'état*, sponsored by Britain and the USA, that overthrew Mossadegh in 1953.

Nigeria

Within **OPEC** Nigeria is the sixth largest oil producer, while, in world terms, the country ranks seventh. Revenues from oil constitute the principal source of Nigeria's foreign exchange earnings and contribute some 95% of the country's annual revenue. In 1965, Nigeria's first oil refinery, whose capacity of 38,000 barrels per day (b/d) was sufficient to meet domestic requirements at that time, commenced operations at Alesa Eleme, near Port Harcourt. Refinery output increased to 60,000 b/d after the country's civil war, but failed to keep pace with fast-growing domestic demand. In 1978 a second refinery, with a capacity of 100,000 b/d, was opened at Warri. The new refinery was 100%-owned by the Nigerian National Petroleum Company (NNPC), which, since 1979, had also held an 80% share in the first refinery. In 1979, oil refined by the two facilities totalled, on average, 89,000 b/d, sufficient to meet more than 80% of domestic demand. In addition to oil, Nigeria possessed considerable reserves of natural gas. Consumption of natural gas grew steadily from the late 1970s, and in 1990 provided more than 20% of Nigeria's total commercially-sourced energy. Even so, far more natural gas was available than was used. In 1988, Nigeria produced 21,200m. cu m per day, of which 2,900m. cu m was utilized by the National Electric Power Authority (NEPA) and other domestic customers, 2,600m. cu m by foreign oil companies, and 15,700m. cu m (more than 75%) was flared. In 1999, after almost 16 years of military rule, a new constitution was adopted. Nigeria's transition to civilian government has been peaceful, but the country is now confronted by the immense challenge of reforming its oil-based economy, which has long been subject to corruption and mismanagement.

Nobel Brothers in Baku

Alfred Nobel was born in Stockholm, Sweden. In 1842, he went with his family to St Petersburg, **Russia**, where his father established a torpedo factory. Having returned to Sweden after the bankruptcy of the family business, Alfred Nobel studied explosives, in particular the safe manufacture of nitroglycerine. In 1876, Alfred's brothers, Ludvig and Robert, founded the oil company Branobel in Baku, **Azerbaijan**. During the late 19th century Branobel became one of the world's largest oil companies, distributing its oil products throughout Russia by train and in **Central Asia** and Europe by ship. Following the Russian Revolution in October–November 1917, the Nobel family partly fled to Stockholm, forfeiting their Russian assets to the Bolsheviks. The companies that they still owned in Europe were sold. In 1920 the Red Army entered Baku. Later that year, half of the Nobels' oil company shares were sold to Standard Oil of New Jersey, thus securing their economic future.

The Nobel Prize

The Nobel Prize, whose award is recognized as the most prestigious international recognition of intellect, is linked to oil production, in particular to the oilfields of Baku, **Azerbaijan**. The Prize was established in 1901, using funds bequeathed by Alfred Nobel, who had been the largest single stockholder in the **Nobel Brothers'** Oil-Producing Company, which operated in Azerbaijan. On his death, Alfred Nobel's wealth was calculated at 31m. Swedish crowns, some 12% of which was estimated to have been derived from oil.

North Sea Oil

Although sizeable reserves of oil and natural gas reserves were discovered there in the 1960s, it was not until the 1980s and 1990s that the full potential of the North Sea as a significant, non-**OPEC** source of oil began to be fully realized. North Sea production of oil and gas, which has required technological innovation in order to overcome the disadvantages (climate, depth of reserves, etc.) of its location, is only achievable at high cost, but against this may be weighed such advantages as the stability of the states involved in exploiting the resource and easy distribution to major European markets. Thus, the region has been able to occupy an important position in world markets for oil and natural gas, enriching the economies of the United Kingdom and **Norway** and helping Europe reduce its reliance on **petroleum** sourced from the Middle East. North Sea oil has made a major contribution to the rise in non-OPEC output since the 1980s. Currently, however, output from many of the region's major oilfields is in decline. Although the United Kingdom and Norway will remain important producers in the medium term, and high oil prices, in combination with enhanced recovery technology, may slow the decline of their major fields, significant new discoveries would be required to arrest the anticipated decline in the long term.

Norway

Norway possesses about one-half of the reserves of oil and natural gas that remain to be exploited in Europe. Norwegian supplies of natural gas are sufficient to meet some 10% of European consumption. Norway's exports of natural gas are forecast to rise significantly in the near future, to the point where they will account for about 30% of Europe's total imports of natural gas. Norwegian gas is distributed by pipelines that extend from the North and Norwegian Seas to Belgium, France, Germany and the United Kingdom. Norway's network of submarine natural gas pipelines is the largest in the world and the country is well placed to meet the challenges that will arise from the liberalization of European natural gas markets. By the end of the second decade of the 21st century it is anticipated that natural gas will have overtaken oil as the principal source of revenue in Norway's oil and gas sector. Co-operation between the oil sectors of Norway and **Russia** may be initiated in the future, possibly in connection with a resolution of the issue of the so-called delimitation line in the Barents Sea, which has been subject to negotiation for some 30 years. Since 1995 Norway has been able to maintain oil production at some 3m. barrels per day (b/d). Average output is forecast to total 2.8m. b/d in 2006—rather lower than production in 2005. Output is forecast to rise in both 2007 and 2008, but the long-term outlook is for it to decline.

O

Odessa–Brody Pipeline

The Odessa–Brody pipeline carries crude oil between the Ukrainian cities of Odessa, situated on the Black Sea, and Brody, close to the Ukrainian-Polish border. The extension of the pipeline to Brody was completed in 2002. The Odessa–Brody pipeline is 674 km in length and has an annual design throughput capacity of 14m. metric tons. In May 2003, Ukraine, Poland and the European Commission issued a statement on the extension of the pipeline to Plock, and established an expert working group for this purpose. In November, the Ukrainian and Polish governments concluded an agreement of intent regarding the use of the pipeline and its connection to the Polish pipeline system. In 2004, the Ukrainian and Polish state pipeline operators established a joint company, Sarmatia, to construct the extension to Plock. The pipeline has attracted international attention owing to its geopolitical significance, with regard to both its usage and its direction. Originally it was planned to extend the pipeline to Gdańsk, Poland, in order to transport oil from the Caspian Sea to that country and onwards, to other destinations in Europe. However, largely in response to pressure from **Russia** and its oil companies, which are closely connected to the Russian government, the Ukrainian government determined its reverse flow, making it transfer Russian oil southwards to the Black Sea and, thereafter, to Mediterranean destinations. Since 2005, however, the interest of the (new) Ukrainian government in using the pipeline as originally intended, to transfer oil from the Caspian to Europe, has revived.

Oil and Conflict in the Middle East

After the British Navy had replaced coal with oil as its fuel in 1911, and following the development, post-**Second World War**, of petrochemical industries, oil acquired military and economic significance for the leading Western powers. They thus became dependent on the oilfields of the Middle East, especially those of the Persian (Arabian) Gulf region. In the 20th century the Western powers resorted to both military and political intervention in order to increase their influence in the Middle East. Following the collapse of the Ottoman Empire in the aftermath of the **First World War,** Western power in the Middle East increased as a result of the mandates granted to Britain and France to establish nation states in the region. Britain's presence in the Gulf region (**Iraq, Iran** and **Saudi Arabia**) had significant socio-economic repercussions, giving rise, for instance, to instability and dissatisfaction among large sections of the population and provoking anti-Western sentiment among the urban populations of Iraq and Iran. Such consequences were aggravated by the rapid development of oil production in the region. Generally, the oil industry benefited from the stability in the Gulf states that was brought about through the domination of small, conservaties élites. By the time of the Second World War—and thereafter—it could be argued that the revenues accruing to the region's rulers from the oil companies were used mainly to preserve their regimes from potential social crises. The oil boom of the 1970s and increased state control over oil production in the Gulf retarded the social consequences of the contradictions that existed in Iran, Iraq and Saudi Arabia. In Iran and Iraq the use of state revenues to pre-empt popular unrest took the form of investment in economic development. In Saudi Arabia, however, where the social structure reflected the old tribal system, there was only minimal social and economic development. Generous welfare benefits and a proliferation of 'white collar' state employment merely adapted traditional social relations to the prevailing oil bonanza. Together with the carrot of state patronage, the regimes of all oil-rich countries in the Gulf used the stick of repression against left-wing, religious and secularist opposition. In particular, Iran and Iraq developed powerful and ruthless security services, which prevented the reorganization of mass parties. But, while the Baa'thist regime in Iraq used its patronage of whole sections of the population to divide the opposition, the Shah of Iran carried out a programme of systematic and brutal repression which united most of his enemies. The high price of oil in the 1970s had led to increased investment in developing and expanding oil production. The first Gulf War, between Iran and Iraq in 1981–88, served to deal with the threat of social unrest in both countries. The mass deaths on the war fields and the state of national emergency within both countries allowed the two regimes to crush their internal oppositions easily. For Saudi Arabia, the 1980s were a period of social and political crisis that the regime could not easily defuse. Despite the generosity of Saudi welfare provisions in the previous decade, the distribution of wealth amongst the population had remained unequal and continued to reflect old patterns of privilege and hierarchies. When oil prices fell in the 1980s, the state was obliged to cut back on its welfare provisions. As a result, the already existing discontent of the Saudi population deepened. In the face of the various waves of pan-Arabism and anti-imperialism, it had been important for the Saudi regime to stress its Islamic origins. To do this, it manipulated the more moderate section of the clergy, those willing to accept modernization. However, the fervent and coherent anti-US and Islamic stance of the Shi'i Iranian leadership served to expose Saudi Arabia's distinctly un-Islamic foreign policy and led to growing criticism. This criticism would reach its climax during the Gulf War in 1990, when Saudi Arabia had to resort to US military support, subsequently allowing its territory to be used as a base for attacking Iraq.

The Afghan War, where the local Muslim population opposed the occupying Soviet force in 1979, offered many Middle Eastern states the opportunity to try to rid themselves of their indigenous Islamist 'troublemakers'. Many Arab states, including Saudi Arabia, encouraged zealous Muslim youth to leave their country and to martyr themselves in a *jihad* against the Communist 'infidel' in Afghanistan. US government agencies played an important role in training and sponsoring these Islamist militant forces. In this period, it was the Saudi government that sent Osama bin Laden to Afghanistan, and funded his operations there. With the withdrawal of Soviet forces from Afghanistan in 1992 and a change in American policy, the USA ceased its support for the Islamist militant groups. The Middle Eastern states, afraid that the Islamist extremism would now be directed against them, closed their borders to the militants. This left groups of exiled *jihadi*, with a growing resentment of the USA which had 'used' them for its own ends, to find new causes to fight in other countries on behalf of fellow Muslims. With the attack on Iraq in the 1990s, these Muslim groups directed their efforts against the USA, turning the *jihad* into guerrilla actions. This process created international links, one of which was al-Qa'ida. As a result, the most strategically significant area of the world for the industrialized countries became its most troublesome. By 1991, Iran was governed by an Islamist regime and Iraq by the secular national-socialist Ba'ath party. Both Iranian and Iraqi regimes were virulently anti-Western. Similarly, Saudi Arabia was in profound social and political crisis, which deepened following the regime's commitment to the USA during the second Gulf War. This crisis would later lead to the world-wide emergence of small Islamist guerrilla groups. This state of affairs in the Middle East is not just a coincidental misfortune, but the result of contradictions created by the subsumption of the Middle East into the global economic system, the effect of the arbitrary creation of new nation states and deep-rooted oil interests in the region.

Oil & Gas Journal

The *Oil & Gas Journal*, published since 1902, is the most widely read international oil industry publication, supplementing its news coverage of the sector with economic and political analysis, technological features and statistical information.

'Oil imperialism'

'Oil imperialism' refers to the assertion contained in numerous political science theories, that the struggle for control, both direct and indirect, of the world's oil reserves underlies many contemporary and recently historical political events. Such theories tend to highlight the role of oil imperialism in international politics since the **First World War**. More recently, it has been argued that oil imperialism was the underlying motive for the Gulf War and the invasion, in 2003, of Iraq. The significance of access to oil has also been asserted in explanation of the rise to sole superpower status of the USA and of the Soviet Union's (and, subsequently, **Russia**'s) ability to cope with long-term economic mismanagement. The so-called '**petrodollar** theory' claims that the recent conflicts in Iraq have been motivated to some extent at least by the USA's desire to retain the status of international currency for the US dollar—*see* **Iraq**.

Oil Pipelines

Among the many forms of transportation that are used to distribute oil to marketplaces, pipelines are the most secure, most efficient and most economical. Pioneered by Vladimir Shukhov and the Branobel company (*see* **Nobel Brothers in Baku**) in the late 19th century, pipeline transport offers lower costs per unit and higher capacity than transportation by rail. Pipelines may be used to move both crude oil and refined liquid **petroleum** products over both short and long distances. They may also connect oil platforms to loading rigs or to main pipelines onshore, and underground pipelines are used to carry petroleum products from refineries to airports, inland terminals, etc. Submarine pipelines can be constructed, but only at high cost and to exacting technical requirements, so the transport of oil overseas is usually undertaken by tanker. The length of all the pipelines laid world-wide amounts to thousands of kilometres. One of the world's largest pipelines is the **Trans-Alaska pipeline** system, which extends for 1,300 km across three mountain ranges and 800 rivers or streams, and has a diameter of 122 cm and a daily capacity of 350m. litres of crude oil. Oil pipelines are constructed out of steel or plastic tubes, whose diameters generally range between 30–120 cm. The flow of oil through pipelines, at a speed of 1–6 m per second, is maintained by pumping stations located along them. Multi-product pipelines exist for the transportation of two (or more) different products in sequence through the same pipeline. Multi-product pipelines do not usually separate the different products and some mixing of adjacent products occurs, producing interface, which is removed at receiving destinations and isolated to avoid contamination. Smaller pipelines are used to distribute natural gas for domestic and commercial purposes. In Canada and the USA it is a legal requirement for underground pipelines to be protected against corrosion, frequently by means of coating in combination with cathodic protection. Transnational pipelines have been in use for more than 100 years, but low prices and abundant supplies gradually eroded their strategic significance. So-called super tankers were first launched in the early 1950s, allowing oil producers to distribute their products world-wide and broadening the range of sellers available to consumers. Some two-thirds of trade in oil now takes place via tankers. In recent years increased demand for oil have placed pressure on energy networks, supplies have struggled to keep pace with consumption, and tensions have risen accordingly. The role of pipelines in a time of increased restriction in energy markets, terrorist threats to energy infrastructure, and the political use of energy resources is critical.

'Oil Shocks'

'Oil shocks' have perplexed macroeconomists since they first arose in the 1970s, making 'geopolitics of oil' the byword to describe the sources of ambiguity surrounding oil supplies and prices. The oil price 'spikes' of that time clearly had significant macroeconomic implications, marking one of the rare times that higher prices in an individual industry have had an important effect on the global political economy. Oil shocks have serious effects on the economy because they immediately raise prices for an important production input—oil—and important consumer goods, such as gasoline and heating oil. They are also likely to cause prices in other energy markets to rise. These price increases are significant enough to, typically, show up as temporary bursts in the overall rate of inflation. They may even be passed through to continuing rates of inflation if they become incorporated into price- and wage-setting mechanisms. Increases in oil prices also reduce consumer spending power, in much the same way as when a new excise tax is passed along by oil producers. To the extent that these producers are foreign, there should be a corresponding drop in domestic demand. Even if the oil producers are domestic, a drop in domestic demand could still occur if the producers do not spend as much of their new income as consumers would have or if they do not recycle their profits to shareholders. Currently, for the first time in the history of the modern oil industry, global demand continues to rise faster than the world's capacity to produce more crude. That is very different from the last major oil shocks of the 1970s, which were the result of a decision by the newly formed **OPEC** to withhold supplies in order to drive up prices.

Oil Transit 'Chokepoints'

A significant volume of oil is traded internationally by means of oil tankers and **oil pipelines**. About two-thirds of the world's oil trade (both crude oils and refined products) moves by tanker. About 43m. barrels per day of that trade is in crude oil. Tankers have made the intercontinental transportation of oil possible, as they are low-cost, efficient, and extremely flexible. Oil transported by sea generally follows a permanent set of maritime routes. Along the way, tankers come across several geographic 'chokepoints', or narrow channels, such as the Strait of Hormuz leading out of the Persian (Arabian) Gulf and the Turkish Strait linking the Black Sea (and oil coming from the Caspian Sea basin) with the Mediterranean (and major consuming markets in the West). Other important maritime chokepoints include the Panama Canal and the Panama Pipeline connecting the Pacific and Atlantic Oceans; and the Suez Canal and the Sumed Pipeline connecting the Red and Mediterranean Seas. Chokepoints are critically important to world oil trade because so much oil passes through them, yet they are narrow and theoretically could be blocked or jammed. In addition, chokepoints are susceptible to attacks by pirates and shipping accidents in their narrow channels.

OPEC – *see* Organization of the Petroleum Exporting Countries

Organization of the Petroleum Exporting Countries (OPEC)

The Organization of the Petroleum Exporting Countries (OPEC) is a permanent, intergovernmental organization that was created at the Baghdad Conference, held in September 1960, by **Iran**, **Iraq**, **Kuwait**, **Saudi Arabia** and **Venezuela**. Subsequently, Qatar (1961), Indonesia (1962), the Socialist People's Libyan Arab Jamahiriya (**Libya**, 1962), the United Arab Emirates (1967), Algeria (1969), **Nigeria** (1971), Ecuador (1973–92) and Gabon (1975–94) jointed the Organization. For the first five years of its existence OPEC's headquarters were located in Geneva, but were transferred to Vienna, Austria, in September 1965. OPEC aims to co-ordinate and unify **petroleum** policies among its members, as part of the pursuit of fair and stable prices for petroleum producers; an efficient, economic and regular supply of petroleum to consuming nations; and a fair return on capital to those investing in the industry. In its early years, in international terms, OPEC remained a relatively low-profile organization. During the 1970s, however, it acquired increased international significance as its members took control of their domestic petroleum industries and gained decisive influence over the pricing of crude oil on world markets. Oil pricing crises were triggered, notably, by the Arab oil embargo of 1973 and by the outbreak of the Iranian Revolution in 1979—both events caused the price of oil to rise sharply. Prices peaked at the beginning of the 1980s and thereafter, throughout the decade, declined dramatically, collapsing in 1986—the third oil-pricing crisis. At the beginning of the 1990s a fourth pricing crisis was avoided on the outbreak of hostilities in the Middle East, when a sudden sharp increase in prices was arbitrated by increased production by OPEC Members. Thereafter, prices remained relatively stable until about 1998, when economic downturn in South-East Asia triggered another collapse. Collective action by OPEC, together with some leading non-OPEC producers, brought about a recovery.

P

'Peak Oil'

Until early modern times (approximately the 16th century), miners, scientists, natural philosophers and other experts dealing with natural resources believed that most minerals were vegetable-like, and that when mined they would grow back like mown grass. This belief, in the case of coal and other hydrocarbon fuels in gaseous and liquid form, was not wrong in principle, because they are the residues of ancient organisms, but it was wrong as a practical maxim. It would be completely mistaken to assume that coal, natural gas and **petroleum** can grow back, and that they are therefore infinite resources, for the time it would take normal geological processes to transform organic matter into these carbon fuels is of the order of millions of years. Therefore, these hydrocarbon fossil fuels are, to all intents and purposes, non-renewable, finite resources. Before oil is exhausted in a given field, it will reach a production peak, which is the highest production level in the history of oil production in that field. After this peak point has been reached, a structural decline in oil production will begin. The term 'peak oil' was first introduced by M. King Hubbert, a US geologist working for the Shell oil company. On 8 March 1956, at a meeting of the **American Petroleum Institute** in San Antonio, Texas, Hubbert predicted that production from the US lower 48 states would peak during the next 10 to 15 years (i.e. in 1966–71). Shell oil company, concerned about a panic in the financial markets, tried to prevent Hubbert from making his calculations and projections public. Most experts working in the oil industry at this time were also quick to dismiss Hubbert's predictions. He was accused of being non-scientific and his calculations were not recognized for many years. He was spot on: US continental oil did indeed peak in 1970. Since then, Hubbert's method, and his bell-shaped curve, has been considered a powerful predictive tool and has been widely used to forecast the timing of the peak all over the world. Even though the exact timing of the peak is difficult to pinpoint, mainly due to a lack of reliable data, it has generally been agreed that of the 65 largest oil-producing countries in the world, at least 54 have already passed their peak point of production and are now in permanent decline. The modern world economic system was built on ever more readily available cheap fossil fuels (first coal and then oil and gas). Because all industrial societies are now extremely dependent on oil, the amount of oil we consume increases every year, while the quantity of oil in the ground diminishes. In a real economic sense, peak oil means 'running out of cheap oil'. When commercial oil production first started, oil companies began by extracting the oil that was easiest to reach, which was the oil on land and near the surface. This oil was (and still is) called 'cheap oil'. Once the 'cheap oil' has been exhausted, the remainder is generally off shore, or deep under the ground, or technically too difficult to extract, or of lower quality. These conditions apply to much of the new crude oil currently reaching the market, which is at the root of high oil prices. According to industry estimates, a global economic crisis, related to dramatically rising oil prices, is likely to happen between 2005 and 2010. It is also estimated that continued price increases will become a structural problem after 2010.

Petrodollar

The petrodollar is a notional unit of currency earned by a country from the export of **petroleum**. In 1972–74 the USA and **Saudi Arabia** concluded a series of agreements in which the USA undertook to support the House of Saud with technical and military assistance as long as Saudi Arabia agreed to accept only US dollars in payment for its oil. The little-publicized agreement served the dual purpose of securing Saudi Arabia's ruling family and obtaining for the USA an alliance with **OPEC**'s largest producer. Saudi Arabia is in fact the only OPEC member that is not allocated a production, retaining the role of **'swing producer'**, whereby it may may raise or reduce oil production to regulate market supplies. Accordingly, Saudi Arabia exerts the strongest influence on oil prices. Since the conclusion of the US-Saudi Arabian agreement and its acceptance by OPEC, all oil traded world-wide has been priced in US dollars. Hence the oil standard became the dollar standard.

Petrodollar Warfare

Petrodollar warfare is a hypothesis which asserts that many of the international manoeuvres undertaken in recent decades have been pursued in support of the current fiat money system under which the pricing (in dollars) of key commodities (including oil and natural gas) preserves the prestige and the international value of the US currency. As a consequence, many countries maintain substantial dollar reserves which they can use to purchase these commodities without currency conversion. If the price of commodities were to be denominated in another currency, the euro for example, many countries would sell dollars and cause the banks to adjust their reserves. This would cause the value of the dollar against the euro to fall, in accordance with the law of supply and demand. The term 'oil currency wars' was coined by William R. Clark, but he did not, however, invent the theory. US Congressman Ron Paul has promoted the idea that empires have been upheld by continuing expansions and exploitations, and when they have no longer been able to do that they have collapsed. According to Paul, the USA behaves similarly, by issuing to the world dollars whose value is not tied to a commodity such as gold. Paul foresees US economic collapse if the dollar hegemony is not upheld, and proposes that the dollar should once again be backed by gold. He further asserts that wars and coups in oil-producing states are occurring partly to support dollar hegemony. Since 1971, when the US dollar ceased to be redeemable in gold, its value has not been explicitly linked to any commodity. Implicitly, however, it has been linked to Middle Eastern oil as a result of agreements concluded between the USA and **Saudi Arabia** in the early 1970s (*see* **Petrodollar**). In 2000, **Iraq** began to price all of its oil transactions in euros. Following the US-led invasion of Iraq in 2003 the dollar was restored as the currency in which Iraqi oil is priced.

Petroleum

Petroleum, or 'rock oil'—from the Greek petros (rock) and oleum (oil)—consists of varying combinations of carbon and hydrogen atoms, referred to as hydrocarbons. Petroleum is formed over millions of years from the organic remains of animals and plants and is found trapped in large sedimentary basins in porous rock formations. The discovery of such oil and gas 'traps' and the extraction of petroleum from its reservoir usually involves considerable technical ingenuity and expense. Potential traps may be located through seismic surveys, but the presence of petroleum can only be established with certainty by drilling. The most familiar petroleum products are liquefied petroleum gas, petrol (gasoline), aviation fuels, kerosene, diesel oil, lubricating oils and bitumen. Refined petroluem may be used as a petrochemical feedstock for the production of industrial and domestic plastic goods, synthetic rubber, packaging, fabrics, dyes, adhesives and paint.

Production Sharing Agreement (PSA)

The Production Sharing Agreement (PSA) is a common model for the structure of the oil industry in many oil-producing countries, particularly in developing and transitional economies. In this system, the state retains ownership and therefore ultimate control of the country's oil resources. The foreign company (or a consortium of companies) provides the capital investment, in terms of technical and financial services, and in return receives the right to extract and process oil under contract. The essential part and main distinguishing characteristic of this system is production sharing. That is why it is called Production Sharing Agreement. An early version of this system was first used in Bolivia in the early 1950s. However, a more sophisticated legal agreement, similar to its current form, was employed in Indonesia in the 1960s. Since then, in a large number of countries, PSAs have been used to define the main form of arrangement between a foreign investor and a state (generally the state's national oil company) in terms of oil exploration and development operations. Currently, this system is used in more than 40 countries, including **Angola**, Egypt, **Equatorial Guinea**, **Libya**, Malaysia, Peru, the Philippines, Syria, **Viet Nam** and Yemen. After the collapse of the state-socialist regimes in Eastern Europe and the Soviet Union in 1989–91, the world oil industry witnessed a dramatic rise in the number and range of PSAs in the former communist oil-producing countries. Even the oil-rich Russian Federation adopted a federal law 'on Agreements about Production Sharing' in 1995. According to the **International Energy Agency**, about 12% of the world's oil reserves are operated under the PSA system. A PSA is a kind of legal contract which defines the relations between the oil-producing state and a contractor (generally a foreign investor company). Even though PSAs come in a variety of styles, according to a typical PSA, the investor is supposed to recover all or most of the initial investment costs from the sales of the first proportion of oil. The oil used for this purpose is called 'cost oil'. The contracts generally specify what proportion of oil extracted in any year can be considered as 'cost oil'. This proportion is generally 50%–50% or 40%–60% depending on the special characteristics of the oilfield. Once the initial costs have been recovered, the remainder of the oil produced is divided between the state and the foreign investor in agreed proportions. This portion of oil is called 'profit oil'. The PSA system is desirable for a developing or transitional economy, because it is a convenient and easy way of attracting substantial levels of foreign investment. Because the state upholds national ownership of resources, the negative political implications of a PSA agreement are quite limited. This is a desirable system for the foreign investor, because it provides a greater level of flexibility while the profit margins are generally high.

R

Reserve Currency

In economics, reserve currency refers to national holdings, in the form of major foreign currencies or gold, of internationally acceptable means of payment. Similarly, central banks maintain reserves of money for their domestic banking sectors. To be eligible for reserve status a currency must be fully convertible and widely accepted. It should have extensive and liquid financial markets, for both domestic assets and foreign exchange. Its value should be fairly stable. And, finally, it should be the medium for a substantial amount of trade and financial business. Once a currency's role as the dominant medium has been established, business tends to be transacted in it, and this explains the contemporary significance of the US dollar. There are signs, however, of change. In Asia, in the context of fundamental dollar weakness, massive reserve holdings are being built up at the same time as the euro is emerging as a credible alternative to the dollar. Nevertheless, not all of the criteria that qualify a currency to fulfil the role of reserve currency need be met simultaneously. There can also be time lags of significant duration. The British pound sterling, for example, fulfilled such a role long after the British economy had begun to decline in the post-**Second World War** period, partly because of the depth and liquidity of sterling markets, but also because of the United Kingdom's enduring political influence and its reputation for fairness in economic matters. By the same token, there are many countries with sizeable economies which fail to meet other key criteria, for example China, whose currency, the renminbi, is far from being able to assume the role of reserve currency in spite of China's huge presence in world trade and the rank of its economy as the world's second largest.

Red Line Agreement

In the early 1920s, when the American oil companies first became interested in oil concessions in the Middle East, they placed great emphasis on what was termed the 'open door' policy, and, in fact, made the recognition of this policy a *sine qua non* of their participation in the **Iraq Petroleum Company (IPC)**. In this, they were actively backed by the US government. In its initial stages the 'open door' policy was generally understood to mean lack of restrictions for any company to obtain, without discrimination, oil concessions, in mandated areas, above all in Mesopotamia. The 'open door' policy which had been so strongly advanced was abandoned in succeeding years without a single test of its sufficiency as a practical functioning standard. Competition among the owners themselves was not allowed by retaining the 'self-denying' clause of the 1914 Foreign Office agreement. Within an area restricted on a map by a 'Red Line' encompassing most of the old Ottoman Empire (including Turkey, **Iraq**, **Saudi Arabia**, and adjoining sheikhdoms, but excluding **Iran, Kuwait**, Israel, and Trans-Jordan), the owners decided to be involved in oil only through the IPC. When Gulf Oil, a member of the American group, sought permission to employ an option to acquire a concession in Bahrain, the IPC rejected the demand. The Red Line Agreement is an exceptional example of a restrictive mixture for the control of a large portion of the world's supply by a group of companies which together control the world market for this commodity. In a confidential memorandum, France portrayed the objectives of the agreement thus: 'the execution of the Red Line Agreement marked the beginning of a long-term plan for the world control and distribution of oil in the Near East'. The IPC was so functioned as 'to avoid any publicity which might jeopardize the long-term plan of the private interests of the group ...'.

Rockefeller Family

Of German origin, the Rockefeller family achieved prominence in US industry in the late 19th century through the Standard Oil Company. The family also became celebrated for its philanthropy and several of its members held high public office in the USA. John D. Rockefeller achieved control of one-tenth of the US oil industry by exploiting the lack of regulation in the industry in the late 19th century to outmanoeuvre the competitors of Standard Oil. Notable among the methods employed to achieve this control were secret arrangements concluded with railway operators, whose co-operation with Standard Oil and its partners prevented rival oil companies and refineries from transporting their oil by rail. Since oil was free at source, the cost of transporting it was the only cost companies incurred after they had invested in extraction and refining. Standard Oil ensured the co-operation of railway operators through the secret payment of rebates on the transportation of oil. The resulting low price at which Standard Oil was able to market its oil mystified its competitors for many years and it remains unclear even now precisely how the collusion of the railway operators was secured and kept secret for so many years. The Standard Oil company obtained business intelligence from its own network of spies. While Rockefeller considered that a little knowledge could be a decisive factor in commerce, he became known for his unwillingness to offer any public comment on the conduct of his business.

Romania

Romania, with proven reserves of 956m. barrels, is the largest producer of oil in Central and Eastern Europe. However, the country's output has declined sharply in recent decades, from 252,000 barrels per day (b/d) in 1980 to 125,000 b/d in 2002, a fall of about 50%. This decline may be largely attributed to the deep political and economic upheaval that resulted from the post-communist transition. Romania also dominates south-eastern Europe's downstream **petroleum** industry, operating 10 of the 11 regional refineries. The country's refining capacity is far in excess of domestic demand for refined petroleum products, creating an exportable surplus of a wide range of oil products and petrochemicals. However, almost all of Romania's refineries operate well below capacity for want of crude oil supplies, and most remain state-owned. Low investment over many years has left Romania's refining sector in need of huge amounts of capital in order to modernize and improve efficiency. The national oil company, PETROM, is 93% state-owned although there are plans to allow private investment in about one-half of the company. Companies known to be interested in buying into PETROM include **Russia**'s LUKoil, Hungary's MOL, US Occidental Petroleum, Austria's OMV, Switzerland's Glencore, Greece's Hellenic Petroleum and Poland's PKN. The sale is complicated, however, by the leading role PETROM plays in the Romanian economy and the assistance of the International Monetary Fund and the European Union has been sought to ensure that the privatization proceeds smoothly.

Russia

Founded in the 12th century, the Principality of Muscovy was able to emerge from more than 200 years of Mongol domination (13th–15th centuries) and to gradually defeat and capture nearby principalities. In the early 17th century, a new Romanov Dynasty sustained this policy of expansion across Siberia to the Pacific. Under Peter I (ruled 1682–1725), Russian control was extended over the Baltic Sea and the whole country was renamed the Russian Empire. During the 19th century, more territorial acquisitions were made in Europe and Asia. Repeated devastating defeats of the Russian army in the **First World War** led to extensive rioting in the key cities of the Russian Empire and to the overthrow, in 1917, of the imperial household by a revolution. The Bolsheviks, under Vladimir Lenin, seized power and established the Union of Soviet Socialist Republics (USSR). After 70 years of one-party rule, the Soviet economy and society stagnated in the 1980s. Despite the heroic attempt in 1985–91 of Mikhail Gorbachev to modernize the state-socialist economy, a deep economic, social and political crisis led to the disintegration of the USSR into 15 independent republics by December 1991. Since then, Russia has struggled in its efforts to build a democratic political system and a functioning market economy to replace the strict social, political, and economic controls of the communist period. While some progress has been made in economic reform, there has taken place in recent years a recentralization of power under Vladimir Putin and the erosion of nascent democratic institutions. A determined guerrilla conflict is still being waged in **Chechnya** that threatens to destabilize the North Caucasus region. Russia has significant oil and gas resources. Indeed, the first oil well in the world was drilled in the Russian Empire, at Bibi-Aybat near Baku in 1846, more than a decade before the drilling of the first well in the USA. This event marked the beginning of the modern oil industry. The Baku region contained many large fields which were relatively easy to exploit, but transporting the oil to market was difficult and expensive. The **Nobel brothers** and the Rothschild family played a major role in the development of the oil industry in Baku, which was at that time part of the Russian Empire. The industry grew rapidly, and by the beginning of the 20th century Russia accounted for more than 30% of oil production world-wide. Shell Transport & Trading, which later became part of Royal Dutch/Shell, began by ferrying oil produced by the Rothschilds to Western Europe. Later in the 19th century, oil was also discovered in other parts of the Russian Empire. In 1864, a well drilled in Krasnodar Krai produced the first 'gusher'. Four years later, the first oil well was drilled on the banks of the Ukhta River, while in 1876 commercial production commenced on the Cheleken peninsula in present-day **Turkmenistan**. The rapid development of oil production was accompanied by the construction of various plants for processing crude oil, including a lubricants plant which opened in 1879 near Yaroslavl and a similar facility which opened in the same year in Nizhny Novgorod. Oil production suffered as a result of the Russian Revolution in 1917, and the situation worsened with the nationalization of the oilfields by the Bolsheviks in 1920. The Nobels sold a significant part of their Russian holdings to Standard Oil of New Jersey, which was later to become Exxon. Standard Oil protested against the decision to nationalize the oilfields and refused to co-operate with the new Soviet government. Other companies, how-ever, including Vacuum and Standard Oil of New York, which was later to become Mobil, invested in Soviet Russia. The continued inflow of Western funds helped Russian oil production to recover, and by 1923 exports had been restored to their pre-revolutionary levels. The Caspian and North Caucasus remained the centre of the Soviet oil industry until the **Second World War**, with rising production feeding the country's rapid drive to industrialize. Securing control over oil production in Baku was a centrepiece of German strategy during the war, and for a time the Soviet Union found itself cut off from access to its oil. Caspian oil production once again began to increase after the end of the war, and reached a new record high point of some 850,000 barrels per day (b/d) in 1951. Baku remained the centre of the industry and nearly two-thirds of Soviet oilfield equipment was manufactured in the area. By 1950, the new fields accounted for 45% of Soviet oil production. Massive investments in the region were rewarded by a substantial increase in Soviet oil production. The extra barrels were used to supply the many new refineries which were brought on stream in the period between the 1930s and the 1950s. The growth in production also allowed the Soviet Union to increase its exports of oil. The Soviet Union was keen to maximize its earnings of hard currency from oil exports, and priced aggressively in order to boost its market share. By the early 1960s, the Soviet Union had replaced **Venezuela** as the second largest oil producer in the world. The arrival of abundant supplies of Soviet oil on the market forced many Western oil companies to reduce their posted prices for Middle Eastern oil, thus reducing royalty revenues for governments of the Middle East. This reduction in revenues was one of the driving forces behind the formation of the **Organization of Petroleum Exporting Countries (OPEC)**. By the mid-1970s, the Soviet Union was already aware of an impending decline in output. The first such decline occurred in 1977 as a result of chronic under-investment in exploration in Western Siberia, but the authorities managed to reverse the decline through increased spending on drilling. The second fall occurred in the period between 1982 and 1986. This time, too, the Soviet Union managed to avert a crisis through increased investment. In 1988, Soviet output rose to a new record level of some 11.4m. b/d. At this point, it was the largest producer in the world, with output significantly higher than that of either the USA or **Saudi Arabia**. It was also in 1988 that output from Western Siberia peaked, at 8.3m. b/d. By then, however, a sustained decline in production was inevitable—thanks to poor reservoir management techniques, the Soviet Union managed to raise production only marginally during the first part of the 1990s, despite a dramatic increase in capital expenditure. Thereafter, Russian production declined continuously for a decade, falling to only about one-half of its original level. The collapse of the Soviet economy in 1991 initially resulted in a big drop in the domestic consumption of oil, but export capacity restraints meant that companies were forced to continue selling a large portion of their output on the domestic market, often to insolvent customers. The companies' financial difficulties forced a complete halt to all new exploration and drilling activity, and even work-overs of existing wells, a situation which aggravated the collapse in production. The slide in Russian oil production was finally halted in 1997. Today, estimates of proven reserves in Russia vary wildly, ranging from the US *Oil & Gas Journal*'s 48,600m. barrels to analyst estimates which are three times higher. Experts agree on one thing, however. Russia's oil reserves are big enough to support a boom in exports for many decades. In 2005 Russia achieved a seventh successive year of economic growth, which has averaged 6.4% annually since the financial crisis of 1998. Although high oil prices and the relatively low value of the Russian rubl have been important drivers of this economic recovery, investment and consumer-driven demand have played a noticeably increasing role since 2000. Real fixed capital investments have averaged gains greater than 10% over the last five years, and real personal incomes have realized average increases of more than 12%. Russia has also improved its international financial position since the 1998 financial crisis, with its foreign debt declining from 90% of gross domestic product to around 36%. Strong oil export earnings have allowed Russia to increase its foreign reserves from only US $12,000m. to some $180,000m. at the end of 2005.

S

Sakhalin Island Oil

Sakhalin, formerly Saghalien, island (*c.* 76,400 sq km), located off the coast of Asian **Russia**, between the Sea of Okhotsk and the Sea of Japan, is divided from the Russian mainland on the west by the Tatar Strait and from Japan's Hokkaido island by the Soya Strait. Together with the Kuril Islands it forms the Sakhalin region of the Russian Far East. The principal industries of Sakhalin include offshore gas production. In the north east there are oilfields and pipelines have been extended to Nikolayevsk and Komsomolsk Amur on the mainland. Offshore oilfields are also under development. Sakhalin's reserves of oil and natural gas have been assessed, respectively, at 14,000m. barrels and about 2,720,000m. cu m. Since the collapse of the Soviet Union and Russia's subsequent pursuit of economic reform, there has been an oil boom in Sakhalin in which most of the multinational oil companies have conducted extensive exploration. Since the beginning of the 21st century the development of offshore oilfields has created a booming economy. By 2005, the island had become Russia's principal target for foreign investment, followed by Moscow.

Saudi Arabia

Saudi Arabia is the world's leading producer and exporter of oil. The Saudi Arabian state arose from the puritanical Wahhabi movement, to which the powerful Saud family of the Nejd, in central Arabia, gave its allegiance. With the support of a large Bedouin following, the Sauds were able to gain control of most of the Arabian Peninsula, apart from Yemen and the Hadhramaut in the extreme south. In 1902, Abd al-Aziz bin Abd ar-Rahman as-Saud, a descendant of the Wahhabi rulers, took control of Riyadh and initiated a campaign to unify the Arabian Peninsula, creating an absolute monarchy that instituted rule under strict Islamic law. Today Saudi Arabia is ruled by one of Abd al-Aziz's sons, and the country's Basic Law decrees that the throne shall remain in the hands of the sons and grandsons of the kingdom's founder. In 1990, following **Iraq**'s invasion and annexation of **Kuwait**, the Saudi authorities permitted Western and Arab troops to used its territory as a base from which to launch the campaign to liberate Kuwait, thereby fuelling tensions between the Saudi monarchy and its subjects. Terrorist attacks in Saudi Arabia in May and November 2003 prompted the Saudi government to increase its efforts to tackle terrorism and extremism. At the same time, constraints applied to the media were relaxed somewhat and plans were announced to gradually introduce a degree of political representation. In February–April 2005 the government allowed nation-wide elections to be held for one-half of the members of 179 municipal councils. Saudi Arabia's economy is overwhelmingly based on oil, and the government exercises strong control over the principal forms of economic activity. The country possesses about one-quarter of all proven reserves of **petroleum** world-wide, is the world's largest exporter of petroleum, and plays a dominant role in **OPEC**. About 75% of budget revenue, 45% of gross domestic product (GDP) and 90% of export earnings are derived from the petroleum sector. Private-sector growth is being fostered as part of an attempt to reduce the country's dependence on oil and to create jobs for the rapidly growing population. High budget surpluses resulting from increased oil revenues have allowed the government to increase spending on education and vocational training, the development of infrastructure and on public-sector remuneration. Oil was first discovered in 1936 by the US-owned Arabian Standard Oil Company, which subsequently became the Arabian American Oil Company (Aramco). Commercial production commenced in 1938. In 1972 the government demanded greater control over its oil industry and participation in the oil concessions of foreign companies. In 1974 an agreement was concluded under which the government would acquire 60% majority ownership of Aramco's concessions and assets. The concept of participation was developed as an alternative to nationalization. Although Saudi Arabia had played only a minimal role in the Arab wars waged against Israel in 1948, 1967 and 1973, King Faisal was instrumental in organizing the Arab oil embargo of 1973 that was directed against the USA and other supporters of Israel. Relations with the USA improved as a result of the conclusion, in 1974, of cease-fire agreements between Israel and Egypt and Israel and Syria, and of a visit by US President Nixon to Saudi Arabia. Having succeeded King Faisal, who was assassinated in 1975, Crown Prince Khalid initiated the expansion of the Saudi economy, social programmes and its education system. Saudi Arabia's regional relations were complicated by the fall of the Shah of **Iran** in 1979, owing to the Iranian Revolution, and by the resultant wave of Islamic fundamentalism that emanated from Iran. Together with the USA and the United Kingdom, Saudi Arabia supported Iraq in its war with Iran during most of the 1980s, but was able to avoid direct involvement in the hostilities. Saudi Arabian armed forces participated in the Gulf War (1991) to liberate Kuwait from Iraqi occupation on a large scale. Despite the recent growth in the income it receives from oil, the Saudi economy is confronted by a number of serious long-term challenges, including a high rate of population growth and high unemployment that has given rise to the need for increased government spending. Efforts to diversify the economy away from oil have so far met with little success and the country is likely to remain the world's largest net exporter of oil for the foreseeable future.

Second World War (and Middle Eastern Oil)

The Second World War was an important turning point, tipping the balance in the race for oil completely in the favour of the USA in the oil-producing regions of the Middle East. By the end of the war, Europe was devastated and Germany was destroyed. France and Great Britain, the major imperial powers in the region, emerged much weaker from the war, while the USA emerged relatively intact and controlling more than one-half of the world's industrial output. This helped the USA claim the mantle of the dominant power in the West, while France and Britain had to become its junior partners. This change in the pecking order of the world's global powers was reflected in the control of oil resources after the war. In 1940, the US share of Middle East oil was 10%. By 1950, it had risen to 50%. Some of this increase was due to new concessions gained by the USA. However, the USA took over Britain and France's oil holdings, broke up the British monopoly in **Iran**, and marginalized France in **Iraq**. For example, after Iran's nationalist Prime Minister Mohammed Mossadegh nationalized the operations of the British-controlled Anglo-Iranian Oil Company (AIOC) in 1951, the US Central Intelligence Agency organized a coup to overthrow Mossadegh, replacing him with the Shah, who became a loyal ally of the USA. After Mossadegh had been overthrown, Iranian oil was not returned to the British AIOC. Instead, it was divided up among Exxon, Mobil, Gulf Oil and other American oil companies, with AIOC now holding a minority share of 40%.

Sibneft

Sibneft, established by presidential decree in 1995 and subsequently, over the following two years, privatized, is **Russia**'s fifth largest oil-producing and refining company. Privatization was carried out through auctions and Roman Abramovich and Boris Berezovsky both used 'front companies' as a means of acquiring shares in Sibneft. These transactions received the approval of Russian President Boris Yeltsin, despite having been widely condemned as unlawful. Yeltsin was reportedly on good terms with Berezovsky and, in particular, Abramovich, who was stated by Gen. Alexander Korzhakov, the former chief of Yeltsin's security service, to have managed Yeltsin's family's financial affairs. At first, Sibneft operated an oil-refining complex—Russia's largest—at Omsk, together with an oil and gas production business located in the city of Noyabrsk in the Yamal-Nenets autonomous district. Sibneft also conducted geological exploration and distributed oil products. In recent years the company has divested itself of peripheral businesses and has taken steps to improve the efficiency of its international operations. It collaborates closely with prominent international oilfield services companies. Two unsuccessful attempts were made (in 1998 and 2003) by Sibneft to merge with Yukos, the first failing owing to a management dispute and the second after Sibneft's shareholders halted the merger in response to action taken by the Federal Government's against Yukos. In September 2005, in Russia's largest ever corporate takeover, Gazprom purchased 72.663% of Sibneft shares for US $13,010m.

Sierra Club

The Sierra Club is the USA's most effective advocate for environmental protection, both locally and globally. In its first conservation campaign, the Club, which was founded in 1892, led efforts to defeat a proposed reduction in the boundaries of Yosemite National Park. The Sierra Club has helped to preserve wilderness, wildlife and wild places (including, in the USA, Yosemite National Park, Grand Canyon National Park, the Florida Everglades and the Sequoia National Monument) for more than 100 years. In early 2006, the Club took the decision to make energy policy its top priority, in reflection of an increased focus by the environmental movement on questions concerning energy, including the nexus between energy and climate change. The Sierra Club favours policies that reduce US reliance on foreign fossil fuels, supplied, in many instances, by (sometimes unstable) Middle Eastern sources. The Club claims that the national security of the USA would benefit from a more extensive use of alternative sources of energy.

State Oil Company of the Azerbaijan Republic (SOCAR)

The State Oil Company of the Azerbaijan Republic (SOCAR), together with its numerous subsidiaries, is responsible for oil and natural gas production in **Azerbaijan**. SOCAR also operates the country's two refineries, administers the national pipeline system and is responsible for managing Azerbaijan's foreign trade in oil and natural gas. Although government ministries are responsible for Azerbaijan's exploration and production agreements with foreign companies, SOCAR participates in all of the international consortia that are developing new oil and gas projects in the country.

SOCAR was established in 1992 by the merger of Azerineft and Azneftkimiya, Azerbaijan's two national oil companies. In 1994 SOCAR was a signatory to the so-called 'Contract of the Century' in respect of oil extraction from the Caspian Sea. The company has also taken a 25% stake in the Baku-Tbilisi-Ceyhan pipeline project.

'Swing Producers'

Generally, the term 'swing producer' is used with reference to a country which extracts more oil than it consumes, or a supplier with a huge available surplus of oil. When oil prices are (perceived as) excessively high and threaten economic chaos, a 'swing producer' may saturate the market, depressing prices and restoring economic order. **Saudi Arabia**, for example, maintains idle capacity amounting to several million barrels per day (b/d) for emergencies, and, as a consequence, the ability to moderate oil-price spikes. Examples of successful moderation include during the **Iran–Iraq War**, when Iranian and Iraqi production was disrupted; during and after the Gulf War (1991), in the absence of Iraqi and Kuwaiti production; and in response to the reduction of Venezuelan and Nigerian production as a consequence of civil unrest in those countries prior to the US-led invasion of **Iraq** in 2003. Having fulfilled the role of the world's swing producer for many years, in 2005 Saudi Arabia declared that it would no longer do so—for reasons of financial self-interest rather than due to any shortage of oil. The potential instability of Saudi Arabia's oil supply remains a weak point for the world economy.

Syriana

Syriana is a term used both with reference to Syria (as in *Pax Syriana*), and, in contexts other than Middle Eastern international relations, as an indicator of resemblance to Syria. *Pax Syriana* is Latin for 'Syrian peace', a successor to the historical terms *Pax Romana* and *Pax Britannica*. *Pax Syriana* is generally used with reference to the period of reduced conflict in Lebanon in 1990–April 2005 that was brought about by Syria's military occupation of and pervasive influence in that country. Use of the term may also suggest Syria's perceived ambition to annex Lebanon. A 2005 Academy Award-winning geopolitical thriller film written and directed by Stephen Gaghan was named *Syriana*. *Syriana*'s central theme is US reliance on oil. Like Gaghan's screenplay for *Traffic*, *Syriana*'s multiple storylines depict a world-wide epidemic. The film focuses on the influence of the oil industry as experienced, in its political, economic, legal, and social facets, by a US Central Intelligence Agency operative (played by George Clooney), an energy analyst (played by Matt Damon), an attorney (Jeffrey Wright), and a young unemployed Pakistani immigrant in an unnamed Persian Gulf emirate (Mazhar Munir). *Syriana*'s screenplay is based loosely on Robert Baer's memoir, *See No Evil*. The film suggests that the USA is willing to assassinate reformists in order to ensure chaos in the Middle East, with the aim of reinforcing its control of the region's oil.

T

The Taliban and Central Asian Oil

The Taliban Movement, often referred to simply as the Taliban, is a Sunni Islamist nationalist pro-Pashtun Movement which effectively held power in most of Afghanistan in 1996–2001. Only three states (the United Arab Emirates, Pakistan, and **Saudi Arabia**), as well as the unrecognized government of the Chechen Republic of Ichkeria, granted the Taliban diplomatic recognition. The Movement's most influential members, including its leader, Mullah Mohammed Omar, were junior Islamic religious scholars (village mullahs) who had usually studied at *madrassas* in Pakistan. Mainly derived from the Pashtuns of Afghanistan and Pakistan's North-West Frontier Province, the ranks of the Taliban were also boosted by numerous non-Afghan volunteers from the Arab world, **Central Asia**, South Asia, and South-East Asia. Following the collapse of the Soviet-backed Democratic Republic of Afghanistan in 1992, Afghanistan descended into civil war waged by rival warlords. The Taliban was eventually able to assert itself as a force capable of restoring order to Afghanistan. The Movement's ascent to power benefited the economy by abolishing the taxes that had been imposed by the warlords on local businesses. Political benefits included the elimination of most factional fighting and restoration of order to a chaotic society. However, the radical ideology of the Taliban subsequently alienated observers who had initially viewed its emergence in a positive light. Many sources have asserted that Pakistan supplied the Taliban with arms, military training and economic assistance. Some have even claimed that this support was orchestrated by the USA, whose preference was for a Pakistan-installed government in Afghanistan rather than the Iranian/Russian-backed Northern Alliance. Having combined military and diplomatic victories to take power in Kandahar and its environs, in September 1995 it initiated an ultimately successful military campaign against the forces of Ismail Khan in the west of Afghanistan. In the ensuing months, the Taliban besieged the capital, Kabul, capturing the city in September 1996 and establishing the Islamic Emirate of Afghanistan. In May 1997, on the same day that Taliban forces entered Mazar-i Sharif, Pakistan granted the Taliban diplomatic recognition. Saudi Arabia similarly recognized the Taliban as the government of Afghanistan on the following day. In late May, however, the Taliban was engaged in street battles by Malik's forces and comprehensively defeated. It was not until

15 months later, on 8 August 1998, that the Taliban was able to re-capture Mazar-i Sharif. The terrorist attacks that took place in the USA on 11 September 2001 redirected US attention to Afghanistan once more. Already, on 20 August 1998, US President Bill Clinton had ordered a naval attack with cruise missiles on targets near Khost, in Afghanistan, which the USA claimed were the locations of terrorist training camps. At the time of these attacks (known as 'Operation Infinite Reach'), the Taliban controlled the whole of Afghanistan, apart from some small regions in the north east where the Northern Alliance prevailed. Both Saudia Arabia and Pakistan supplied the Taliban with logistical and humanitarian assistance. Relations with **Iran**, meanwhile, were poor owing to the Taliban's anti-Shi'a character, and deteriorated further in 1998 following the seizure by Taliban forces of the Iranian consulate in Mazar-i Sharif and their execution of Iranian diplomats. In response, Iran increased its support for the Northern Alliance. The Taliban was involved in some negotiations with US and Argentinian oil companies concerning the transportation through Afghanistan of oil and gas from the Caspian Sea basin to the Indian Ocean. In 1997, a Taliban delegation travelled to Texas, USA, to take part in talks on the construction of a gas pipeline running from **Turkmenistan** to Pakistan via Afghanistan, spending several days at UNOCAL's company headquarters in Sugar Land, Texas. Although civil war was being waged in Afghanistan at that time, both UNOCAL and Argentina's Bridas were seeking to construct the pipeline.

The Tanker War and the USA

The USA had been suspicious of the Islamic Republic of **Iran** ever since the Iranian Revolution of 1979, not least as a result of the **Iran hostage crisis** in 1979–81. From 1982 US support for **Iraq** in the **Iran–Iraq War** was increased, incorporating intelligence, economic aid, normalized relations with the government (which had been severed during the 1967 Six-Day War—*see* **Arab–Israeli Wars**), and also the supply of weapons. From 1981, both Iran and Iraq had targeted oil tankers and merchant vessels, including those of neutral nations, in an effort to deprive each other of trade. Following successive Iraqi attacks on Iran's main oil-exporting facility on Khark (Kharg) Island, in May 1984 Iran attacked a Kuwaiti tanker near Bahrain, and a Saudi Arabian oil tanker in Saudi waters. A sharp increase in attacks on the ships of non-combatant nations sailing in the Persian (Arabian) Gulf subsequently occurred, and this phase of the war came to be known as the 'Tanker War'. Lloyd's of London, a British insurance market, estimated that a total of 546 commercial vessels were damaged and some 430 civilian mariners were killed as a result of the Tanker War. The most serious attacks were those carried out by Iran on Kuwaiti vessels, and in November 1986 **Kuwait** formally requested foreign assistance to safeguard its shipping. In 1987 the Soviet Union agreed to charter tankers, and the USA offered to protect tankers flying the US flag ('Operation Earnest Will' and 'Operation Prime Chance'). Under international law, an attack on such ships would be considered as an attack on the USA, obliging the USA to respond with military action. Such 'assistance' would safeguard ships destined for Iraqi ports, effectively guaranteeing Iraq's revenue stream for the course of the war.

In October 1987, the USA attacked Iranian oil platforms in retaliation for an Iranian attack on a US-flagged tanker, *Sea Isle City*. In April 1988, the frigate USS *Samuel B. Roberts* was seriously damaged by an Iranian mine. In response, the USA launched 'Operation Praying Mantis', which constituted the US Navy's largest engagement of surface warships since the **Second World War**, in which two Iranian ships were destroyed, and an American helicopter was shot down. During these escorts by the US Navy, on 3 July 1988 the cruiser USS *Vincennes* shot down Iran Air Flight 655 with the loss of all 290 passengers and crew. The US government stated that the airliner had been mistakenly identified as an Iranian F-14 *Tomcat*, and that the *Vincennes* was operating in international waters at the time and believed itself to be under attack. Iran, however, insisted that the *Vincennes* had been in Iranian territorial waters, and that the Iranian passenger jet was turning away from it and increasing altitude after take-off. US Adm. William J. Crowe also accepted that the *Vincennes* had been located in Iranian waters at the time of the attack. Conspiracy theories have subsequently proliferated. US observers, for instance, have pointed to several unusual aspects of the crash, such as the fact that none of the victims' corpses recovered were clothed, and that none of the passengers' relatives or friends have ever been named by the Iranian government. There has been speculation that the airliner may have been filled with criminals, political prisoners, hostages, or perhaps even corpses, and deliberately flown to a location where it would be bound to be shot down by US forces. These views remain current, and controversial. Although the USA paid compensation for the incident, it has never apologized for it. In 1985 and 1986, officials of the US Reagan Administration sold weapons to Iran in the hope that Iran would assist in obtaining the release of US hostages held in Lebanon, and, illegally, gave financial support to right-wing Nicaraguan rebels, or Contras. The ensuing scandal became known as the Iran-Contra Affair.

Teapot Dome

Teapot Dome refers to an oilfield on public land in Wyoming, USA, so named because of a rock resembling a teapot which overlooks the field. It is also a term used with reference to a scandal that beset the US Administration of President Warren G. Harding. Elk Hills and Buena Vista Hills in California, and Teapot Dome in Wyoming, were oilfields sited on public land and reserved for emergency use by the US Navy only when regular supplies began to decline. This restriction had encountered opposition from both private oil interests and politicians with interests in the oil business, on the grounds that it was unnecessary as US oil companies would always be able to meet the Navy's needs. The restriction was strongly opposed, in particular, by a Republican Senator from New Mexico, Albert B. Fall. Fall had previously used covert means to pursue his interests. In 1912 his election to the Senate for the first time was effected by means of a political alliance; Fall's allies were later, in 1921, able to secure his appointment as US Secretary of the Interior. In 1922, the reserves in question remained the responsibility of Edwin C. Denby, the US Secretary of the Navy. However, Denby was subsequently prevailed upon by Fall himself to transfer responsibility for them to Fall's own government department. Thereafter, rights to the oil were legally leased to Harry F. Sinclair of Mammoth Oil (later Sinclair Oil) with no involvement of rival bidders. At the same time, Fall leased the naval oil reserves at Elk Hills to Edward L. Doheny of Pan American Petroleum, receiving in exchange personal loans at no interest. In total, for issuing the leases Fall received gifts of some US $404,000. It was Fall's receipt of gifts rather than the leases themselves that were subsequently deemed to have been illegal. In April 1922, the *Wall Street Journal* published a report on clandestine arrangements under which the **petroleum** reserves had been leased to a private oil company without competitive bidding. Fall refuted the allegations, and, superficially, the leases to the oil companies appeared to have been legal. On the day after the *Wall Street Journal* published its claims, however, John B. Kendrick, a Democratic Senator from Wyoming, initiated one of the Senate's most important investigations. Wisconsin Republican Senator Robert La Follette, who, to begin with, was convinced of Fall's innocence, arranged for the affair to be investigated by the Senate Committee on Public Lands. The Committee's investigation continued inconclusively until 1924, when evidence of a loan by Doheny of $100,000 to Fall was uncovered. Ultimately, in 1927, the US Supreme Court determined that the oil rights had been granted corruptly and cancelled both the Elk Hills lease and the Teapot lease in the same year. The US Navy assumed control over the Teapot Dome and the Elk Hills reserves once more owing to the Court's decision. In 1929 Fall was convicted of bribery, fined $100,000 and sentenced to one year's imprisonment, thereby becoming the first ever member of the presidential Cabinet to be jailed for illegal conduct while in office. Sinclair, who had declined to co-operate with government investigators, was charged with offences of contempt and jury tampering, convicted, fined $100,000, and sentenced to a short period of imprisonment. In 1930 Doheny was acquitted of having attempted to bribe Fall. The Teapot Dome scandal caused only one political casualty: Holm O. Bursum, Fall's chosen successor who was guilty only of his association with Fall, failed to be re-elected to the Senate in 1924. In later years the Teapot Dome affair came to be included in a series of scandals that damaged big-business Republicans. The attention focused on the scandal caused it to be viewed as the first true symbol of government corruption in the USA. In fact, such scandals had occurred previously—Teapot Dome was simply the first time such corruption had been revealed nationally. President Harding was not aware of the scandal in any capacity, public or private. However, as a result of Teapot Dome his administration has been characterized as one of the most corrupt ever to have occupied the White House.

Tibet

Chinese geologists have undertaken extensive preliminary investigations, studies and research on Tibet's Qiangtang Basin, which is the basis for further understanding of the evolution of the basin and appraisal of its potential gas/oil reserves. The uninhabited Qiangtang Basin is located at a height of more than 5,100 m above sea level and remains the least exploited basin on the Chinese mainland hitherto. Research has revealed that hydrocarbon source rock at the basin is thick and well developed, thus constituting a robust material basis for substantial oil- and gasfields. A **petroleum**-bearing belt extending 100 km has also been discovered to the south of the Qiangtang Basin, and this is regarded as further evidence that the process of oil/gas gathering has taken place in the basin. Covering some 160,000 sq m, the Qiangtang Basin is a marine facies basin, the geological land type which has yielded most of the world's oil and gas resources. (The oilfields of the Middle East and the Caspian Sea are of the same geological type as the Qiangtang Basin.) Chinese researchers believe that this region of northern Tibet, together with the Tarim Basin, will become the source of important strategic oil reserves for China in the 21st century. However, exploration for and eventual exploitation of these reserves is impeded by insufficient transportation links. The Tibet highway (into Tibet) has recently been expanded and the construction of a railway is planned. However, building a railroad through the glaciers of Tibet represents a formidable engineering challenge.

Trans-Alaska Pipeline

The Trans-Alaska pipeline is one of the world's largest pipeline systems and the only means of transporting crude oil from **Alaska**'s North Slope fields to tankers in Valdez. Constructed in the 1970s after the discovery of oil at Prudhoe Bay in 1968, the 1.2-m diameter, 1,287-km pipeline connects Prudhoe Bay on the Arctic Ocean with the terminal at Valdez, the northernmost ice-free port in the Western Hemisphere. The flow from this pipeline constitutes approximately 20% of annual US oil output. The pipeline is buried for less than half of its length, where the ground is well-drained gravel or solid rock, and thawing does not represent a problem. In places where the warm oil would cause the icy soil to thaw (and thus lead to sinking or 'heaving') the pipeline, whose construction cost US $8,000m., rests on 78,000 aboveground supports at 18-m intervals. Aboveground sections of the pipeline are insulated and covered. Elsewhere, the pipeline has been elevated in order to span rivers or to permit wildlife to cross beneath it. The flow of oil through the pipeline was originally controlled by 12 pumping stations and a system of valves. The pipeline system is operated from an Operations Control Centre located in Valdez, but may also be operated independently at each pumping station.

Trans-Balkan Pipeline Project

In March 2001 the US Congress conducted a debate on the construction of an oil pipeline to extend from the Black Sea port of Burgas through Bulgaria and Macedonia to the Albanian port of Valona on the Adriatic Sea. Caspian Sea oil would be transported via this pipeline to supply the US market. Control of the future route of this pipeline from **Central Asia** towards the West is considered to be of strategic importance for the USA. The pipeline is regarded as likely to become one of the main routes to the West for oil and gas currently being extracted in Central Asia. Its potential throughput has been estimated at 750,000 barrels per day (b/d), worth some US $600m. a month at current prices. Discussion of the project is long-standing. The US administration views the Trans-Balkan pipeline as part of the region's future critical east-west *Corridor 8* infrastructure. An initial feasibility study on the pipeline, backed by the US government, was carried out in 1996. In July 1993, before the corridor project had received initial formal approval, the USA had dispatched peace-keeping troops to the Balkans. The fact that they were deployed not in the conflict zones of Bosnia, Croatia and Serbia, but on the northern borders of Macedonia was interpreted by some observers as a first step aiming to secure the area where the Trans-Balkan pipeline construction project would proceed. In 2005, Bulgaria, Greece and **Russia** concluded a 522m.-euro agreement for the construction of the pipeline. Funding for the project was to be provided by companies interested in running and exploiting the pipeline, however, not by the governments of those three countries. Later in 2005, the Macedonian, Bulgarian and Albanian Prime Ministers signed a political declaration confirming their countries' support for the pipeline's construction.

Turkish Straits

Turkey's high rate of economic growth during much of the 1990s, as well as resulting in booming industrial production, led to higher levels of energy consumption, imports, air and water pollution, and increased risks to the environment. Furthermore, increased oil exports from the Caspian Sea region to Russian and Georgian ports and, thereafter, to markets in the West across the Black Sea have led to increased oil tanker traffic through the narrow Turkish Straits. The development of Caspian and Central Asian oil and gas resources, in addition to Russian resources, has transformed Turkey into a major hub of the world's energy supply routes. The Turkish Straits system, comprising the two narrow straits of Istanbul and the Dardanelles, connected by the inner sea of Marmara, accounts for the greatest part of this traffic and will continue to do so in the next few years. The increase in shipping traffic through the Bosphorus Straits has raised fears of a major accident and the possible consequences of such an accident for the environment and the 12m. residents of Istanbul. Currently, annual traffic through the Straits amounts to some 50,000 vessels. About one in 10 of these are tankers carrying oil or liquefied natural gas. The rise in congestion has resulted in an increase in accidents. In 1988–92 155 collisions occurred in the Straits. The construction of a comprehensive radar and vessel control system for the waterway commenced in 2001. The need for such a system had already been highlighted in 1994, when a collision involving the Greek-Cypriot tanker *Nassia* killed 30 seamen and led to the spillage of 20,000 tons of oil into the Straits. Disastrous consequences for Istanbul were only avoided because the collision occurred several kilometres north of the city. Subsequently, Turkey adopted regulations that oblige vessels transporting hazardous cargoes to report to the national ministry of environmental protection. However, Turkey's ability to control commercial shipping through the Straits is restricted by the 1936 Treaty of Montreux, under which the Straits are designated as an international waterway. By virtue of subsequent international agreements Turkey has the right to regulate the right of passage through the Straits in order to guarantee the safe and steady flow of traffic, but, owing to pressure from some Black Sea border countries, shipping legislation adopted in 1994 has not been strictly enforced. In December 1999, a Russian tanker, the *Volgoneft-248*, ran aground and split in two close to the southwestern shores of Istanbul, spilling more than 800 tons of the 4,300 tons of fuel oil on board into the Marmara Sea. Stocks of fish in the Straits subsequently declined to one-sixtieth of their former levels. Meanwhile, the ecosystem of the Black Sea has been damaged by overfishing and pollution from surrounding countries. It has been estimated that it would cost as much as US $15,000m. to rid the Black Sea of pollution, but this is far beyond the means of the six countries which border the Sea. The Black Sea Strategic Action Plan of 1996 proposes the establishment of a Black Sea Environmental Fund to be funded through levies on activities in the Black Sea, but such levies would probably not meet the costs of the Fund. In June 2002, the ministers of the environment of Turkey and other Black Sea coastal states convened in Bulgaria to discuss plans to restore the Black Sea environment and protect it from further damage.

Turkmenistan

Having been annexed by **Russia** in 1865–85, in 1924 Turkmenistan became a Soviet republic. It gained independence after the collapse of the USSR in 1991. Turkmenistan's territory is largely comprised of desert. In irrigated oases there intensive cultivation is undertaken. There are also substantial reserves of oil and gas. One-half of Turkmenistan's irrigated land is planted with cotton, of which it was formerly the 10th largest producer in the world. In recent years cotton exports have fallen by almost 50% as a result of poor harvests, however. Turkmenistan's authoritarian ex-communist regime and tribally based social structure have dictated a cautious approach to economic reform. It is hoped that revenues from sales of natural gas and cotton will improve the country's economic performance, but only a limited degree of privatization is envisaged. In 1998–2005, however, economic progress was impeded by the continued absence of adequate export routes for natural gas and by the need to service extensive short-term debt. More positively, the value of exports rose by 20%–30% annually in 2003–05, owing mainly to higher international prices for oil and gas. In 2005, the government sought to raise the price of natural gas exported to Russia and Ukraine, its main customers, from US $44 per 1,000 cu m to $66 per 1,000 cu m. The prospects for economic improvement are hampered by extensive domestic poverty, burdensome foreign debt, the government's failure to make the best use of oil and gas revenues, and its reluctance to pursue market-oriented reforms.

V

Venezuela

Venezuela, one of South America's most stable democracies, disposes of reserves of oil that are among the largest in the world, in addition to vast reserves of coal, iron ore, bauxite and gold. Consequently, the country's economic fortunes remain closely linked to fluctuations in the international price of oil. The oil boom that occurred in the early 1970s largely benefited Venezuela's middle class and the subsequent collapse of world oil prices reduced many members of this class to poverty, causing a further deterioration in the standard of living of poorer social sectors. Official figures have assessed some 60% of the country's households as poor. In 1998, populist left-winger **Hugo Chávez Frías**, a former army officer, was elected as the country's President. Chávez has proclaimed a 'Bolivarian revolution', and his presidency has been characterized by radical reform, political unrest and deep social divisions. Under Chávez, Venezuela has attempted to increase its regional influence in what has been viewed as an effort to counteract US influence in South America and the Caribbean. Oil is unquestionably the fuel of the Venezuelan economy, accounting for about one-third of the country's gross domestic product and for about 80% of export earnings. In 2002, Venezuelan output of oil represented about 4.3% of total world production and Venezuela ranked as the world's eighth largest producer. In the previous year Venezuela had ranked as the world's sixth largest producer, its output representing 4.8% of global output. The decline occurred as a result of a national strike in December 2002 which interrupted the country's oil trade. Venezuela supplies about 10% of the USA's total oil imports. The oil business in Venezuela is administered by the state-run *Petróleos de Venezuela* SA (PDVSA), from which the government derives more than one-half of all of its revenues. Chávez has strongly supported **OPEC**'s policy of seeking to maintain international oil prices at a high level. In February 2002, Chávez appointed PDVSA's board of directors, leading some to suggest that he was attempting to take direct control of Venezuela's oil industry. The appointments were the focus of demonstrations held in April, at which Chávez's resignation was called for. Violent unrest prompted military commanders to place Chávez in custody for several days. Meanwhile, the head of Venezuela's largest business association, Pedro Carmona, was installed as the country's transitional leader. After only two days in power, however, Carmona resigned under pressure from Chávez's supporters, and Chávez was restored to the presidency. The importance of Venezuela's oil to both the country itself and to the rest of the world is such that the army is regularly deployed to defend installations, tankers and refineries, which have become the targets of attacks. A key objective of the Chávez regime has been to achieve full government control over the oil industry and to use earnings from oil to counter poverty. As a result, Venezuela has clashed with both US oil corporations and the US government. Chávez has announced that his government will begin to enforce legislation enacted in 2001 that provides for a substantial increase in the royalties levied on foreign corporations by the Venezuelan government for the extraction of oil in the country. The Venezuelan government is also attempting to eradicate corporate tax evasion, fining and temporarily closing down businesses that break the law. The anti-tax evasion campaign so far brought about a 50% increase in the government's tax revenue, which the government has used in turn to fund an increase of 24% in the minimum wage.

Viet Nam

Output of crude oil and natural gas by Viet Nam was in its early stages in the late 1980s and estimates of commercially recoverable reserves were not available to Western analysts. With Soviet assistance, Viet Nam began exploiting a reported discovery of 1,000m. metric tons of offshore oil to the south east of the Vung Tau-Con Dao Special Zone. By early 1987, Viet Nam had begun to export oil for the first time, to Japan. Production remained relatively low, however, at an estimated 5,000 barrels per day (b/d), while Viet Nam's minimum domestic oil requirement amounted to 30,000 b/d. Viet Nam's output declined in the early 1980s, falling below the level achieved in 1976–80. Viet Nam's estimated proven oil reserves of 600m. barrels are likely to rise as exploration proceeds. Output of crude oil averaged 403,300 b/d in 2004, Viet Nam thus ranking as Asia's third largest oil producer. The country's principal oilfields are Bach Ho (White Tiger), Rang Dong (Dawn), Hang Ngoc, Dai Hung (Big Bear) and Su Tu Den (Ruby). Although it has become a significant producer, Viet Nam continues to rely on imports of **petroleum** products due to the inadequacy of its own refining capacity. Net exports totalled 193,300 b/d in 2004. Markets for Vietnamese oil include the USA, Japan, Singapore and the Republic of Korea. The country's largest producer is Vietsovpetro (VSP), a joint venture between PetroViet Nam and **Russia**'s Zarubezhneft. VSP operates Bach Ho, Viet Nam's largest oilfield. In late 2004, VSP received government permission to develop some 10.5m. tons of crude oil in the following year, mainly from the Bach Ho field. Additional foreign partners include Conoco-Phillips, BP, Petronas, and Talisman. Since drilling operations were initiated in the Su Tu Den (Black Lion) crude field in October 2003, PetroViet Nam has reported increased production. PetroViet Nam's discovery in April 2003 of a deposit in Dai Hung with an estimated capacity of 6,300 b/d was expected to increase output further; and production is likely to be boosted further by the development of new oilfields over the next few years.

Meanwhile, new oil resources continue to be discovered in Viet Nam. For instance, substantial reserves of oil and gas were found in the Ca Ngu Vang (Golden Tuna) and Voi Trang (White Elephant) fields in 2002. In 2004, VSP discovered new oil resources of oil in its Dragon field. Provided the current rate of development can be maintained, Viet Nam will become the 30th largest oil-producing country in the world.

White House Energy Task Force

The US Administration of George W. Bush has fought a long-running battle to withhold from the public information concerning the membership of the US National Energy Policy Development Group—sometimes referred to as the 'Cheney Energy Task Force'. The Task Force was formed in May 2001 under US Vice-President Dick Cheney, a former CEO of Halliburton. From the beginning of his first tenure of the presidency, in early 2001, the foreign policy priority of President Bush was to increase supplies of foreign **petroleum** to US markets. In the months before he assumed office, severe shortages of oil and natural gas had occurred in many parts of the USA, in addition to sporadic electrical power blackouts in the state of California. Moreover, oil imports had risen to account for more than 50% of total US consumption for the first time ever, giving rise to considerable concern over the security of the country's supplies of energy in the long term. The problems the USA had experienced in energy supply in 2000–01 led to the establishment by President Bush of a task force responsible for developing long-term plans to meet the country's energy needs. On the recommendation of his close friend and largest campaign contributor, Enron CEO Ken Lay, Bush chose Vice-President Dick Cheney as head of the Energy Task Force. The Task Force's main function is to 'work with and monitor Federal Agencies' efforts to expedite their review of permits or take other actions as necessary to accelerate the completion of energy-related permits, while maintaining safety, public health, and environmental protections'. The Task Force is comprised of staff members of the Council on Environmental Quality (CEQ) and experts from the departments of agriculture, energy, the interior, and from the Environmental Protection Agency. Precisely what the Energy Task Force does remains classified information, even though Freedom of Information Act (FOIA) requests (since 19 April 2001) have sought to gain access to its materials. Critics of the Bush Administration's energy policies have alleged that energy industry representatives received preferential access to the Task Force's deliberations compared with that granted to representatives of environmental groups, consumer advocates, and others who pursued agendas that were at variance with those of Enron, Exxon and other oil multinationals. Committees established to advise the government on issues of policy which include individuals who are not employed by the government are obliged to observe the Federal Advisory Committee Act (FACA), which, *inter alia*, stipulates that their membership should be balanced and their meetings open. The Energy Task Force has been criticized for apparently failing to meet either of these requirements. For its part, the Bush Administration has denied that the FACA applied to the Energy Task Force—according to the White House, it had no non-government members. However, the office of the Vice-President and other federal agencies connected with the Energy Task Force have refused requests—including one by the General Accounting Office—to disclose the documents about the Task Force's activities that would be necessary to determine the issue. President Bush and Vice-President Cheney have claimed that the advice they received via the Task Force could be withheld from the public in accordance with executive privilege. A White House document has revealed that that oil company executives met with the Energy Task Force in 2001, as long suspected by environmentalists but denied as recently as late 2005 by industry officials in evidence to Congress. The document in question, which was published in November 2005 by *The Washington Post*, shows that officials from Exxon Mobil Corpn, Conoco (before it merged with Phillips), Shell Oil Co and BP America Inc. met with Cheney's aides to pursue the development of a national energy policy.

Woodside Petroleum

Established in 1954, Woodside Petroleum (WPL) has grown to become Australia's leading oil and gas company. WPL is currently Australia's largest publicly traded oil and gas exploration and production company, with a market capitalization of more than A$30,000m. (US $21,000m.). WPL, which is 34%-owned by Royal Dutch/Shell, operates a number of offshore wells in the North West Shelf, a huge new oil- and gasfield off the north-western coast of Western Australia, and is conducting exploration in a number of other areas off Western Australia and Victoria. The company is also the major shareholder in the Greater Sunrise field, in partnership with ConocoPhillips and Japan's Osaka Gas. The rich oil and gas reserves of the Great Sunrise Field, which lies in the Timor Sea, is expected to generate huge revenues for East Timor in the long term. The area is believed to contain as much gas as the nearby North West Shelf, which is also operated by WPL. The North West Shelf has identified reserves of some 2,831,685m. cu m, sufficient to make about 2,000m. metric tons of liquefied petroleum gas, enough to meet world demand for more than a decade.

Y

Yamani, Sheikh Ahmed Zaki

For 24 years Sheikh Yamani was responsible for **Saudi Arabia**'s oil affairs, thereby becoming, arguably, the most prominent Arab personality in the world. Yamani, who had been educated in the USA and Egypt, was appointed by King Faisal as legal adviser to the Saudi Arabian Council of Ministers. In 1962, reflecting the high esteem in which he held his abilities, Faisal appointed Yamani as Minister of Petroleum and Mineral Resources. In this role, thanks to his mastery of his brief and his talent for strategy and negotiation, Yamani's influence, both domestic and foreign, grew, in particular after oil prices increased threefold in 1973–74, raising Saudi Arabia's status to that of a financial super-power. By dominating **OPEC**, however, Yamani was able to limit damage to the global economy by excessive fluctuations in the price of oil. Yamani was also a leading proponent of OPEC governments' efforts to obtain shares in the concessions of the major oil companies. In 1977, a full Saudi take-over was achieved. King Fahd, who succeeded Faisal in 1975, continued to rely on Yamani's knowledge and experience, but their relationship was never as close as that between Faisal and Yamani. At the time of the **Iran–Iraq War** (1980–88) and the 1980s oil recession the moderate policies pursued by Yamani until 1986 (when King Fahd dismissed him) contrasted with those of the so-called OPEC 'hawks'.

Maps

MAP 1: MAJOR OIL PIPELINES

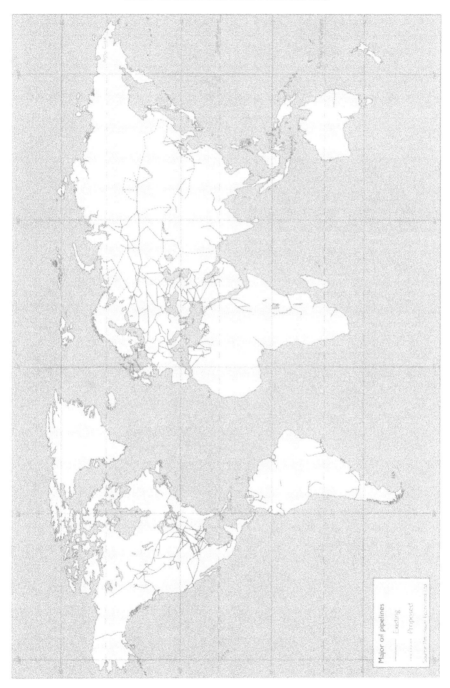

MAP 1A: MAJOR OIL PIPELINES IN EUROPE AND EURASIA

MAP 1B: MAJOR OIL PIPELINES IN THE MIDDLE EAST

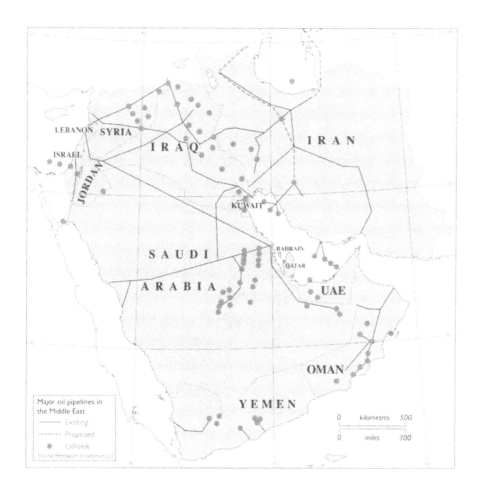

MAP 1C: MAJOR OIL PIPELINES IN NORTH AMERICA

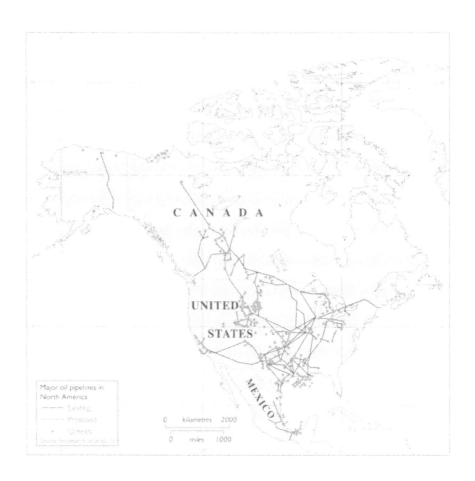

MAP 2: PROVEN RESERVES

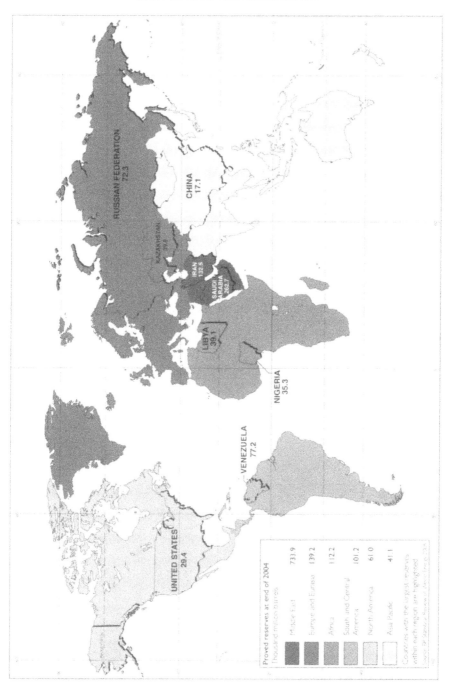

MAP 3: OIL PRODUCTION

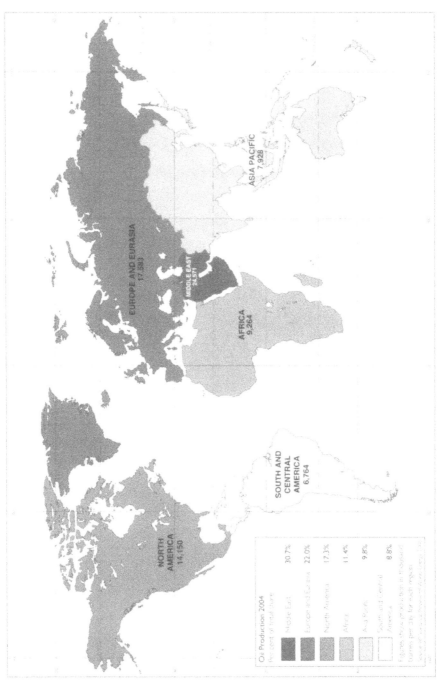

MAP 4: MAJOR OILFIELDS AND REFINERIES IN THE MIDDLE EAST AND CENTRAL ASIA

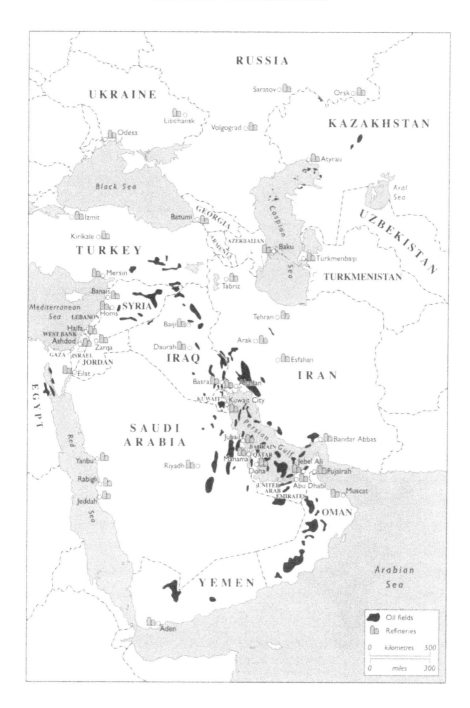

MAP 5: OIL CONSUMPTION

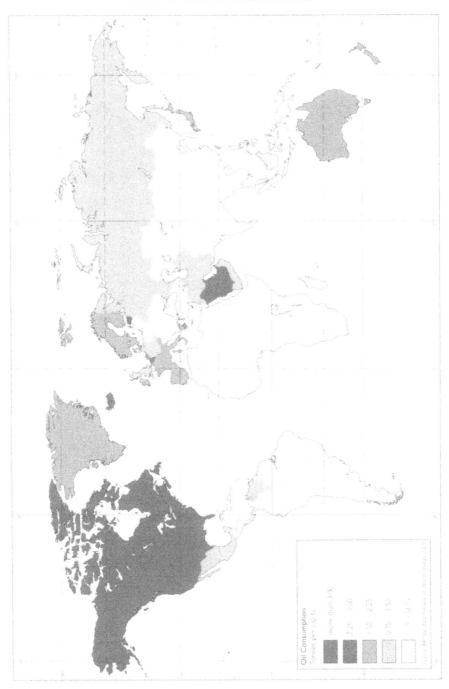

Oil Consumption
Tonnes per capita

MAP 6: TRADE FLOWS

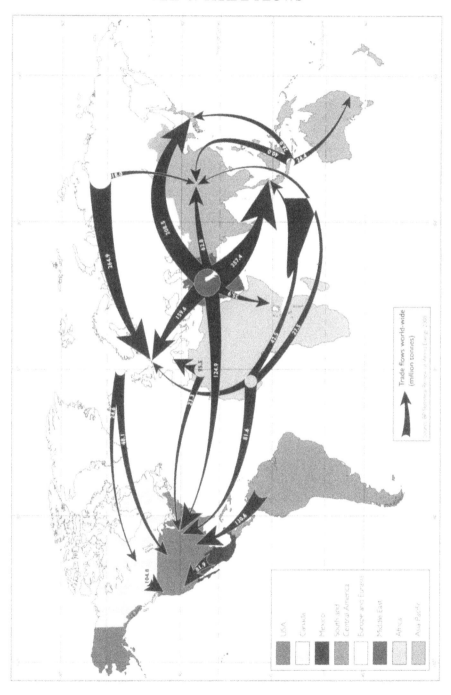

Statistics

Proven reserves of petroleum at end 2005

	'000m. Tons	'000m. Barrels	Share of total (%)	Reserves to production ratio
USA	3.6	29.3	2.4	11.8
Canada	0.5	16.5	1.4	14.8
Mexico	1.9	13.7	1.1	10.0
Total North America	7.8	59.5	5.0	11.9
Argentina	0.3	2.3	0.2	8.7
Brazil	1.6	11.8	1.0	18.8
Colombia	0.2	1.5	0.1	7.3
Ecuador	0.7	5.1	0.4	25.6
Peru	0.1	1.1	0.1	27.1
Trinidad & Tobago	0.1	0.8	0.1	13.0
Venezuela	11.5	79.7	6.6	72.6
Other S. & Cent. America	0.2	1.3	0.1	24.8
Total S. & Cent. America	14.8	103.5	8.6	40.7
Azerbaijan	1.0	7.0	0.6	42.4
Denmark	0.2	1.3	0.1	9.3
Italy	0.1	0.7	0.1	17.0
Kazakhstan	5.4	39.6	3.3	79.6
Norway	1.3	9.7	0.8	8.9
Romania	0.1	0.5	◆	11.3
Russian Federation	10.2	74.4	6.2	21.4
Turkmenistan	0.1	0.5	◆	7.8
United Kingdom	0.5	4.0	0.3	6.1
Uzbekistan	0.1	0.6	◆	12.9
Other Europe & Eurasia	0.3	2.2	0.2	12.9
Total Europe & Eurasia	19.2	140.5	11.7	22.0
Iran	18.9	137.5	11.5	93.0
Iraq	15.5	115.0	9.6	*
Kuwait	14.0	101.5	8.5	*
Oman	0.8	5.6	0.5	19.6
Qatar	2.0	15.2	1.3	38.0
Saudi Arabia	36.3	264.2	22.0	65.6
Syria	0.4	3.0	0.2	17.5
United Arab Emirates	13.0	97.8	8.1	97.4
Yemen	0.4	2.9	0.2	18.3
Other Middle East		0.1	◆	4.6
Total Middle East	101.2	742.7	61.9	81.0
Algeria	1.5	12.2	1.0	16.6
Angola	1.2	9.0	0.8	19.9

contd	'000m. Tons	'000m. Barrels	Share of total (%)	Reserves to production ratio
Chad	0.1	0.9	0.1	14.3
Rep. of Congo (Brazzaville)	0.3	1.8	0.1	19.3
Egypt	0.5	3.7	0.3	14.6
Equatorial Guinea	0.2	1.8	0.1	13.6
Gabon	0.3	2.2	0.2	25.8
Libya	5.1	39.1	3.3	63.0
Nigeria	4.8	35.9	3.0	38.1
Sudan	0.9	6.4	0.5	46.3
Tunisia	0.1	0.7	0.1	25.2
Other Africa	0.1	0.6	◆	12.0
Total Africa	15.2	114.3	9.5	31.8
Australia	0.5	4.0	0.3	20.0
Brunei	0.2	1.1	0.1	14.9
China	2.2	16	1.3	12.1
India	0.8	5.9	0.5	20.7
Indonesia	0.6	4.3	0.4	10.4
Malaysia	0.5	4.2	0.3	13.9
Thailand	0.1	0.5	◆	5.2
Viet Nam	0.4	3.1	0.3	21.8
Other Asia Pacific	0.1	1.0	0.1	13.2
Total Asia Pacific	5.4	40.2	3.4	13.8
Total World	163.6	1,200.7	100.0	40.6
OECD	10.6	80.6	6.7	11.2
OPEC	123.2	902.4	75.2	73.1
Non-OPEC†	23.5	175.4	14.6	13.6
Former Soviet Union	16.8	122.9	10.2	28.4

* More than 100 years.
◆ Less than 0.05%.
† Excludes Former Soviet Union.
n/a not available.
Notes: Proved reserves of oil – Generally taken to be those quantities that geological and engineering information indicates with reasonable certainty can be recovered in the future from known reservoirs under existing economic and operating conditions.
Reserves/Production (R/P) ratio – If the reserves remaining at the end of any year are divided by the production in that year, the result is the length of time that those remaining reserves would last if production were to continue at that level.
Source of data: The estimates in this table have been compiled using a combination of primary official sources, third party data from the OPEC Secretariat, World Oil, Oil & Gas Journal and an independent estimate of Russian reserves based on information in the public domain.
The reserves figures shown do not necessarily meet the definitions, guidelines and practices used for determining proved reserves at the company level, for instance those published by the United States Securities and Exchange Commission or recommended for the purposes of UK SORP, nor do they necessarily represent BP's view of proved reserves by country. The figure for Canadian oil reserves

includes an official estimate of Canadian oil sands 'under development'. Oil includes gas condensate and natural gas liquids as well as crude oil.

For the purposes of this table, shares of total are calculated using thousand million barrels figures.

Source: *BP Statistical Review of World Energy 2006.*

Petroleum production* ('000 barrels daily)

	2003	2004	2005	Change 2005 over 2004 (%)	2005 share of total (%)
USA	7,400	7,228	6,830	−5.5	8.0
Canada	3,004	3,085	3,047	−1.3	3.7
Mexico	3,789	3,824	3,759	−1.6	4.8
Total North America	14,193	14,137	13,636	−3.5	16.5
Argentina	806	754	725	−3.9	0.9
Brazil	1,555	1,542	1,718	11.1	2.2
Colombia	564	551	549	−0.4	0.7
Ecuador	427	535	541	1.1	0.7
Peru	92	94	111	11.5	0.1
Trinidad & Tobago	164	152	171	13.6	0.2
Venezuela	2,607	2,972	3,007	1.1	4.0
Other S. & Cent. America	153	144	142	−2.4	0.2
Total S. & Cent. America	6,367	6,745	6,964	3.0	9.0
Azerbaijan	313	317	452	42.8	0.6
Denmark	368	390	377	−3.3	0.5
Italy	107	105	118	12.2	0.2
Kazakhstan	1,111	1,297	1,364	4.3	1.6
Norway	3,264	3,188	2,969	−7.5	3.5
Romania	123	119	114	−4.5	0.1
Russian Federation	8,544	9,287	9,551	2.7	12.1
Turkmenistan	202	193	192	−0.5	0.2
United Kingdom	2,257	2,028	1,808	−11.0	2.2
Uzbekistan	166	152	126	−16.9	0.1
Other Europe & Eurasia	509	496	463	−6.8	0.6
Total Europe & Eurasia	16,965	17,572	17,534	−0.3	21.7
Iran	3,999	4,081	4,049	−0.8	5.1
Iraq	1,339	2,010	1,820	−9.5	2.3
Kuwait	2,329	2,481	2,643	6.5	3.3
Oman	823	785	780	−0.6	1.0
Qatar	917	990	1,097	9.0	1.3
Saudi Arabia	10,222	10,588	11,035	4.3	13.5
Syria	562	529	469	−11.4	0.6
United Arab Emirates	2,611	2,656	2,751	3.7	3.3
Yemen	448	420	426	1.3	0.5
Other Middle East	48	48	48	◆	0.1
Total Middle East	23,296	24,588	25,119	2.0	31.0

contd	2003	2004	2005	Change 2005 over 2004 (%)	2005 share of total (%)
Algeria	1,852	1,946	2,015	3.8	2.2
Angola	885	986	1,242	26.0	1.6
Cameroon	68	62	58	–6.1	0.1
Chad	24	168	173	3.0	0.2
Rep. of Congo (Brazzaville)	243	240	253	5.5	0.3
Egypt	749	721	696	–3.9	0.9
Equatorial Guinea	234	329	355	7.9	0.5
Gabon	240	235	234	–0.2	0.3
Libya	1,486	1,607	1,702	5.9	2.1
Nigeria	2,263	2,502	2,580	3.1	3.2
Sudan	255	325	379	16.6	0.5
Tunisia	68	72	74	3.4	0.1
Other Africa	71	75	72	–3.0	0.1
Total Africa	8,438	9,266	9,835	6.2	12.0
Australia	624	541	554	2.0	0.6
Brunei	214	211	206	–2.0	0.3
China	3,401	3,481	3,627	4.2	4.6
India	798	816	784	–4.1	0.9
Indonesia	1,183	1,152	1,136	–1.4	1.4
Malaysia	831	857	827	–4.3	0.9
Thailand	223	220	276	25.2	0.3
Viet Nam	364	427	392	–8.2	0.5
Other Asia Pacific	195	186	199	6.9	0.2
Total Asia Pacific	7,832	7,890	8,000	1.2	9.8
Total World	77,091	80,198	81,088	1.0	100.0
OECD	21,156	20,716	19,763	–4.7	23.8
OPEC	30,806	32,985	33,836	2.5	41.7
Non-OPEC†	35,787	35,805	35,408	–1.1	43.4
Former Soviet Union	10,499	11,409	11,844	3.7	14.8

* Includes crude oil, shale oil, oil sands and NGLs (natural gas liquids – the liquid content of natural gas where this is recovered separately). Excludes liquid fuels from other sources such as coal derivatives.
† Excludes Former Soviet Union.
◆ Less than 0.05.
Notes: Annual changes and shares of total are calculated using million tons per annum figures rather than thousand barrels daily.
Growth rates are adjusted for leap years.
Because of rounding some totals may not agree exactly with the sum of their component parts.
Source: *BP Statistical Review of World Energy 2006.*

Petroleum production* (million metric tons)

	2001	2002	2003	2004	2005
USA	349.2	346.9	338.4	329.2	310.2
Canada	126.1	135.0	142.7	147.6	145.2
Mexico	176.6	178.4	188.8	190.7	187.1
Total North America	651.9	660.2	669.8	667.4	642.5
Argentina	41.5	40.9	40.2	37.8	36.2
Brazil	66.3	74.4	77.0	76.5	84.7
Colombia	31.0	29.7	27.9	27.3	27.1
Ecuador	21.2	20.4	21.7	27.3	27.6
Peru	4.8	4.8	4.5	4.4	4.9
Trinidad & Tobago	6.5	7.5	7.9	7.3	8.3
Venezuela	161.6	149.9	134.2	153.4	154.7
Other S. & Cent. America	6.9	7.8	7.8	7.3	7.1
Total S. & Cent. America	339.8	335.3	321.1	341.3	350.6
Azerbaijan	14.9	15.4	15.5	15.7	22.4
Denmark	17.0	18.1	17.9	19.1	18.4
Italy	4.1	5.5	5.6	5.5	6.1
Kazakhstan	40.1	48.2	52.4	60.6	63.0
Norway	162.0	157.3	153.0	149.9	138.2
Romania	6.2	6.1	5.9	5.7	5.4
Russian Federation	348.1	379.6	421.4	458.8	470.0
Turkmenistan	8.0	9.0	10.0	9.6	9.5
United Kingdom	116.7	115.9	106.1	95.4	84.7
Uzbekistan	7.2	7.2	7.1	6.6	5.5
Other Europe & Eurasia	22.2	23.7	24.0	23.4	21.8
Total Europe & Eurasia	746.6	786	818.9	850.2	845
Iran	184.4	168.6	197.9	202.6	200.4
Iraq	116.7	99.9	65.7	99.2	89.5
Kuwait	101.9	98.2	114.8	122.5	130.1
Oman	47.5	44.5	40.7	38.9	38.5
Qatar	38.4	35.1	41.2	44.9	48.8
Saudi Arabia	442.9	427.3	487.9	506.1	526.2
Syria	28.9	27.1	28.0	26.4	23.3
United Arab Emirates	118.3	108.5	122.2	124.7	129.0
Yemen	21.5	21.6	21.1	19.9	20.1
Other Middle East	2.2	2.2	2.2	2.2	2.2
Total Middle East	1,102.8	1,033.0	1,121.7	1,187.3	1,208.1
Algeria	65.8	70.9	79.0	83.6	86.5
Angola	36.6	44.6	43.6	48.7	61.2
Cameroon	4.1	3.8	3.5	3.2	3.0

contd	2001	2002	2003	2004	2005
Chad	–	–	1.3	8.8	9.1
Rep. Of Congo (Brazzaville)	14.0	13.3	12.5	12.4	13.1
Egypt	37.3	37.0	36.8	35.4	33.9
Equatorial Guinea	8.6	10.4	11.6	16.3	17.6
Gabon	15.0	14.7	12.0	11.8	11.7
Libya	66.8	64.6	69.9	75.8	80.1
Nigeria	110.8	102.3	110.3	121.9	125.4
Sudan	10.4	11.5	12.6	16.1	18.7
Tunisia	3.4	3.5	3.2	3.4	3.5
Other Africa	2.5	3.0	3.5	3.6	3.5
Total Africa	375.2	379.6	399.6	441.0	467.1
Australia	31.8	31.6	26.6	23.0	23.3
Brunei	9.9	10.2	10.5	10.3	10.1
China	164.8	166.9	169.6	174.1	180.8
India	36.0	37.0	36.9	37.9	36.2
Indonesia	68.0	63.0	57.7	55.9	55.0
Malaysia	33.8	35.4	37.4	38.5	36.8
Thailand	7.0	7.8	9.2	9.0	11.2
Viet Nam	17.1	17.3	17.7	20.8	19.1
Other Asia Pacific	9.1	9.0	9.1	8.7	9.2
Total Asia Pacific	377.5	378	374.5	378.1	381.7
Total World	3,593.7	3,572.0	3,705.8	3,865.3	3,895.0
OECD	999.6	1,005.4	995.6	976.0	927.7
OPEC	1,475.6	1,388.2	1,480.8	1,590.5	1,625.5
Non-OPEC†	1,693.6	1,717.6	1,711.4	1,716.2	1,692.0
Former Soviet Union	424.5	466.2	513.6	558.6	577.4

* Includes crude oil, shale oil, oil sands and NGLs (natural gas liquids – the liquid content of natural gas where this is recovered separately).
Excludes liquid fuels from other sources such as coal derivatives.
† Excludes Former Soviet Union.
Notes: Growth rates are adjusted for leap years.
Because of rounding some totals may not agree exactly with the sum of their component parts.
Source: *BP Statistical Review of World Energy 2006.*

Consumption* ('000 barrels daily)

	2003	2004	2005	Change 2005 over 2004 (%)	2005 share of total (%)
USA	20,033	20,732	20,655	–0.2	24.6
Canada	2,132	2,248	2,241	–0.2	2.6
Mexico	1,885	1,898	1,978	3.3	2.3
Total North America	24,050	24,877	24,875	0.1	29.5
Argentina	372	394	421	7.6	0.5
Brazil	1,785	1,776	1,819	2.4	2.2
Chile	229	244	257	5.5	0.3
Colombia	222	223	230	3.7	0.3
Ecuador	137	144	148	2.7	0.2
Peru	140	152	139	–9.6	0.2
Venezuela	479	525	553	5.3	0.7
Other S. & Cent. America	1,173	1,188	1,208	1.6	1.5
Total S. & Cent. America	4,537	4,647	4,776	2.8	5.8
Austria	293	285	294	3.4	0.4
Azerbaijan	86	92	103	11.3	0.1
Belarus	152	153	137	–10.4	0.2
Belgium & Luxembourg	748	785	809	3.1	1.0
Bulgaria	98	102	109	6.7	0.1
Czech Republic	185	203	211	4.1	0.3
Denmark	193	189	189	0.2	0.2
Finland	239	224	233	4.2	0.3
France	1,965	1,978	1,961	–0.7	2.4
Germany	2,664	2,634	2,586	–1.7	3.2
Greece	404	435	429	–1.5	0.5
Hungary	132	136	151	10.6	0.2
Iceland	18	20	19	–2.4	◆
Republic of Ireland	178	185	196	5.4	0.2
Italy	1,927	1,873	1,809	–3.5	2.2
Kazakhstan	183	188	208	11.4	0.3
Lithuania	51	54	57	4.0	0.1
Netherlands	962	1,003	1,071	7.7	1.3
Norway	219	210	213	1.8	0.3
Poland	435	460	478	4.1	0.6
Portugal	317	322	320	–0.5	0.4
Romania	199	230	240	4.5	0.3
Russian Federation	2,645	2,714	2,753	1.4	3.4

contd	2003	2004	2005	Change 2005 over 2004 (%)	2005 share of total (%)
Slovakia	71	68	73	9.6	0.1
Spain	1,559	1,593	1,618	1.7	2.1
Sweden	332	319	315	−1.2	0.4
Switzerland	259	258	262	2.1	0.3
Turkey	668	688	650	−5.9	0.8
Turkmenistan	95	103	110	6.8	0.1
Ukraine	286	293	294	0.4	0.4
United Kingdom	1,717	1,764	1,790	1.7	2.2
Uzbekistan	148	155	161	4.3	0.2
Other Europe & Eurasia	475	482	502	4.4	0.6
Total Europe & Eurasia	19,903	20,195	20,350	0.9	25.1
Iran	1,513	1,575	1,659	5.4	2.0
Kuwait	238	266	280	5.2	0.4
Qatar	77	84	98	17.1	0.1
Saudi Arabia	1,684	1,805	1,891	4.5	2.3
United Arab Emirates	333	355	376	5.5	0.5
Other Middle East	1,394	1,407	1,436	1.9	1.8
Total Middle East	5,238	5,492	5,739	4.4	7.1
Algeria	231	240	254	6.0	0.3
Egypt	550	567	616	9.3	0.8
South Africa	513	523	529	0.6	0.6
Other Africa	1,274	1,315	1,363	3.6	1.7
Total Africa	2,568	2,646	2,763	4.4	3.4
Australia	851	856	884	2.7	1.0
Bangladesh	78	80	82	2.8	0.1
China	5,803	6,772	6,988	2.9	8.5
China Hong Kong SAR	269	314	285	−9.6	0.4
India	2,420	2,573	2,485	−3.5	3.0
Indonesia	1,132	1,150	1,168	1.4	1.4
Japan	5,455	5,286	5,360	1.4	6.4
Malaysia	480	493	477	−3.3	0.6
New Zealand	148	150	152	1.1	0.2
Pakistan	321	325	353	8.8	0.5
Philippines	330	336	314	−6.9	0.4
Singapore	668	748	826	11.0	1.1
South Korea	2,300	2,283	2,308	0.8	2.7
Taiwan	868	880	884	0.2	1.1

contd	2003	2004	2005	Change 2005 over 2004 (%)	2005 share of total (%)
Thailand	836	913	946	4.0	1.2
Other Asia Pacific	400	427	445	4.3	0.5
Total Asia Pacific	22,359	23,586	23,957	1.5	29.1
Total World	78,655	81,444	82,459	1.3	100.0
European Union 25	14,546	14,687	14,772	0.7	18.3
OECD	48,289	49,082	49,254	0.4	59.2
Former Soviet Union	3,752	3,861	3,936	1.9	4.9
Other EMEs	26,614	28,501	29,270	2.6	36.0

* Inland demand plus international aviation and marine bunkers and refinery fuel and loss.
◆ Less than 0.05%.
Notes: Annual changes and shares of total are calculated using million tonnes per annum figures rather than thousand barrels daily.
Growth rates are adjusted for leap years.
Differences between these world consumption figures and world production statistics are accounted for by stock changes, consumption of non-petroleum additives and substitute fuels, and unavoidable disparities in the definition, measurement or conversion of oil supply and demand data.
Source: *BP Statistical Review of World Energy 2006.*

Consumption* (million tons)

	2001	2002	2003	2004	2005	Change 2005 over 2004 (%)	2005 share of total (%)
USA	896.1	897.4	912.3	948.8	944.6	−0.2	24.6
Canada	90.5	92.2	95.9	100.6	100.1	−0.2	2.6
Mexico	85.0	81.5	83.7	85.2	87.8	3.3	2.3
Total North America	1,071.6	1,071.1	1,091.8	1,134.6	1,132.6	0.1	29.5
Argentina	19.1	17.1	17.6	18.7	20.1	7.6	0.5
Brazil	87.5	85.5	82.0	81.9	83.6	2.4	2.2
Chile	10.5	10.4	10.5	11.3	11.9	5.5	0.3
Colombia	11.1	10.0	10.0	10.1	10.4	3.7	0.3
Ecuador	5.9	5.9	6.2	6.4	6.6	2.7	0.2
Peru	7.0	6.9	6.5	7.2	6.4	−9.6	0.2
Venezuela	24.8	27.0	22.0	24.2	25.4	5.3	0.7
Other S. & Cent. America	55.6	56.1	57.2	58.1	58.8	1.6	1.5
Total S. & Cent. America	221.5	219.0	212.0	217.9	223.3	2.8	5.8
Austria	12.8	13.0	14.1	13.8	14.2	3.4	0.4
Azerbaijan	4.0	3.7	4.3	4.6	5.1	11.3	0.1
Belarus	7.3	7.1	7.4	7.5	6.7	−10.4	0.2
Belgium & Luxembourg	32.2	33.5	36.4	38.4	39.5	3.1	1.0
Bulgaria	4.0	4.1	4.5	4.7	5.0	6.7	0.1
Czech Republic	8.3	8.2	8.7	9.5	9.9	4.1	0.3
Denmark	9.8	9.6	9.2	9.1	9.1	0.2	0.2
Finland	10.5	10.9	11.4	10.6	11.0	4.2	0.3
France	95.5	92.9	93.1	94.0	93.1	−0.7	2.4
Germany	131.6	127.4	125.1	124.0	121.5	−1.7	3.2
Greece	20.1	20.2	19.6	21.3	20.9	−1.5	0.5
Hungary	6.7	6.4	6.1	6.3	7.0	10.6	0.2
Iceland	0.9	0.9	0.9	1	0.9	−2.4	◆
Republic of Ireland	9.0	8.8	8.5	8.9	9.4	5.4	0.2
Italy	92.8	92.9	92.1	89.7	86.3	−3.5	2.2
Kazakhstan	8.9	9.3	8.8	9.0	10.0	11.4	0.3
Lithuania	2.7	2.5	2.4	2.6	2.7	4.0	0.1
Netherlands	43.7	43.8	44.1	46.2	49.6	7.7	1.3
Norway	9.7	9.4	9.9	9.6	9.8	1.8	0.3
Poland	19.2	19.4	19.9	21.1	21.9	4.1	0.6
Portugal	15.8	16.2	15.2	15.4	15.3	−0.5	0.4
Romania	10.6	10.6	9.4	10.9	11.3	4.5	0.3
Russian Federation	122.3	123.5	124.7	128.5	130.0	1.4	3.4
Slovakia	3.2	3.5	3.3	3.2	3.5	9.6	0.1
Spain	72.7	73.8	75.5	77.6	78.8	1.7	2.1
Sweden	15.2	15.2	15.9	15.3	15.1	−1.2	0.4
Switzerland	13.1	12.4	12.1	12.0	12.2	2.1	0.3
Turkey	29.9	30.6	31.2	32.0	30.0	−5.9	0.8
Turkmenistan	3.7	3.8	4.2	4.6	4.9	6.8	0.1

contd	2001	2002	2003	2004	2005	Change 2005 over 2004 (%)	2005 share of total (%)
Ukraine	12.7	13.1	13.5	13.9	13.9	0.4	0.4
United Kingdom	78.4	78.0	79.0	81.7	82.9	1.7	2.2
Uzbekistan	6.5	6.3	7.2	7.5	7.8	4.3	0.2
Other Europe & Eurasia	20.6	21.8	22.9	23.3	24.3	4.4	0.6
Total Europe & Eurasia	934.3	933.0	940.8	957.6	963.3	0.9	25.1
Iran	63.5	67.9	71.8	74.6	78.4	5.4	2.0
Kuwait	10.5	11.4	12.2	13.7	14.4	5.2	0.4
Qatar	2.1	3.2	3.0	3.3	3.8	17.1	0.1
Saudi Arabia	71.9	72.7	77.7	83.7	87.2	4.5	2.3
United Arab Emirates	14.6	15.9	16.3	17.4	18.3	5.5	0.5
Other Middle East	68.7	68.9	67.4	68.1	69.2	1.9	1.8
Total Middle East	231.4	239.9	248.3	260.7	271.3	4.4	7.1
Algeria	8.8	9.7	10.1	10.6	11.2	6.0	0.3
Egypt	26.1	25.2	25.9	26.8	29.2	9.3	0.8
South Africa	23.0	23.6	24.2	24.8	24.9	0.6	0.6
Other Africa	58.3	58.9	59.8	61.9	64.0	3.6	1.7
Total Africa	116.2	117.5	120.1	124.2	129.3	4.4	3.4
Australia	38.1	38.0	38.3	38.8	39.7	2.7	1.0
Bangladesh	3.9	3.9	3.8	3.9	4.0	2.8	0.1
China	227.9	247.4	271.7	318.9	327.3	2.9	8.5
China Hong Kong SAR	11.7	12.9	13.0	15.3	13.8	−9.6	0.4
India	107	111.3	113.1	120.2	115.7	−3.5	3.0
Indonesia	51.9	53.1	53.9	54.7	55.3	1.4	1.4
Japan	247.5	243.6	248.9	241.4	244.2	1.4	6.4
Malaysia	20.6	22.5	22.2	22.8	22.0	−3.3	0.6
New Zealand	6.3	6.5	6.9	7.0	7.0	1.1	0.2
Pakistan	18.3	17.9	15.8	16.0	17.4	8.8	0.5
Philippines	16.5	15.6	15.5	15.8	14.7	−6.9	0.4
Singapore	36.4	35.5	33.9	38.1	42.2	11.0	1.1
South Korea	103.1	104.7	105.6	104.9	105.5	0.8	2.7
Taiwan	39.2	40.1	41.1	41.7	41.6	0.2	1.1
Thailand	33.1	36.4	40.0	44.0	45.6	4.0	1.2
Other Asia Pacific	18.4	19.4	19.0	20.3	21.1	4.3	0.5
Total Asia Pacific	980.0	1,008.5	1,042.6	1,103.6	1,116.9	1.5	29.1
Total World	3,554.9	3,589.0	3,655.6	3,798.6	3,836.8	1.3	100.0
European Union 25	688.4	684.6	688.2	697.3	700.4	0.7	18.3
OECD	2,197.6	2,190.9	2,223.0	2,267.3	2,270.7	0.4	59.2
Former Soviet Union	172.6	174.1	177.3	183.2	186.3	1.9	4.9
Other EMEs	1,184.7	1,224.0	1,255.3	1,348.1	1,379.9	2.6	36.0

* Inland demand plus international aviation and marine bunkers and refinery fuel and loss.
◆ Less than 0.05%.
Notes: Growth rates are adjusted for leap years.

Differences between these world consumption figures and world production statistics are accounted for by stock changes, consumption of non-petroleum additives and substitute fuels, and unavoidable disparities in the definition, measurement or conversion of oil supply and demand data.
Source: *BP Statistical Review of World Energy 2006.*

Trade movements ('000 barrels daily)

	2003	2004	2005	Change 2005 over 2004 %	2005 share of total %
Imports					
USA	12,254	12,898	13,525	4.9	27.1
Europe	11,993	12,538	13,261	5.8	26.6
Japan	5,314	5,203	5,225	0.4	10.5
Rest of World*	16,238	17,471	17,895	2.4	35.8
Total World	45,799	48,110	49,906	3.7	100.0
Exports					
USA	921	991	1,129	14.0	2.3
Canada	2,096	2,148	2,201	2.5	4.4
Mexico	2,115	2,070	2,065	−0.2	4.1
S. & Cent. America	2,942	3,233	3,528	9.1	7.1
Europe	2,066	1,933	2,149	7.8	4.3
Former Soviet Union	6,003	6,440	7,076	9.9	14.2
Middle East	18,943	19,630	19,821	1.0	39.7
North Africa	2,715	2,917	3,070	5.2	6.2
West Africa	3,612	4,048	4,358	7.7	8.7
Asia Pacific†	3,025	3,009	2,967	−1.4	5.9
Rest of World*	1,361	1,631	1,542	−5.5	3.1
Total World	45,799	48,110	49,906	3.7	100.0

* Includes unidentified trade.
† Excludes Japan.
Note: For the purposes of this table, annual changes and shares of total are calculated using thousand barrels daily figures.
Source: *BP Statistical Review of World Energy 2006.*

Imports and exports 2005

	Million tons			
	Crude imports	Product imports	Crude exports	Product exports
USA	500.7	166.0	1.9	52.2
Canada	46.5	13.2	81.8	26.7
Mexico	–	15.7	97.4	5.2
S. & Cent. America	32.7	19.1	109.6	63.5
Europe	524.7	130.3	38.1	66.2
Former Soviet Union	–	4.4	267.6	81.4
Middle East	10.2	6.4	862.9	119.2
North Africa	8.9	8.1	122.6	29.1
West Africa	2.9	8.9	208.7	8.0
East & Southern Africa	27.3	5.6	12.4	0.8
Australasia	24.3	11.2	7.2	3.7
China	127.1	39.8	6.7	14.0
Japan	210.4	47.8	–	5.1
Other Asia Pacific	369.5	99.8	46.3	66.4
Unidentified*	–	–	22.0	34.8
Total World	1,885.2	576.3	1,885.2	576.3

* Includes changes in the quantity of oil in transit, movements not otherwise shown, unidentified military use, etc.
Note: Bunkers are not included as exports. Intra-area movements (for example, between countries in Europe) are excluded.
Source: *BP Statistical Review of World Energy 2006.*

Imports and exports 2005

	'000 barrels daily			
	Crude imports	Product imports	Crude exports	Product exports
USA	10,055	3,470	38	1,091
Canada	934	276	1,643	558
Mexico	–	328	1,956	109
S. & Cent. America	657	399	2,201	1,327
Europe	10,537	2,724	765	1,384
Former Soviet Union	–	92	5,374	1,702
Middle East	205	134	17,329	2,492
North Africa	179	169	2,462	608
West Africa	58	186	4,191	167
East & Southern Africa	548	117	249	17
Australasia	488	234	145	77
China	2,552	832	135	293
Japan	4,225	999	–	107
Other Asia Pacific	7,420	2,086	930	1,388
Unidentified*	–	–	442	727
Total World	37,859	12,047	37,859	12,047

* Includes changes in the quantity of oil in transit, movements not otherwise shown, unidentified military use, etc.
Note: Bunkers are not included as exports. Intra-area movements (for example, between countries in Europe) are excluded.
Source: *BP Statistical Review of World Energy 2006*.

Inter-area movements 2005 (million tons)

From	To												Total
	USA	Canada	Mexico	S. & Cent. America	Europe	Africa	Australasia	China	Japan	Other Asia Pacific	Rest of World	
USA	–	7.4	10.1	15.5	11.6	0.7	–	0.4	4.0	3.5	0.9	54.1
Canada	107.1	–	0.1	0.2	0.8	–	–	–	0.3	–	–	108.5
Mexico	81.8	1.7	–	6.7	10.5	0.1	–	–	–	1.6	0.2	102.6
S. & Cent. America	140.9	5.3	2.1	–	15.1	1.0	–	5.3	0.1	3.3	–	173.1
Europe	53.3	22.0	2.4	2.3	–	12.9	–	0.6	0.3	6.0	4.5	104.3
Former Soviet Union	23.0	–	0.1	3.0	287.0	0.5	–	19.6	2.3	3.5	10.0	349.0
Middle East	116.5	7.1	0.5	7.8	156.1	37.2	5.6	67.4	211.7	369.2	3.0	982.1
North Africa	26.7	8.4	0.3	5.7	97.0	4.1	0.2	3.2	0.1	5.4	0.6	151.7
West Africa	96.5	2.0	–	8.4	34.6	4.4	0.2	28.6	3.0	38.1	0.9	216.7
East & Southern Africa	–	–	–	–	1.3	–	–	6.7	4.0	1.2	–	13.2
Australasia	0.7	–	–	–	–	–	–	1.2	3.2	5.8	–	10.9
China	1.6	0.1	–	1.6	0.2	0.1	0.4	–	2.3	14.0	0.4	20.7
Japan	–	–	–	–	0.4	–	0.4	3.3	–	1.0	–	5.1
Other Asia Pacific	8.3	0.2	0.1	0.3	6.1	0.7	26.8	30.3	24.8	14.6	0.5	112.7
Unidentified*	10.3	5.5	–	0.3	34.3	–	1.9	0.3	2.1	2.1	–	56.8
Total imports	666.7	59.7	15.7	51.8	655.0	61.7	35.5	166.9	258.2	469.3	21.0	2,461.5

* Includes changes in the quantity of oil in transit, movements not otherwise shown, unidentified military use etc.

Source: *BP Statistical Review of World Energy 2006.*

Inter-area movements 2005 ('000 barrels daily)

From	To											
	USA	Canada	Mexico	S. & Cent. America	Europe	Africa	Australasia	China	Japan	Other Asia Pacific	Rest of World	Total
USA	–	154	211	323	242	15	–	8	84	73	19	1,129
Canada	2,172	–	2	4	17	–	–	–	6	–	4	2,201
Mexico	1,647	34	–	135	211	2	–	–	–	32	4	2,065
S. & Cent. America	2,868	109	44	–	309	21	–	107	2	68	–	3,528
Europe	1,100	444	50	48	–	270	–	12	6	125	94	2,149
Former Soviet Union	473	–	2	60	5,811	10	–	398	47	72	202	7,076
Middle East	2,345	143	10	157	3,144	752	113	1,360	4,269	7,466	63	19,821
North Africa	547	169	6	115	1,959	83	4	64	2	109	12	3,070
West Africa	1,943	40	–	169	696	88	4	574	60	765	18	4,358
East & Southern Africa	–	–	–	–	26	–	–	135	80	25	–	266
Australasia	14	–	–	–	–	–	–	25	65	117	–	222
China	32	2	–	33	4	2	8	–	47	289	8	427
Japan	–	–	–	–	8	–	8	69	–	21	–	107
Other Asia Pacific	170	4	2	6	128	15	545	626	511	301	10	2,318
Unidentified*	214	111	–	6	706	–	39	6	44	44	–	1,169
Total imports	13,525	1,210	328	1,056	13,261	1,258	722	3,384	5,225	9,507	431	49,906

* Includes changes in the quantity of oil in transit, movements not otherwise shown, unidentified military use etc.
Source: *BP Statistical Review of World Energy 2006.*

Select Bibliography

Select Bibliography

a) Political Economy of Oil—General

Billingsley, T. 'Non-OPEC Fact Sheet', US Department of Energy, 2001, http://www.nigc/eia/nonopec.asp

Briody, D. *The Halliburton Agenda: The Politics of Oil and Money*. Wiley, 2004.

Brown, Michael Barratt. *The Economics of Imperialism*. Penguin, 1974.

Caravale, G. A., and Tosato, Domenico A. *Ricardo and the Theory of Value, Distribution and Growth*. London, Routledge & Kegan Paul, 1980.

Cohen, Benjamin J., 'The Triad and the Unholy Trinity: Problems of International Monetary Cooperation', in Frieden, Jeffry A., and Lake, David A. (Eds), International Political Economy (4th Edn), Boston, Bedford/St Martins, 2000, pp. 245–256.

Cox, Robert, 'Global *Perestroika*', in Crane, George T., and Amawi, Abla (Eds), The Theoretical Evolution of International Political Economy (2nd Edn), Oxford, Oxford University Press, 1997, pp. 158–172.

Duncan, Richard C. *The Peak of World Oil Production and the Road to the Olduvai Gorge*. Seattle, WA, Institute on Energy and Man, 2000.

Duncan, Richard C., and Youngquist, Walter. *The World Petroleum Life-Cycle*. Seattle, WA, Institute on Energy and Man, 1998.

Eichengreen, Barry, 'Hegemonic Stability Theories of the International Monetary System' in Frieden, Jeffry A., and Lake, David A. (Eds), International Political Economy (4th Edn), Boston, Bedford/St Martins, 2000, pp. 220–244.

Energy Information Administration. *Monthly Energy Review*. Washington, DC, US Department of Energy, 2005.

Erdman, Paul. *Tug of War*. New York, St. Martin's Griffin, 1996.

Fouskas, K. Vassilis, and Gökay, B. *The New American Imperialism: Bush's War on Terror and Blood for Oil*. Praeger, 2005.

Helleiner, Eric. *States and the Reemergence of Global Finance*. Ithica, Cornell University Press, 1994.

   The Making of National Money. Ithica, Cornell University Press, 2003.

Henning, C. Randall. *Currencies and Politics in the United States, Germany, and Japan*. Washington, DC, Institute for International Economics, 1994.

Karl, Terry Lynn. *The Paradox of Plenty: Oil Booms and Petro-states* (Studies in International Political Economy). University of California Press, 1997.

Lake, David A., 'British and American Hegemony Compared: Lessons for the Current Era of Decline', in Frieden, Jeffry A., and Lake, David A. (Eds), International Political Economy (4th Edn), Boston, Bedford/St Martins, 2000, pp. 127–139.

Macrae, J. C. *An Introduction to the Study of Fuel.* Elsevier, 1966.

Odell, Peter R. *Oil and World Politics: Background to the Oil Crisis.* Penguin, 1975.

Organization of Petroleum Exporting Countries. *The Petroleum Industry,* 2005, http://www.opec.library/FAQ/Petrol Industry.htm

Parra, Francisco. *Oil Politics: A Modern History of Petroleum.* I. B. Tauris, 2003.

Perkins, John. *Confessions of an Economic Hit Man.* San Francisco, Berrett Koehler, 2004.

Phillips, Kevin. *American Theocracy: The Peril and Politics of Radical Religion, Oil, and Borrowed Money in the 21st Century.* Viking Books, 2006.

Roberts, Paul. *The End of Oil.* Boston, Houghton Mifflin Company, 2004.

Ruppert, Michael C. *Crossing the Rubicon: The Decline of the American Empire at the End of the Age of Oil.* New Society Publishers, 2004.

Sampson, Anthony. *The Seven Sisters. The History, the Companies and the Politics of Oil.* Coronet Books, 1993.

Strange, Susan. *Sterling and British Policy.* London, Oxford University Press, 1971.

States and Markets. London, Pinter, 1994.

The Retreat of the State: the Diffusion of Power in the World Economy. Cambridge, Cambridge University Press, 1996.

Tempest, Paul. *World Petroleum at the Crossroads.* PTA, 1999.

Turner, Louis. *Oil Companies in the International System.* The Royal Institute of International Affairs, 1980.

United States Energy Information Agency. *World Petroleum Consumption (Btu), 1980–Present.* Washington, DC, US Department of Energy, 2003.

United States Energy Information Agency. *Future and Options Markets Changed Energy Marketing.* Washington, DC, US Department of Energy, 2005.

b) Peak Oil/Energy Security

Campbell, Colin J., and Laherrere, Jean H., 'The End of Cheap Oil', in Scientific American, Vol. 278, No. 3, March 1998.

Deffeyes, Kenneth S. *Beyond Oil: The View from Hubbert's Peak*. Hill & Wang, 2005.

 Hubbert's Peak: The Impending World Oil Shortage. Princeton University Press, 2001.

Hartshorn, J. E. *Oil Trade: Politics and Prospects*. Cambridge, Cambridge University Press, 1993.

Klare, Michael T. *Resource Wars: The New Landscape of Global Conflict*. New York, Owl Books, 2002.

 Blood and Oil: The Dangers and Consequences of America's Growing Oil Dependency. New York, Henry Holt and Co, 2004.

Kurth, James, 'The Decline and Fall of Almost Everything', in Foreign Affairs, Vol. 72: 2, 1993.

Leggett, Jeremy. *Half Gone: Oil, Gas, Hot Air and the Global Energy Crisis*. Portobello Books Ltd, 2005.

Roberts, Paul. *The End of Oil: On the Edge of a Perilous New World*. Boston, Houghton Mifflin Co, 2004.

Sempa, Francis P. *Geopolitics: From the Cold War to the 21st Century*. Transaction Publishers, New Brunswick, 2002.

c) African Oil

Apter, Andrew. *The Pan-African Nation: Oil and the Spectacle of Culture in Nigeria*. University of Chicago Press, 2005.

De Capua, J. 'Niger Delta Crisis Affecting Crude Oil Prices and supplies to US, China, Japan and Europe', in *VOA Washington News*, 24 February 2006.

El-Khawas, Mohamed A., and Ndumbe, J. Anyu. *Democracy, Diamonds and Oil: Politics in Today's Africa*. Nova Science Publishers Inc., 2006.

Ford, Mark, and Godier, Kevin. *Africa Oil and Gas Report: Politics, Investment,and Hydrocarbon Prospects in 54 Countries*. CWC Publishing, 1999.

Forrest, T. *Politics and Economic Development in Nigeria*. Boulder, Colorado, Westview Press, 1995.

Hoyle, D., '"We made it peaceful": oil politics in the Niger delta', *Open Democracy*. Article In Print, 2005.

Ibeanu, O., 'Oiling the Friction: Environmental Conflict Management in the Niger Delta, Nigeria', in *Environmental Change and Security Report* 6, 1998, pp. 19–32.

Idahosa, D. A., 'Issues and Problems in Nigerian Politics – Tribes, Ethnicism and Regionalism', in Ola, R. F. (Ed.), Nigerian Political System: Inputs, Outputs and Environment, Benin City, Mbik Press, 1999.

Katz, Menachem. *Lifting the Oil Curse, Improving Petroleum Revenue Management in Sub-Saharan Africa.* International Monetary Fund, 2004.

Nnoli, O. *Ethnic Politics in Nigeria.* Enugu, Fourth Dimension Publishers, 1978.

Obi, C., 'The Impact of Oil on Nigeria's Revenue Allocation System: Problems and Prospects for National Reconstruction', in Amuwo, K., et al. (Eds), Federalism and Political Restructuring in Nigeria, Ibadan, Spectrum Books, 1998.

Odiniyi, M., and Ezigbo, O., 'Delta Threat Raises Oil Prices to $70 Per Barrel', in This Day, 13 April 2006.

Oknota, I., and Oronto, D. *Where the Vultures Feed: Forty Years of Shell in the Niger Delta.* USA, Sierra Club Publishing, 2001.

Osadolor, B. O., 'The Development of the Federal Idea and the Federal Framework, 1914–1960', in Amuwo, K., et al. (Eds), Federalism and Political Restructuring in Nigeria, Ibadan, Spectrum Books, 1998.

Rowell, Andrew, Marriott, James, and Stockman, Lorne. *The Next Gulf: London, Washington and Oil Conflict in Nigeria.* Constable and Robinson, 2005.

Tamuno, T. N., 'Nigerian Federalism in Historical Perspectives', in Amuwo, K., et al. (Eds), Federalism and Political Restructuring in Nigeria, Ibadan, Spectrum Books, 1998.

US Energy Information Administration. *Nigeria Country Analysis Brief,* December 1997.

Vanderwalle, Dirk. *Libya Since Independence: Oil and State Building.* I. B. Tauris, 1998.

Wiwa, K. *In the Shadow of a Saint.* London, Black Swan, 2000.

d) America(s) and Oil

Anderson, A. *US Oil and Gas Industry Outlook Survey.* Arthur Andersen & Co, 2000.

Brown, Jonathan C., and Knight, Alan (Eds). *The Mexican Petroleum Industry in the Twentieth Century* (Symposia on Latin America Series). University of Texas Press, 1992.

Bryce, Robert. *Cronies: Oil, the Bushes, and the Rise of Texas, America's Superstate.* Hardie Grant Publishing, 2005.

Colby, Gerard, and Dennett, Charlotte. *Thy Will Be Done: The Conquest of the Amazon: Nelson Rockefeller and Evangelism in the Age of Oil.* HarperCollins, 1995.

Coronil, Fernando. *The Magical State: Nature, Money and Modernity in Venezuela.* University of Chicago Press, 1997.

Ewell, Judith. *Venezuela and the United States: From Monroe's Hemisphere to Petroleum's Empire (United States & the Americas S.).* University of Georgia Press, 1996.

Gerlach, Allen. *Indians, Oil, and Politics: A Recent History of Ecuador (Latin American Silhouettes S.).* Scholarly Resources Inc., 2003.

Hodel, Donald P., and Deitz, Robert. *Crisis in the Oil Patch: How America's Energy Industry Is Being Destroyed and What Must Be Done to Save It.* Regnery Publishing, 1994.

Pelletiere, Stephen C. *America's Oil Wars.* Praeger Publishers Inc., 2004.

Petzinger, Thomas, Jr. *Oil and Honor: the Texaco-Pennzoil Wars: Inside the US $11 Billion Battle for Getty Oil.* Beard Books, 1999.

Sabin, Paul. *Crude Politics: The California Oil Market, 1900–1940.* University of California Press, 2004.

Sawyer, Suzana. *Crude Chronicles: Indigenous Politics, Multinational Oil, and Neoliberalism in Ecuador (American Encounters/Global Interactions S.).* Duke University Press, 2004.

Thuro, Catherine, and Bell, Ken (Illustrator). *Oil Lamps: The Kerosene Era in North America.* Collector Bks, 1998.

Waterman, Jonathan. *Where Mountains Are Nameless: Passion and Politics in the Arctic National Wildlife Refuge.* W. W. Norton & Co Ltd, 2005.

Wirth, John D. (Ed.). *The Oil Business in Latin America - The Early Years.* Beard Books, 2001.

Yergin, Daniel (Ed.). *The Dependence Dilemma: Gasoline Consumption and America's Security.* University Press of America, 1980.

e) Caspian Oil

Adeebfar, Tamine. *Geopolitical Dimensions of the Main Export Pipeline in the Caspian Region.* Tehran, IIES, 2005.

Amineh, Mehdi Parvizi, and Houweling, Henk, 'Caspian Energy : Oil and Gas Resources and the Global Market', in Amineh, Mehdi Parvizi, and Houweling,

Henk (Eds), Central Eurasia in Global Politics : Conflict, Security and Development, Koninklijike Brill, Leiden, 2004.

Bahgat, Gawdat, 'Pipeline Diplomacy: The Geopolitics of the Caspian Sea Region', in International Studies Perspectives, Vol. 3, 2002.

Blank, Stephen J., 'The United States: Washington's New Frontier in the Transcaspian', in Croissant, Michael P., and Aras, Bülent (Ed.), Oil and Geopolitics in the Caspian Sea Region, Greenwood Press, 2000.

Blouet, Brian W., 'Halford Mackinder and the Pivotal Heartland', in Blouet, Brian W. (Ed.), *Global Geostrategy : Mackinder and the defence of the West*, Frank Cass Publishers, London, 2005.

Dekmejian, R. H., and Simonian, H. H. *Troubled Waters. The Geopolitics of the Caspian Region*. I. B. Tauris, 2001.

Gökay, Bülent, (Ed.), *Battle of the Black Gold: Oil, War and Geopolitics from Kosovo to Afghanistan*, special issue of Journal of Southern Europe and the Balkans, Vol. 4, No. 1, May 2002.

'The Most Dangerous Game in the World: Oil, War and US Global Hegemony', in Alternatives: Turkish Journal of International Relations, Vol. 1, No. 2, Summer 2002.

Gökay, Bülent (Ed.). *The Politics of Caspian Oil*. Palgrave, 2001.

Shaffer, Brenda, 'From Pipedream to Pipeline: A Caspian Success Story', in Current History: A Journal of Contemporary World Affairs, 104, No. 684 (October 2005), at http://bcsia.ksg.harvard.edu/BCSIA_content/documents/ShafferCurrentHistoryOct2005.pdf, Retrieved on 29 December 2005.

'US Policy in the South Caucasus in the Second George W. Bush Administration', in Nursin Atesoglu Guney and Fuat Aksu (Ed.), The Prospects for Cooperation and Stability in the Caucasus, Foundation For Middle East and Balkan Studies (OBİV), 2005.

Torbakov, Igor, 'Reexamining Old Concepts About The Caucasus and Central Asia', 2 April 2004, at http://www.eurasianet.org/departments/insight/articles/eav020404a.shtml, Retrieved on 28 February 2006.

f) Middle Eastern Oil

Ahmed, Nafeez Mosaddeq. *Behind the War on Terror*. Clairview, 2003.

Ali, Tariq. *The Clash of Fundamentalists*. London, Verso, 2002.

Amuzegar, Jahangir. *Managing the Oil Wealth*. London, I. B. Tauris, 1999.

Andersen, Roy, Siebert, Robert F., and Wagner, Jon G. *Politics and Change in the Middle East: Sources of Conflict and Accommodation*. Englewood Cliffs, Prentice Hall, 1992.

Askari, Hossein, 'Oil, Not Islam, Is At Fault in the Middle East', in The National Interest, January 2004.

Bamford, James. *A Pretext for War*. New York, Doubleday, 2004.

Benmansour, Hacène. *Politique Économique en Islam*. Paris, Éditions Al-Qalam, 1995.

Cappelen, Ådne, and Choudhury, Robert. *The Future of the Saudi Arabian Economy*. Oslo, Statistics Norway, 2000.

Cause, F. Gregory III. *Oil Monarchies*. New York, Council on Foreign Relations, 1994.

Al-Chalabi, Fadhil, and Al-Janabi, Adnan, 'Optimum Production and Pricing Policies', in Journal of Energy and Development, Spring 1979, pp. 229–258.

Chaudhry, Kiren Aziz. *The Price of Wealth*. London, Cornell University Press, 1997.

'Economic Liberalisation and the Lineages of the Rentier State', in Hopkins, Nicholas S., and Ibrahim, Saad Eddin (Eds), Arab Society, Cairo, The American University in Cairo Press, 1997.

Chevalier, Jean-Marie. *Les grandes batailles de l'énergie*. Paris, Gallimard, 2004.

Choudoury, Musul Alam, and Abdul Malik, Uzir. *The Foundations of Islamic Political Economy*. London, Macmillan, 1992.

Contributions to Islamic Economic Theory. London, Macmillan, 1986.

Choueiri, Youssef M. *Arab Nationalism*. London, Blackwell, 2000.

Dam, Kenneth W. *Oil Resources*. London, University of Chicago Press, 1976.

Dasgupta, Partha S., and Heal, Geoffrey M. *Economic Theory and Exhaustible Resources*. Cambridge, Cambridge University Press, 1979.

Dekmejian, R. Hrair. *Islam in Revolution*. Syracuse, Syracuse University Press, 1995.

Denison, Edward F. *Why Growth Rates Differ*. Washington, DC, Brookings, 1967.

Droz-Vincent, Philippe, and Salamé, Ghassan. *Moyen Orient : pouvoirs autoritaires, sociétés bloquées*. Paris, Presses Universitaires de France, 2004.

El Mallakh, Ragaei. *Kuwait*. Chicago, The University of Chicago Press, 1968.

Fargues, Philippe, 'Demographic explosion or social upheaval', in Salamé, Ghassan (Ed.), Democracy without Democrats, London, I. B. Tauris, 1994, pp. 156–79.

Gran, Peter. *Islamic Roots of Capitalism*. New York, Syracuse University Press, 1998.

Halliday, Fred. *Nation and Religion in the Middle East*. London, Saqi Books, 2000.

Hammad, Alam E. *Islamic Banking - Theory and Practice*. Cincinnati, Ohio, Zakat and Research Foundation, 1989.

Huband, Mark. *Brutal Truths, Fragile Myths*. Boulder, Col, Westview Press, 2004.

Ismael, Jacqueline S. *Kuwait: Dependency and Class in a Rentier State*. Gainesville, FL, University Press of Florida, 1993.

Jabarti, Anwar, 'The Oil Crisis: A Producer's Dilemma, US and World Energy Resources: Prospects and Priorities, El Mallakh, Ragaei, and McGuire, Carl (Eds), Boulder, Col, ICEED, 1997, pp. 130–131.

Khalidi, Rashi. *Resurrecting Empire*. Boston, Beacon Press, 2004.

Lacey, Robert. *The Kingdom*. Fontana/Collins, 1981.

Lapidus, Ira M., 'The Separation of State and Religion in the Development of Early Islamic Society', in *International Journal of Middle East Studies*, No. 6, 1975, pp. 363–385.

Lindholm, Charles. *The Islamic Middle East Tradition and Change*. London, Blackwell Publishers, 2002.

   The Islamic Middle East. London, Blackwell, 2004.

Looney, Robert, 'Iraq's Economic Transition: The Neoliberal Model and its Role', in The Middle East Journal, Autumn 2003, Vol. 57, No. 3, pp. 568–587.

Mannan, Muhammad Abdul. *Islamic economic principles: Theory and Practice*. Boulder, Col, Westview Press, 1987.

Manning, Jean P. (Ed.). *Iraq: Government, US Forces and Oil*. Nova Science Publishers Inc., 2005.

Mills, Paul S., and Presley, John R. *Islamic Finance: Theory and Practice*. London, Macmillan, 1999.

Naqvi, Syed Nawab Haider. *Islam, Economics and Society*. London, Kegan Paul International, 1994.

Owen, Roger, and Pamuk, Sevket. *A History of the Middle East Economies in the Twentieth Century*. Cambridge, MA, Harvard University Press, 1999.

Penrose, Edith, and Penrose, E. F. *Iraq, International Relations and National Development*. London, Ernest Benn, 1978.

Richards, Alan, and Waterbury, John. *A Political Economy of the Middle East: State, Class and Economic Development*. Boulder, CO, Westview Press, 1990.

Roberts, John. *Visions and Mirages*. Edinburgh, Mainstream Publishing, 1995.

Oil and the Iraq War of 2003. Boulder, CO, ICEED, 2003.

Ruthven, Malise. *Islam in the World*. Oxford, Oxford University Press, 2000.

Rutledge, Ian. *Addicted to oil*. London, I. B. Tauris, 2005.

Shirley, Edward G., 'Is Iran's Present Algeria's Future', in Foreign Affairs, May–June 1995, pp. 28–58.

Stelzer, Irwin M., 'Can We Do Without Saudi Oil?', in The Weekly Standard, 19 November, 2001.

g) Russian Oil

Brunstad, Bjorn, Eivind, G. B., Magnus, Philip Swanson, Honneland, Geir, and Overland, Indra. *Big Oil Playground, Russian Bear Preserve or European Periphery?: The Russian Barents Sea Region Towards 2015*. Eburon B V, 2005.

Cohen, Ariel. *Kazakhstan: Energy Cooperation with Russia – Oil, Gas and Beyond (Russian Foreign Energy Policy Reports)*. GMB Publishing Ltd, 2006.

Considine, Jennifer I., and Kerr, William A. *The Russian Oil Economy*. Edward Elgar, 2002.

Dorian, James P. *Oil and gas in Russia and the Former Soviet Union*. Financial Times Energy, 1998.

Ellman, Michael. *Russia's Oil and Natural Gas: Bonanza or Curse* (Anthem Studies in Development & Globalization). Anthem Press, 2006.

Goldman, Marshall I. *The Enigma of Soviet Petroleum: Half-full or Half-empty?* HarperCollins, 1980.

Grace, John. *Russian Oil Supply: Performance and Prospects*. Oxford University Press, 2005.

Hill, Fiona. *Energy Empire: Oil, Gas and Russia's Revival*. Foreign Policy Centre, 2005.

Kryukov, Valery, and Moe, Arild. *The Changing Role of Banks in the Russian Oil Sector* (RIIA Special Paper). Royal Institute of International Affairs, 1998.

'Russia Drills Less Oil, OPEC Keeps It Cheap', *Economist*, 8 June 1985, p. 65.

'Statoil, BP, Aim to Develop Soviet Caspian Oilfield', *Reuters*, 23 October 1990.

Walde, Thomas. *Oil and Gas Legislation in Russia*. University of Dundee, 1992.

The Politics of Series

This new series from Routledge provides a fresh perspective on various political issues worldwide. Subjects including **Terrorism, Oil, Migration, the Environment, Water** and **Religion** are analysed in detail, with statistics and maps providing a thorough examination of the topic.

Each book comprises an A-Z glossary of key terms specific to the subject, as well as relevant organizations, individuals and events.

A selection of 8-10 chapters in essay format, each around 5,000 words in length, written by a group of acknowledged experts from around the world provide in-depth comment on some of the issues most relevant to each title.

Key Features:

- This mixture of analytical and statistical information is a unique aspect of this series, and provides the reader with a comprehensive overview of the subject matter
- Information can now be found on each of these topics in these one-stop resources
- This series provides the only detailed examination of politics relating to specific subjects currently available.

For more information on this series, including a full list of titles, please contact reference@routledge.co.uk

Routledge
Taylor & Francis Group

The Europa Political and Economic Dictionary series

This series provides extensive, up-to-date regional information, examining some of the major political and economic issues of modern international affairs.

Each book in the series reflects the unique perspective of each of the world's regions, providing invaluable information specific to that particular area. They provide, in one easy-to-use format, information that might otherwise take time and many resources to locate.

Each volume offers:

- Concise and cross-referenced entries, providing contact details where appropriate
- Entries on the history and economy of each constituent country of the region
- Entries detailing distinct territories, ethnic groups, religions, political parties, prime ministers, presidents, politicians, businesses, international organizations, multinationals and major NGOs.

Each of these titles is compiled by acknowledged experts in the political economy of the region, and will be a great asset to any reference library.

For more information on this series, including a full list of titles please contact info.europa@tandf.co.uk

Routledge
Taylor & Francis Group

For Product Safety Concerns and Information please contact our EU
representative GPSR@taylorandfrancis.com
Taylor & Francis Verlag GmbH, Kaufingerstraße 24, 80331 München, Germany